A Ukrainian Chapter

The New Approaches to Russian and East European Jewish Culture series aims to bring to the public the finest scholarship on Russian and East European Jewish culture. Drawing on Yiddish, Hebrew, and Slavic studies, the series emphasizes questions of the culture and intellectual history of the Jews in Russia and Eastern Europe. Of particular focus are the unexplored relationships between Jews and their neighbors and among Jews themselves. The editor hopes to publish works that challenge conventional or simplistic ideas regarding the role of Jews in the relevant literatures (Russian, Polish, Czech, etc...), cosmopolitanism and national identity, and the intersection of religious and secular conceptions of self. This series has the goal of becoming a central location for the development of new approaches, including work on the history of ideas, postmodernism, and gender issues.

The New Approaches to Russian and East European Jewish Culture Series

1. Ber Boris Kotlerman, *In Search of Milk and Honey: The Theater of "Soviet Jewish Statehood,"* 1934–49 (2009)
2. Brian Horowitz, *Empire Jews: Jewish Nationalism and Acculturation in 19th- and Early 20th-Century Russia* (2009)
3. Seth L. Wolitz, *Yiddish Modernism: Studies in Twentieth-Century Eastern European Jewish Culture* (2013)
4. Brian Horowitz and Shai Ginsburg, eds., *Bounded Mind and Soul: Russia and Israel, 1880–2010* (2013)
5. Ber Kotlerman, *Disenchanted Tailor in "Illusion": Sholem Aleichem behind the Scenes of Early Jewish Cinema, 1913–16* (2014)
6. Yakov Leshchinsky, *The Jewish Worker in Russia* (2018)
7. Eli Gumener, *A Ukrainian Chapter: A Jewish Aid Worker's Memoir of Sorrow (Podolia, 1918–20)*

Series General Editor: Marat Grinberg (Reed College)

A Ukrainian Chapter
A Jewish Aid Worker's Memoir of Sorrow
(Podolia, 1918–20)

Eli Gumener

Translated from the Yiddish and with an Introduction by
Michael Eli Nutkiewicz

Bloomington, Indiana, 2022

SLAVICA

ISBN 978-089357-511-3

Library of Congress Cataloging-in-Publication Data

Names: Gumener, Eli, 1886-1941, author. | Nutkiewicz, Michael Eli, 1949-
    translator.
Title: A Ukrainian chapter : an aid worker's memoir of sorrow (Podolia,
    1918-20) / Eli Gumener ; translated from the Yiddish and with an
    introduction by Michael Eli Nutkiewicz.
Other titles: Ḳapiṭl Uḳraine. English
Description: Bloomington, Indiana : Slavica, [2022] | Series: New
    approaches to Russian and East European Jewish culture; 7 | Includes
    bibliographical references.
Identifiers: LCCN 2022039221 | ISBN 9780893575113 (paperback)
Subjects: LCSH: Gumener, Eli, 1886-1941--Travel--Ukraine. | Jews--
Ukraine.
    | Humanitarian aid workers--Ukraine--Podillia--Biography. |
    Pogroms--Ukraine--Podillia--History. |
    Jews--Persecutions--Ukraine--Podillia. | Ukraine--History--Revolution,
    1917-1921. | Podillia (Ukraine)--History--20th century.
Classification: LCC D639.J4 G813 2022 | DDC 947.708/4092
    [B]--dc23/eng/20220823
LC record available at https://lccn.loc.gov/2022039221

Slavica Publishers   [Tel.] 1-812-856-4186
Indiana University   [Toll-free] 1-877-SLAVICA
1430 N. Willis Drive   [Fax] 1-812-856-4187
Bloomington, IN 47404-2146   [Email] slavica@indiana.edu
USA   [www] http://www.slavica.com/

Contents

Preface ix

Acknowledgments xv

About the Cover xvii

Note on Transliteration and Translation xix

Figure 1. Eli Gumener, 42 years old. Nowogrodek, 1928 xxi

Figure 2. Gumener family, Nowogrodek, 1938 xxii

Figure 3. Text on the reverse of the Gumener family photo xxii

Introduction xxiii

Figure 4. The Jewish Pale of Settlement, 1905 lxi

Figure 5. Pale of Settlement, 1791–1917 lxii

Brief Chronology lxiii

A Ukrainian Chapter:
A Jewish Aid Worker's Memoir of Sorrow (Podolia, 1918–20)

Title page from the 1921 edition 3

Introduction 5

Komenetz and Podolia 6

February 15, 1919 (Proskurov Pogrom) 7

Order 12

Pogrom Terror in Komenetz and in the District 14

Bolsheviks in Podolia (Spring 1919)... 22

Orinin 26

Vinitza 28

Proskurov 29

Khmelnik 29

Petliura's Army Attacks Podolia (Summer 1919)............................... 32

The Ukrainian Movement and the Jewish Pogroms (Summer 1919) 41

Aid Activity for the Victims 52

The Mood of the Jewish Population under the
Soviet Regime (Summer 1919).. 55

The Situation of the Jews in the Komenetz Period of the UNR 57

The Jewish Ministry in August–November 1919 (Komenetz Period) 61

The Second Death Throes of the UNR 65

Under the Polish Occupation (End of 1919–July 1920)...................... 70

The Komenetz Jewish-American Aid Committee for Pogrom Victims 72

The Polish Assault on Kiev (April–May 1920) 78

Bolsheviks Again in Podolia (Summer 1920) 81

The Ukrainians Retake Komenetz-Podolsk and
the Region (September 1920) 85

Bolsheviks in Komenetz-Podolsk (End of 1920–Beginning of 1921) 87

Our Wanderings in Galicia and Poland 95

Conclusion 96

Appendix No. 1: From the Directory of the
Ukrainian National Republic 98

Appendix No. 2: A Declaration from the Working Group
(Artisans) of the Komenetz Jewish Kehillah (July 6, 1919)............................. 99

Appendix No. 3: The Unification of the Bund with
the Fareynikte in Ukraine.. 101

Appendix No. 4: Circular 102

Appendix No. 5: Petition to the Jewish Ministry 103

Selected Bibliography 105

Preface

Children of Holocaust survivors often sense missing family members who remain abstractly among the living; they are a presence that is not present. In my case, one of these lost relatives was my mother's brother, Elijahu/Ilia (Eli) Gumener (1886–1941?). He was present in my middle name, and he appeared among my mother's photographs. And he was present in a slim clothbound book that stood virtually unnoticed among hundreds of Yiddish volumes in my parents' library. That unassuming book, entitled *A kapitl Ukraine: Tsvey yor in Podolye* (A Ukrainian Chapter: Two Years in Podolia), is an account of my Uncle Eli's experience as an aid worker during the pogroms in Podolia, Ukraine between 1918 and 1920. The title suggests that the book is more than a report; it is a lament for the victims. The word *kapitl* itself brings to mind the Jewish custom of reciting chapters (*kapitlin*) from Psalms at gravesites.

My mother, Betty Gumener Nutkiewicz (1908–85), had told me her brother was a lawyer who was murdered in the Holocaust. But she never mentioned that he had been an aid worker in Ukraine during the Russian Civil War. Nor had she mentioned that he had published a book about his experiences. This book must have had tremendous meaning for my mother as a physical reminder of her dear elder brother. But as with many survivors/refugees, her sadness made it impossible for her to share his full story with me in her lifetime. My discovery of the book after my parents' death illuminated how little I knew of my family who perished.

Even before I began to translate the memoir, a Yiddish inscription on the title page revealed how it came into my mother's hands. The dedication reads: "My friend and colleague I. Drakhler. A memento of joint experiences in Ukraine. A present from the author. November 16, 1921." Yisroel Drakhler was a Russian Jew who also served as a relief worker in Podolia. In 1922 he emigrated to Canada and then moved to Detroit, where he was an educator in Yiddish-speaking circles.[1] My parents lived in Canada and in Detroit during overlapping years. The Nutkiewiczs and Drakhler most certainly were members of the same social circles in both cities, and it was then that Drakhler

---

[1] "Yisroel Drakhler," www.yleksikon.blogspot.com, last modified 6 December 2015.

must have given Eli's memoir to my mother. But how did it come about that by 1941 the Nutkiewiczs were safely in North America and Eli Gumener and his family were murdered in the Soviet Union?

Reconstructing the choices made by Jews in 1930s Europe is complex. Before the concentration camps, ghettos, mass shootings, and death camps, how could they know about the imminent dangers? And even if they "smelled gunpowder in the air," as Eli poignantly notes about Podolia even before the pogrom period, what were the options for leaving? And to what destinations?

Indeed, a chilling glimpse into Eli Gumener's mind barely a year before WWII appears in a photograph among dozens my parents had saved. It depicts his family in April 1938. He wrote on the back: "Who knows if it would not have been better had I emigrated in 1921." Such a thought must have been on the minds of the hundreds of thousands of Jews who had lived through revolution, wars, and the horrific pogroms in Eastern Europe between the two world wars. Working in the border areas of Ukraine, Bessarabia (Romania), and Galicia, Gumener had seen and reported how nearly impossible it was for Jews to escape the war zone. Most hoped to migrate to Western Europe, the United States, or Palestine. But Poland and Romania were not eager to be transit sites for Jewish refugees fleeing west, the United States had passed restrictive emigration quotas in 1921 (and would again in 1924 and 1927) that favored immigrants from northern and western Europe, and Palestine had just become a British mandate. Now Gumener, like the entire Jewish world, was anxiously watching the ominous unfolding events in the 1930s.

My parents Betty and Sergei (1903–88) decided to leave Poland on the eve of the German occupation in 1939. Sergei had been a well-known leader in the Bund, the Jewish socialist party. From 1935 to 1938 he was a member of the Łodz city council elected on the Bund Party ticket. Fearing that if Nazi Germany invaded Poland, the Germans would target Jewish political leaders, they fled Warsaw for Vilna in August. Vilna was ruled by the Soviet Union after the so-called Molotov-Ribbentrop pact gave Lithuania and eastern Poland (known as the *kresy* or "borderlands") to the Soviets and western Poland to Germany. Betty and Sergei were among approximately 15,000 Polish Jews who fled to Lithuania at the outbreak of the war.

Why did they go first to Vilna? Betty knew the city well, having studied art education at Vilnius University and taught at the Jewish Teachers Institute. But they did not remain there long. They soon joined Eli, who lived about 80 miles away in Nowogrodek. It had been part of Poland but was then included in the Byelorussian Soviet Socialist Republic as a result of the Molotov-Ribbentrop pact.

My parents were determined to leave Europe altogether in hopes of reaching North America. It seems a bold decision since they had no relatives there. In February 1941, Betty and Sergei were lucky to receive two rare transit visas for Japan. They took a train to Moscow, continued by the Trans-Siberian Railway to Vladivostok, boarded a Japanese ship to Tsuruga, and finally went by rail to Kobe. They lived in Kobe from February to June 1941 when they received another stroke of luck: permission to immigrate to Canada just a few months before Pearl Harbor, arriving in Vancouver on the ship *Hikawa Maru* on June 17, 1941, its last voyage before the United States and Japan went to war in December.

I do not know why Eli did not join his sister and Sergei in their flight from Europe to Canada. It may be simply that he was unable to obtain visas for himself, his wife, and two children. Like many people, he probably did not imagine that Germany would invade the Soviet Union. He was active in Nowogrodek's Jewish community and engaged professionally in aid work for refugee children on behalf of the American Jewish Joint Distribution Committee (JDC) in various parts of Eastern Europe. By contrast, Betty and Sergei had already left their home and jobs and did not have children. Thus, Eli was still in Nowogrodek with his family when the Germans entered their city on July 4, 1941. Later that year or in early 1942, the Germans shot him, his wife Rachel (née Czacka), and their 13-year-old daughter Genia. Their son Pinchas, a university student in Lvov (in Russian; Lemberik or Lemberg in Yiddish; Lwow in Polish; Lviv in Ukrainian), escaped the fate of the rest of his family: he joined relatives in Kuibyshev (now Samara) in the lower Volga region, where the German army never reached.

Although I did not know these details about my Uncle Eli's family and history when I discovered his memoir in my parents' library, I was immediately intrigued as I began to explore its contents. I was amazed to learn that Eli and I had more in common than our name and a distant familial connection. Without even knowing about my uncle's work with refugees and survivors of armed conflict, I had spent much of my professional life working in agencies that provide help to refugees and victims of state-sponsored torture. Moreover, Gumener makes the motive for his testimony clear: "I simply want to record what I know for future historians who will want to write the bloody tragedy of a powerless people put to the sword, and of the heroic moments that make up the thorny wreath of martyrdom of Podolia."[2] I had also grappled with narratives of trauma while working for the Shoah Foundation collecting survivor interviews.[3]

---

[2] Eli Gumener, *A kapitl Ukraine: Tsvey yor in Podolye* [A Ukrainian chapter: Two years in Podolia] (Vilna: Sreberk Publisher, 1921), introduction.

[3] Michael Nutkiewicz, "Shame, Guilt, and Anguish in Holocaust Survivor Testimony," *The Oral History Review* 30, 1 (2003): 1–22.

The "thorny wreath" described by Gumener occurred between 1918 and 1920 in Ukraine, which soon after the October 1917 Russian Revolution became the battlefield for competing powers and the scene of an estimated 1,200 to 1,500 pogroms. These armed conflicts and assaults against Jews caused the largest number of Jewish deaths and displacements in Jewish history until the Holocaust.

Why should we care about this century-old memoir that is neither part of the literature of survivors nor even meant to be a complete history of the period? The reason is that Gumener provides a bird's-eye view of the challenges of a problem that still confronts us in the 21st century: how to adequately respond to the suffering and dislocation that inevitably accompanies war and civil strife. *A kapitl Ukraine* presents a unique perspective on the powerlessness of individuals, parties, and organizations to address a humanitarian crisis facing Jewish communities in Ukraine.

His particular focus is the most horrific period of the Russian Civil War and is illustrative of a genre of writing called "microhistory": Gumener describes just two years in Podolia, revealing how he conducted himself within that time frame and geographical space.[4] His book is an ideologically tinged account of Jewish party politics, a perspective we must keep in mind as we read it through. Yet it is set in a broader context: pogroms in a particular region and the experiences of the day-to-day life of an average aid worker "in the trenches."[5] It is one of the few surviving memoirs from this period by a relief worker, and as such, is a highly valuable and rare historical source about men and women who faced constant danger as they tried to alleviate the suffering of their brethren. For those reasons, *A kapitl Ukraine* is a worthy memoir to read and to ponder. I dedicate this work to the memory of Elijahu Gumener and to the hundreds of nameless and unrecognized professionals

---

[4] Some of the better-known works of microhistory include Carlo Ginzburg, *The Cheese and the Worms: The Cosmos of a Sixteenth-Century Miller* (Baltimore: Johns Hopkins University Press, 1980); Natalie Zemon Davis, *The Return of Martin Guerre* (Cambridge, MA: Harvard University Press, 1983); Sarah Maza, *Violette Nozière: A Story of Murder in 1930s Paris* (Berkeley: University of California Press, 2011); Alexandra Garbarini, *Numbered Days: Diary Writing and the Holocaust* (New Haven: Yale University Press, 2006), and her *"A Terrible and Terribly Interesting Epoch": The Holocaust Diary of Lucien Dreyfus* (Lanham, MD: Rowman & Littlefield, 2021).

[5] Jaclyn Granick has recently published the first account of Jewish humanitarian aid in the interwar period. See Jaclyn Granick, *International Jewish Humanitarianism in the Age of the Great War* (Cambridge: Cambridge University Press, 2021).

who toiled in the war zones of Ukraine and indeed across the entire Pale of Settlement between 1914 and 1921.[6]

Michael Eli Nutkiewicz

---

[6] The Russian Empire before the Russian Revolution included the Pale of Settlement—essentially a vast "reservation" of towns and villages where Jews numbered five million and constituted more than 90 percent of the population. The territory included most of what is now Ukraine, parts of Belarus, Poland, and Lithuania.

Acknowledgments

I am grateful to the Archives of the American Jewish Joint Distribution Committee (JDC) for the timely and generous Fred and Ellen Lewis/ JDC Archives Fellowship. Special thanks go to Isabelle Rohr, Manager of Academic Programs and Outreach, and Misha Mitsel, Senior Archivist, for their invaluable help. I thank Slavica Publishers for publishing the memoir, and to Vicki Polonsky for her editorial advice.

I express my deepest appreciation to Beni Warshawsky (Los Angeles) for his indispensable collaboration on a complete first draft of the translation, and to Noah Barrera for reviewing and editing the final draft.

David Engel (NYU), Steven Zipperstein (Stanford University), and David (UC Davis) and Rachel Biale, friends since our graduate school days at UCLA, encouraged me to take on this project, and each gave me invaluable advice. Brian Horowitz's (Tulane University) vast scholarship on late 19th-century Russia was essential preparatory reading for this project. Brian once told me that he has a special fondness for the *klal tuer*, and I hope that this translation and introduction brings one *klal tuer* to life.

When I submitted this manuscript to Slavica Publishers in October 2021, I did not know how Eli Gumener's son, Pinchas, survived the Holocaust. Then in November I received out of the blue an email written in Russian accompanied by the Google translation in English: "Hello. I am the son of Pyotr Gumener.… If there is a desire and an opportunity, please respond. Sincerely, Alexander Klyukin." He had found me through the genealogy website JewishGen. I thank Alexander (Sasha) for the moving revelation that a remnant of Eli's immediate family is thriving.

Polly Zavadivker (University of Delaware) and Jaclyn Granick (Cardiff University) were the first scholars I contacted for information about relief work in Eastern Europe. I regard this translation of Gumener's memoir as a modest contribution to their exemplary scholarship on Jewish aid in the interwar period. I feel lucky to have received Jaclyn's book on Jewish humanitarian aid just weeks before I submitted my manuscript to Slavica Publishers.

A huge thank you goes to Dimitri Tolkatsch (Freiburg), who received an inquiry from a stranger in Albuquerque, and after a generous reply, was showered with many more questions, which he tirelessly answered in detail. Without him, I would have been lost in some of the weeds of Ukrainian history during the revolutionary period. I am grateful to Joshua Myers (Boston) for correspondence about Jewish socialist parties in the interwar period, Vassili Schedrin (Queen's University) for clarifying facts about Soviet Russia during the Civil War, Thomas Chopard (École des Hautes Études en Sciences Sociales) for assistance in chasing down biographical information about the atamans mentioned by Gumener, and Yannay Spitzer (Hebrew University) for clarifying the 1897 Russian census.

Although Gumener's memoir was written in Yiddish, it has scattered Russian and Ukrainian words and references. Tamara Tomasson (Albuquerque) and Yuliya Sofronova (Albuquerque) generously translated Russian documents and explained Russian terms. Heidi Lerner (Stanford University) assisted me with transliteration, both Yiddish and Russian. I express my special gratitude to Dominika Laster (University of New Mexico) for translating Gumener's chilling Polish sentiment on the back of a family photograph, and to Dov-Ber Kerler (Indiana University) for deciphering Gumener's handwritten dedication on the cover of *A kapitl Ukraine*. Warm thanks to Michelle Futornick (Stanford University), friend and editor extraordinaire, for her close reading of the preface and introduction, and for pushing me to go deeper.

Thanks to Laima Lauckaite and Aleksandra Jacovskyte (Vilna Gaon Museum of Jewish History, Vilnius, Lithuania) and Renata Piatkowska (Museum of the History of Polish Jews, Warsaw) for verifying that the bold and terrifying graphic on the cover of Gumener's memoir is indeed that of artist Mojzesz Lejbowski. Richard Pontius of the National Center for Jewish Film sent me the annotation for the 1931 film on Nowodrodek. For leads, suggestions, and contacts, thanks go to Susan DeMasi, Daniel Heller, Sarah Nadia Lipes, David Mazower, Brendan McGeever, Kenneth Moss, David Morris, Leonid Smilovitsky, Darius Staliunas, Mark Von Hagen, Theodore Weeks, and Jacob Wisse.

It would be futile to properly express my thanks to Joan Weissman, my dear partner. She is my sounding board, most perceptive reader, and the model of strength and sanity in an uncertain world. She has my deepest love and admiration.

My earliest motive for translating Eli Gumener's memoir was the desire to transmit family history to my children. But as I wrote in the preface, the memoir became something more than sharing a legacy, and even more than honoring a man who gave his life to his people. In Rivka, Racheli, Malka, Shula, and Noam, I am fortunate to have children who are curious and who care about familial and Jewish history. May the past continue to inspire and to guide them.

About the Cover

Mojzesz Lejbowski (1876–1942)

We do not know whether Eli Gumener or his publisher, Shloyme-Zanvl Sreberk, chose to include the unsettling pen and ink illustration for the cover of *A kapitl Ukraine*. Nor do we know if the artist Mojzesz Lejbowski and Eli Gumener were acquainted. I believe, however, that a word about the artist is important because the lives of Lejbowski and the Gumener family had several intersecting points.

Mojzesz Lejbowski was born in Nowogrodek, the town where Eli Gumener settled in 1925. Lejbowski studied art in Vilna, the city where Gumener's sister Betty (my mother) had attended the University of Vilnius with a major in fine arts. After studying in Paris, Lejbowski returned to Vilna in 1917 to teach art at the Jewish gymnasium and to establish a private art school. He was also chair of the Vilna Society of Jewish Artists. From 1924 to 1927, Betty was taking drawing courses in Vilna—whether in Lejbowski's school is unknown—and taught art at the Jewish Teachers Institute. In 1940, when Betty Gumener and my father Sergei fled Warsaw to Vilna in the face of Nazi Germany's invasion of Poland, Lejbowski was still teaching art in the city.

Lejbowski was forced into the Vilna ghetto in 1941, the year that Betty and Sergei escaped to Japan. He was killed in the ghetto in 1942/3.

The pen and ink drawing depicts a Jewish man—perhaps a prophet—lamenting over the body of a dead woman and her child. Blood drips from the Yiddish word "Ukraine" in the title. The drawing is reminiscent of others on the same theme, including Rembrandt's *Jeremiah Lamenting the Destruction of Jerusalem*, which would be a fitting image for the fate of the Jews of Ukraine.

Note on Transliteration and Translation

Most place names follow the JewishGen "Town Finder" database, which provides the names of towns, districts, provinces, and countries before World War I, between the wars, after World War II, and at present (www.jewishgen.org). I privilege the Yiddish rendition of place names simply because Gumener wrote in Yiddish for Yiddish readers. There are some exceptions: Podolia, Volhynia, Kiev, and a few more. Russian names as they would have been in Gumener's time and modern Ukrainian names are in the footnotes. In addition, I have provided the distance in miles ("as the crow flies") between each town that Gumener mentions and Komenetz-Podolsk to give a sense of the length and breadth of the territory where he worked—and the miles he was sometimes forced to flee. These distances are taken from the FreeMapTools website (www.freemaptools.com) and are included in the footnotes.

The names of Jewish political parties follow the *YIVO Encyclopedia of Jews in Eastern Europe* (www.yivoencyclopedia.org). The names of Ukrainian political parties follow the *Internet Encyclopedia of Ukraine* (www.encyclopediaofukraine.com). I only capitalized names of groups or organizations that I could identify or whom Gumener specified.

I have left most Jewish holidays and religious terms in Yiddish transliteration to give a flavor of the "Jewish" feeling of the narrative. Hence, shabbes, not Shabbat; t'ilm, not the English "Psalms" or the Hebrew "tehillim."

In a few places I added a date or a few words that were not in the text in order to clarify Gumener's meaning. These additions are in brackets. Unless otherwise noted, the footnotes are mine.

Figure 1. Eli Gumener, 42 years old. Nowogrodek, 1928.

Figure 2. Gumener family, Nowogrodek, 1938. Left to right: Pinhas, Betty, Genia, Rachel, Eli.

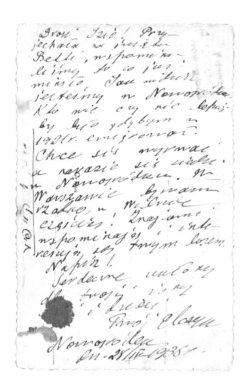

Figure 3. The highlighted passage on the reverse of the above photo reads: "Who knows if it would not have been better had I emigrated in 1921."

Introduction: A Memoir of Sorrow

The Challenges of Navigating *A kapitl Ukraine*

A kapitl Ukraine is set in the Podolia region of Ukraine during the civil wars that followed the Russian Revolution. The Ukrainian-Soviet War, which was fought by Ukrainians to establish sovereignty and by the Bolsheviks to retain control of imperial Russian territory, began after the Bolshevik victory in October 1917. It was one of several overlapping and parallel wars fought wholly or partially on Ukrainian soil: the Red Army against the anti-Bolshevik White Army, the Polish-Ukrainian War for eastern Galicia, and the Polish-Soviet War.[1] It was also a period of pogroms against the Jews, and Gumener's memoir covers the most devastating years, 1918 to 1920.

The desperate years portrayed in Gumener's memoir present substantial challenges to the researcher. Cities, towns, and villages lay open to multiple armies, militias, and bands of fighters that repeatedly occupied, retreated from, and reoccupied the region. Reconstructing the microhistory of individual locations, especially small towns and villages, is very difficult.[2] There were weeks and months in which aid workers could not communicate with their parent organizations such as the Petrograd-based Jewish Committee for Aid

---

[1] For an overview of the period, see Laura Engelstein, *Russia in Flames: War, Revolution, Civil War, 1914–1921* (New York: Oxford University Press, 2018); Timothy Snyder, *The Reconstruction of Nations: Poland, Ukraine, Lithuania, Belarus, 1569–1999* (New Haven: Yale University Press, 2003); John S. Reshetar, Jr., *The Ukrainian Revolution, 1917–1920: A Study in Nationalism* (Princeton, NJ: Princeton University Press, 1952); Serhy Yekelchyk, *Ukraine: Birth of a Modern Nation* (New York: Oxford University Press, 2007); Geoff Eley, "Remapping the Nation: War, Revolutionary Upheaval and State Formation in Eastern Europe, 1914–1923," in *Ukrainian-Jewish Relations in Historical Perspective,* ed. Peter J. Potichnyj and Howard Aster (Edmonton: Canadian Institute of Ukrainian Studies, 1990), 205–46; Paul Robert Magocsi and Yohanan Petrovsky-Shtern, *Jews and Ukrainians: A Millennium of Co-Existence* (Toronto: University of Toronto Press, 2016), 11–65.

[2] On the challenges of reconstructing daily life in wartime, see S. Johnson, "The Daily Lives of Civilians in the Russian Civil War," in *Daily Lives of Civilians in Wartime Twentieth-Century Europe*, ed. Nicholas Atkin (Westport, CT: Greenwood Press, 2008), 49–72.

to War Victims (EKOPO) and the American Jewish Joint Distribution Committee (JDC), whose offices were in Warsaw and other Eastern European cities.[3]

Gumener writes in the preface that he lost his original notes from the field upon which the memoir is based. His recreated manuscript was published by the Vilna publishing house of Shloyme-Zanvl Sreberk, known for issuing popular works in Yiddish, including Simon Dubnow's *World History of the Jewish People*, grammar books by Zalman Reyzen, literature, natural history texts for teachers, and other titles. Although there are moments of poetic anguish, Gumener's work is not an example of literary prose. He wrote in a very idiomatic Yiddish. The work lies somewhere between documentation and memorialization, between a chronicle and a memoir. (I will refer to the work as a "memoir.") He does not offer a sustained detailed narrative. The chronology is compressed and disjointed. We do not get deep portraits of individuals. He is only occasionally meditative and provides virtually no details about his personal life.

In addition, many of the names of aid organizations are generic in Yiddish: e.g., Tsentraln Yidishn Komitet, the "central Jewish committee...." It is often difficult to untangle which organization is being referenced: the committee in Kiev or the one in Komenetz-Podolsk? Another term that is often difficult to pin down is "central" or "the center." It could mean some kind of higher authority in the Ukrainian National Republic or in the Soviet hierarchy. The term might refer to an authority located at the level of a provincial capital, or in Petrograd or Kiev. And, actual political and organizational hierarchies could differ from official ones. For example, Gumener writes about a "Jewish socialist council" in Komenetz that was sanctioned by the local revkom despite the fact that the Soviet authority in Kiev (and Moscow) prohibited supporting Jewish political parties that were deemed "nationalistic" and thus divisive, from the Bolshevik point of view, to the unity of the international proletarian movement.[4]

Gumener was writing for an audience familiar with his references to places, people, and organizations. The contemporary reader, however, will

---

[3] Established in 1914 in Petrograd, EKOPO (Evreiskii komitet dlia pomoshchi zhertvam voiny), also spelled as YEKOPO, was the Jewish Committee for Aid to War Victims. The American Jewish Joint Distribution Committee (the "Joint" or JDC) is an American Jewish relief agency founded in New York in 1914 as an umbrella organization for the distribution of aid to Jews who lived in war-torn regions, as well as the Jewish poor in Palestine. The organization remains one of the most important aid organizations in the Jewish world. For an account of the JDC's work in Ukraine during the Civil War, see Michael Beizer, *Relief in Time of Need: Russian Jewry and the Joint, 1914–24* (Bloomington, IN: Slavica, 2015), 1–51.

[4] Gumener, *A kapitl Ukraine*, 40. In December 1918, the Bolsheviks established revkoms (revolutionary committees) in areas controlled by the Red Army.

find it challenging to navigate this complex history. This introduction and the annotations to the translation serve as a roadmap for the reader by highlighting the memoir's institutional, intellectual, and cultural history, as well as its larger social and political contexts. Specifically, this means identifying and describing the sources, personalities, and institutions mentioned by Gumener. Unfortunately, there are still some persons whom I could not identify. Perhaps historians with access to archives in Russia, Belarus, Lithuania, and Poland will someday uncover more information about them.

Yet even if his chronology is imperfect in its detail, Gumener still relates a story that must be told, namely, the ravages of the pogroms and the tragedy of Jewish communities. And he is also brutally honest, bringing a special, and critical, focus on the role that Jewish politics played in organizing aid for localities devastated by pogroms.

Gumener was a klal-tuer, the Yiddish term for a communal activist. There is little scholarship about lesser-known Jewish activists engaged in aid work between World War I and World War II, and a full biography of an ordinary klal-tuer has yet to be written.[5] It is easy to assume that Gumener was merely a secondary figure. He did not possess the literary power of an activist such as S. An-sky (1863–1920), the renowned author of the play *The Dybbuk*, who was an ethnographer and aid worker; nor was he a compelling narrator like Isaac Babel (1894–1940) who, although not engaged in relief work, wrote a chilling diary about his experiences with the Red Army in Galicia in 1920.[6] Gumener was not a systematic collector of data like Elias Tcherikower, who left Kiev

---

[5] The humanitarian crisis in Eastern European Jewish society brought about by World War I resulted in a new kind of person, namely, the klal-tuer: a secular Jew with professional training (e.g., law, education, journalism) and usually a member of a Jewish political party. Historian Steven Zipperstein termed this cohort "the Third Force." These young professionals slowly superseded the traditional wealthy philanthropists who were based in capital cities (e.g., the St. Petersburg banker and art patron Baron Evzel Gintsburg (1812–78) and the Kiev sugar magnate Lazar Brodsky (1848–1904), emerging as organizers for aid and front-line activists during the interwar period. See Steven Zipperstein, "The Politics of Relief: The Transformation of Russian Jewish Communal Life during the First World War," *Studies in Contemporary Jewry* 4 (1988): 22–40. Brian Horowitz shows that this trend was already beginning in the late 19th century. Brian Horowitz, *Jewish Philanthropy and Enlightenment in Late-Tsarist Russia* (Seattle: University of Washington Press, 2009), 88–93.

[6] *1915 Diary of S. An-sky: A Russian Jewish Writer at the Eastern Front*, trans. Polly Zavadivker (Bloomington: Indiana University Press, 2016). The diary was the basis for his Yiddish memoir, *Der Yudisher Khurban fun poylen galitsye un bukovina, fun tog-bukh 1914–1917* (The Jewish Catastrophe in Polish Galicia and Bukovina from the 1914–1917 Diary). An edited English version was published as *The Enemy at His Pleasure. A Journey through the Jewish Pale of Settlement during World War I*, ed. and trans. Joachim Neugroschel (New York: Metropolitan Books, 2002). For a biography of An-sky, see Gabri-

in 1921 for Berlin with a trove of documentation about the pogroms that became the basis for the massive *In der tkufe fun revolutsye, memuarn, materyaln,
dokumentn* (In the Era of Revolution: Memoirs, Materials, Documents). Other
major contributions were made by Nokhem Shtif, who published his history
of the pogrom in 1922, Joseph Schechtman's 1927 work, *Ver iz farantvortlikh far
di pogromen in ukrayne* (Who Is Responsible for the Pogroms in Ukraine), and
the Latvian-born lawyer Elias Heifetz, who left Russia in 1920 for the United
States, where he compiled the material that would become *The Slaughter of
the Jews in Ukraine in 1919.*[7] It does not follow, however, that Gumener's book
is therefore unimportant to social and political historians and readers interested in the literature of memory. In order to discern the internal dynamics of
Jewish aid work, community organizing, and party relationships at the local
level, we must retrieve and examine the impressions of ordinary workers in
the field.

Several pertinent diaries and memoirs by important writers have recently
been translated into English. But they do not encompass the years described
in Gumener's account, and they are not specifically about Podolia. An-sky's
fragmented diary, translated by Polly Zavadivker, covers only a short period
in 1915 when he was in eastern Galicia and Bukovina and ends well before
1919—the most horrific pogrom year. Isaac Babel's diary, translated from the
Russian by H. T. Willetts, begins in June/July 1920 and ends a few months
later.[8] By contrast, Gumener devotes his work to the period between An-sky's

---

ella Safran, *Wandering Soul: The Dybbuk's Creator, S. An-sky* (Cambridge, MA: Harvard
University Press, 2010).

[7] E. Tcherikower, *In der tkufe fun revolutsye, memuarn, materyaln, dokumentn* [In the era
of revolution: Memoirs, materials, documents] (Berlin: Historical Archive of Eastern
Jewry, 1924). Tcherikower (1881–1943) spent some of the war years in New York. He
lived in Kiev in 1918 and in 1921 left for Berlin. Nokhem Shtif's *Pogromen in ukrayne:
Di tsayt fun der frayviliger armey* (The Pogroms in Ukraine: The period of the Volunteer
Army) was published in Russian in 1922, then in Yiddish in 1923. Shtif (1879–1933)
was active in EKOPO, the main Jewish aid organization in Russia in the interwar
period. In 1922 he moved to Berlin where he published his work on the pogroms.
See Nokhem Shtif, "The Pogroms in Ukraine: The Period of the Volunteer Army,"
trans. Maurice Wolfthal, *In geveb: A Journal of Yiddish Studies*, September 2016, http://
ingeveb.org/texts-and-translations/the-pogroms-in-ukraine-the-period-of-the-volunteer-army; Joseph Schechtman (1891–1970), *Ver iz farantvortlikh far di pogromen in ukrayne* [Who is
responsible for the pogroms in Ukraine] (Paris, 1927); and Elias Heifetz (ca. 1885–?),
The Slaughter of the Jews in the Ukraine in 1919 (New York: Seltzer, 1921), which was published for the People's Relief Committee for Jewish War Sufferers in America.

[8] Isaac Babel traveled with the Cossack cavalry during the Polish-Soviet War of
1919–20. His diary includes descriptions of pogroms perpetrated by the Cossacks that
fought on the side of the Red Army. This experience became the basis for his collection
of stories called *Red Cavalry*. See Isaac Babel, *1920 Diary*, trans. H. T. Willetts (New

and Babel's diaries, and thus constitutes a complementary contribution to the memoir literature of the time.

There are other untranslated Yiddish works, not all written by aid workers, that fill out the picture of life in the pogrom period. For example, Rokhl Faygenberg's (1885–1972) *A pinkes fun a toyter shtot, khurbn dubove* (A Record of a Dead City. The Destruction of Dubove, 1926) focuses on a town in the Minsk district. Her *Bay di bregn fun Dniester* (On the Banks of the Dniester), published in 1925, details her experiences living with Jewish refugees on the Bessarabian-Ukrainian border.[9] Max Sadikov (1893–?), who was an aid worker in Podolia at the same time as Gumener, penned *In yene teg: Zikhroynes vegen der rusisher revolutsye un di ukrayner pogromen* (In Those Days: Memoirs of the Russian Revolution and the Ukrainian Pogroms, 1926).[10] Gumener's fellow klal-tauer, Yisroel Drakhter (1885–1948), wrote sketches about children in the pogrom period: *Mayses fun a kleynem vanderer, erinerungen fun a yidishn yingl in ukrayne beys der milhome un pogromen* (Stories of a Little Wanderer: The Experiences of a Jewish Boy in Ukraine During the War and Pogroms).[11] Itsik Kipnis's (1896–1974) well-known but yet-to-be translated Yiddish work *Khadoshim un teg, a khronik* (Months and Days: A Chronicle), describes the pogrom that engulfed his small Ukrainian town in the Zhitomir district of Volhynia. It was first published in Kiev in 1926 and is a semi-autographical literary work that depicts broader personal and historical events than the pogroms.[12]

Haven: Yale University Press, 1995). For information about Babel, see Gregory Freiden, ed., *The Enigma of Isaac Babel: Biography, History, Context* (Stanford, CA: Stanford University Press, 2009).

[9] Rokhl Faygenberg, *A pinkes fun a toyter shtot: Khurbn dubove* [A record of a dead city: The destruction of Dubove] (Warsaw, 1926); and *Bay di bregn fun Dniester* [On the banks of the Dniester] (Warsaw, 1925).

[10] Max Sadikov, *In yene teg: Zikhroynes vegen der rusisher revolutsye un di ukrayner pogromen* [In those days: Memoirs of the Russian Revolution and the Ukrainian pogroms] (New York, 1926), https://www.yiddishbookcenter.org/collections/yiddish-books/spb-nybc208816/sadikoff-max-in-yene-teg-zikhroynes-vegen-der-rusisher-revolutsye-un-di.

[11] Yisroel Drakhter, *Mayses fun a kleynem vanderer: Erinerungen fun a yidishn yingl in ukrayne beys der milhome un pogromen* [Stories of a little wanderer: The experiences of a Jewish boy in Ukraine during the war and pogroms] (Vilna, 1928).

[12] Itsik Kipnis, *Khadoshim un teg: A khronik* [Months and days: A chronicle] (Vilna: B. Kletskin, 1929; repr., Tel Aviv: Y. L. Perets, 1973). Accessed at National Yiddish Book Center, https://www.yiddishbookcenter.org/collections/yiddish-books/spb-nybc200477/kipnis-itzik-hadoshim-un-teg-un-andere-dertseylungen. I have cited only a small number of Yiddish-language memoirs. There are also Russian-language sources that deserve to be explored by future researchers. A relatively recent discovery of the multivolume Hebrew anthology of survivor testimony collected by Eliezer David Rosenthal (1856–1932) deserves close study. For the history of the anthology and its content, see Gur

Other publications about Ukraine during the pogrom period were written by well-known Jewish politicians who were active during the short-lived Ukrainian National Republic (UNR) and advocated for a Jewish national presence within an independent and sovereign Ukraine.[13] They were politicians, not aid workers, and did not labor in the landscape of destruction.

A rich scholarship has emerged about aid work before the Russian Revolution (1914–17) and after the Red Army conquered Ukraine and pacified the area (1921–37).[14] Gumener's account uniquely augments the investigations of scholars who write about aid in the interwar period. He treats an aspect of the subject that deserves to be rescued from neglect: namely, the role

---

Alroey, "Documenting the Pogroms in Ukraine, 1918–1920: Eliezer David Rosenthal's *Megilat Hatevah*," *Gal-Ed: On the History and Culture of Polish Jewry* 24 (2015): 63–102.

[13] Moshe Silberfarb [Zilberfarb], *The Jewish Ministry and Jewish National Autonomy in Ukraine*, trans. D. Lincoln (New York: Aleph Press, 1993). Silberfarb (1876–1934) served as vice secretary for Jewish affairs in the Central Rada and became the general secretary for Jewish affairs. Solomon I. Goldelman, *Jewish National Autonomy in Ukraine 1917–1920*, trans. Michael Luchkovich (Chicago: Ukrainian Research and Information Institute, 1968). Goldelman (1885–1974) held several offices in the Ukrainian government, including secretary of labor and acting secretary for national minorities. He emigrated to Vienna in 1920, and in 1939 to Palestine. His books *Jewish National Autonomy in Ukraine, 1917–1920* and *Letters from a Jewish Social Democrat about Ukraine* were published in Vienna in 1921. Abraham Revutsky (1889–1946) was minister for Jewish affairs for a short while. He attempted to settle in Palestine in 1920, but the British expelled him the following year. In 1925 he moved to the United States. Revutsky's and Goldelman's memoirs focus on activities related to establishing Jewish national autonomy within the UNR. The pogroms do not play a central role in their accounts. Another source of information about the period comes from memorial books (Yiddish: yizkor bikher). A study of these works would help develop a substantive account of what a klal-tuer meant and did in the interwar period.

[14] Polly Zavadivker, "Fighting 'On Our Own Territory': The Relief, Rescue, and Representation of Jews in Russia during World War I," in *Russia's Home Front in War and Revolution, 1914–22, Book 2: The Experience of War and Revolution*, ed. Adele Lindenmeyr, Christopher Read, and Peter Waldron (Bloomington, IN: Slavica, 2016), 79–105; Jaclyn Granick, "Waging Relief: The Politics and Logistics of American War Relief in Europe and the Near East (1914–1918)," *First World War Studies* 5, 1 (2014): 55–68, https://doi.org/10.1080/19475020.2014.901183; Beizer, *Relief in Time of Need*. For the period after the pacification of Ukraine, see Jaclyn Granick, "The First American Organization in Soviet Russia: JDC and Relief in the Ukraine, 1920–1923," in *The JDC at 100: A Century of Humanitarianism*, ed. Avinoam J. Patt, Atina Grossmann, Linda G. Levi, and Maud S. Mandel (Detroit: Wayne State University Press, 2019), 61–93. Peter Gatrell, *A Whole Empire Walking: Refugees in Russia during World War I* (Bloomington: Indiana University Press, 1999), does not specifically examine the pogrom victims. For the final large-scale aid work in Ukraine, see Allan L. Kagedan, "American Jews and the Soviet Experiment: The Agro-Joint Project, 1924–1937," *Jewish Social Studies* 43, 2 (1981): 153–64.

that Jewish politics played in organizing aid for localities devastated by pogroms. His particular focus is the discord between Jewish political parties in Komenetz-Podolsk (Yiddish) (Kamenets Podolskiy in Russian, Kamyanets-Podilskyy in Ukrainian—the capital of Podolia in imperial Russia from 1797 to 1917 that periodically served as the administrative capital of the Ukrainian National Republic from 1917–20. Gumener repeatedly describes the failure of Jewish parties to work in a concerted manner. "Had there been a greater effort on the part of the party activists among the Jewish population the victims could have been cared for and their terrible trauma somewhat lightened," he states.[15] He describes how ideology often determined who would receive aid, where that aid would go, and how political parties used aid to pursue their political and ideological ends. For Gumener, politics was one of the factors that hindered the aid effort and is a prominent theme in his memoir.[16]

Gumener himself was not neutral in his assessment. His views are presented through the perspective of an anti-Bolshevik socialist. He blames "the

---

[15] Gumener, *A kapitl Ukraine*, 76.

[16] The notion of "political party" was entirely different than the American idea of a political party. In the United States a political party is the vehicle by which candidates are elected to public office. By contrast, the function of political parties in late 19th- and early 20th-century Eastern Europe was infinitely more inclusive of the social and economic needs of its followers. For example, the range of activities of the Jewish Labor Bund included establishing libraries, clubs, evening courses, choral and drama groups, consumer and producer's cooperatives, and national organizations such as Zukunft, Sotsialisticher kinder farband (Socialist Children's Union, SKIF), Yidisher arbiter froy (Jewish Working Women, YAF), and even a central system of Yiddish secular schools in Poland. Zionists and other political parties had many analogous institutions. Before the late 19th century, the kehillah (the local administrative and religious corporate body) was the sole institution that organized Jewish life. Generally run by a wealthy or influential elite, it raised taxes and distributed funds, and supervised the public, private, and ritualistic life of the community through Jewish law (halacha). By the early 20th century, Jewish political parties competed with the traditional kehillah for resources and the right to distribute funds. Thus, the struggle for funds was also related to the desire of parties to attract members of the Jewish community. Gumener's memoir chronicles both the competition for influence between parties and the kehillah, and among parties with different ideological outlooks. For an overview of the Bund's inclusive activities, see Jack Jacobs, *Bundist Counterculture in Interwar Poland* (Syracuse: Syracuse University Press, 2009). On both Bundism and Zionism, see Zvi Gitelman, ed., *The Emergence of Modern Jewish Politics: Bundism and Zionism in Eastern Europe* (Pittsburgh: University of Pittsburgh Press, 2003). For a rich understanding of the kehillah, see Yohanan Petrovsky-Shtern, *The Golden Age Shtetl: A New History of Jewish Life in East Europe* (Princeton, NJ: Princeton University Press, 2014); and Eli Lederhendler, *The Road to Modern Jewish Politics: Political Tradition and Political Reconstruction in the Jewish Community of Tsarist Russia* (New York: Cambridge University Press, 1989).

right" for its self-interested refusal to work with socialists. By "right" he means Zionists and the kehillah, the prewar traditional communal establishment. But it is clear from his narrative that the socialists themselves were not always keen on making alliances with parties from different political orientations.

Reconstructing local Jewish political activities in this period is challenging. Parties generally had left, middle, and right-wing factions that split and formed other parties. The ins and outs of parties vying for power and influence were dizzying. There were breakaway parties that played only short roles in communal affairs. For example, Gumener was a member of the Fareynikte, founded in 1917, which, with the larger Jewish Labor Bund and Poale Tsiyon was the voice of socialism on the Jewish street.[17] But he writes about the creation of a new party, the Fareynikte Bund in spring 1919 in Komenetz-Podolsk. There is no mention of this party in any of the secondary literature.

The divisiveness among parties along competing ideological visions was already in place before the war and is a well-known element in the story of modern Jewish politics.[18] Gumener's memoir contributes to our understanding of the practical consequences of this discord for aid efforts in Jewish communities under stress. From his description, it is easy to conclude that aid was not efficacious during the years he was active. But it is not the contemporary historian's right to judge the efforts of recently established humanitarian organizations working feverishly to provide aid under conditions of unprecedented violence and chaos. Rather, we read *A kapitl Ukraine* simply to understand how one activist in the field framed and understood the relief effort.

---

[17] Founded in 1897 in Vilna, the Bund (Der algemeyner yidisher arbeter bund, General Union of Jewish Workers) was a socialist organization that championed "national cultural autonomy"—an ideology that advocated for rights for minorities dispersed within a given territory or across territories. With such rights in place, the Jewish working class could pursue collective social, educational, and cultural objectives. Established in 1917, the Fareynikte (Fareynikte yidishe sotsialistishe arbiter-partey, United Jewish Socialist Workers' Party) was a socialist party that advocated Jewish "national political autonomy." Like the Bund, it emphasized culture and education but also advocated creating an autonomous political infrastructure that would administer the Jewish community. Both ideologies rejected the idea of a particular territory for the Jews. Poale Tsiyon ("Workers of Zion," the Jewish Social Democratic Labor Party) was a Zionist socialist political party founded in 1906. Its vision was territorial autonomy in Palestine on a socialist basis. Until that goal was achieved, it supported the idea of national cultural autonomy in the lands where Jews lived.

[18] The material on early 20th-century and interwar Jewish politics in Eastern Europe is rich. Some of the more general works include Jonathan Frankel, *Prophecy and Politics: Socialism, Nationalism, and the Russian Jews, 1862–1917* (New York: Cambridge University Press, 1981); Ezra Mendelsohn, *On Modern Jewish Politics* (New York: Oxford University Press, 1993); and Gitelman, *Emergence of Modern Jewish Politics.*

A Biographical Sketch of Eli Gumener

Gumener was born in 1886 in Mariampol (Yiddish and Russian, now Mari-jampole, Lithuania), a town about 76 miles west of Vilna (Vilne in Yiddish and Vilnius in Lithuanian), in the Russian Empire.[19] He trained for the law in St. Petersburg, graduating in 1912, but was prevented from practicing because the reactionary minister of justice, Ivan Grigorievich Shcheglovitov, would not license Jewish lawyers.[20] Barred from the law, Gumener turned to Jewish communal work in his late 20s.

He worked throughout his life for many of the major organizations that addressed the plight of the Jews in the interwar period. In Ukraine, he was a representative of the Petersburg and Kiev EKOPO and the Kultur Lige (Culture League). Gumener was working for EKOPO at least since 1915. The Russian State Historical Archive in St. Petersburg contains a document entitled "Report of the Committee Plenipotentiary Gumener about the Conditions of Expellees and Refugees in Ekaterinoslav and Podolia Provinces, 1915–1916."[21] He was a representative for the Russian Red Cross; he worked with the Jewish Ministry, the governmental institution for Jewish affairs established during the fleeting period of Ukrainian sovereignty; and he was a representative of

---

[19] Details of Gumener's life are found in Sergei Nutkiewicz, "Eliyahu Gumener," *Oy-fun Shvall*, no. 12 (June–July 1947): 12; and Moses Shalit, ed., *Oyf di hurves fun milhomes un mehumes: Pinkes fun Gegnt-komitet "YEKOPO" 1919–1931* [On the ruins of wars and turmoil: Records of the Regional Committee YEKOPO, 1919–1931] (Vilna: Gegnt-komitet "YEKOPO," 1931), 829–34.

[20] Shcheglovitov was the minister who in 1913 indicted Menahem Mendel Beilis in Kiev on the charge of ritual murder. For an understanding of the origins of ethnic restrictions for lawyers, see Benjamin Nathans, *Beyond the Pale: The Jewish Encounter with Late Imperial Russia* (Berkeley: University of California Press, 2002), 311–39.

[21] I have not examined the document in the State Archive and thank Polly Zavadivker for bringing it to my attention. Most of the prewar Jewish welfare organizations contracted with EKOPO. These included ORT (Society for Trade and Agricultural Work Among the Jews of Russia), whose focus was occupational training, OZE (Society for the Protection of the Health of the Jewish Population), and OPE (Society for the Promotion of Culture Among the Jews of Russia). The Kultur Lige (Culture League) was founded in Kiev in 1918 to promote a new Jewish culture based on Yiddish and secular values. EKOPO also coordinated with the American Jewish Joint Distribution Committee. See Y. Pevzner, "Jewish Committee for the Relief of War Victims (1914–1921)," *Pinkas* 1 (2006): 114–42; Z. Szajkowski, "Jewish Relief in Eastern Europe 1914–1917," *The Leo Baeck Institute Yearbook* 10, 1 (1965): 24–56; Zavadivker, "Fighting 'On Our Own Territory,'" 81–107.

Fareynikte, the United Jewish Socialist Workers' Party.[22] He held various administrative positions in the municipality of Komenetz. After he left Ukraine in 1921 he worked on behalf of Jewish war orphans for the American Joint Distribution Committee in Warsaw and Vilna as its representative in the Bialystok region.

In 1925 he moved to Nowogrodek, Poland (Navaredok in Yiddish; now Navahrudak, Belarus) where after the Russian Revolution he was able to practice law and engage in communal affairs, including as a city councilman. *Pinkas Navaredok,* published in 1963 by Holocaust survivors from that town, notes that "from 1926, the lawyer Gumener was helping with official contacts" in support of the orphanage.[23]

We can also document Gumener's work on behalf of refugee children between the period that he left Ukraine and moved to Nowogrodek. A JDC memo dated December 23, 1921, from Abraham Shohan, director of the War Orphans Bureau in Warsaw notes: "Apparently our Mr. Gumener is doing good work in the district of Bialystok."[24] Another JDC memo dated April 24, 1922, requests a visa for Gumener from the consul of the Czechoslovak Republic to travel to "Munkaz" (Mukacevo in Subcarpathian Czechoslovakia) to organize aid for war orphans. We can track his work into the 1930s. A fundraising letter dated September 11, 1938, on behalf of the Nowogrodek Children's Home to the Nowogrodek landsmanshaft in New York is signed by E. Gumener, President. We have evidence of his activities even during World War II. The minutes of a meeting of JDC representatives held in Vilna on November 14, 1939, reveal that during a mission to Soviet-occupied Poland, Dr. B. Horovits gave Gumener JDC funds for beleaguered Jewish communities. At this point it appears that he was still travelling from his home in Nowogrodek to Bialystok—both of which were under Soviet occupation.[25] That is the last

---

[22] Gumener's name is on the list of the Russian Socialist Revolutionary Party candidates from Vinnitsa (Podolia) for the elections to the Russian Constituent Assembly. The elections took place in November 1917 (in utter chaos) when the Bolsheviks were already power in Russia.

[23] *Navaredok Memorial Book (Navahrudak, Belarus)* (Tel Aviv: Navaredker Relief Committee, 1963), 111. The translation can be found online at https://www.jewishgen.org/Yizkor/ Nowogrodek/Nowogrodek.html.

[24] American Jewish Joint Distribution Committee Archives (hereafter JDC Archives), 1921–1932 New York Collection, Poland: Child Care, General, 1921: "Letter from A. Shohan, War Orphan Bureau, Warsaw to M. D. Waldman, European Director, Child Case Department," 23 December 1921, folder 88.1.

[25] JDC Archives, 1933–1944 New York Collection, Poland: Administration, General, 1939 (October–December): "Translation Minutes of a Meeting Held on November 14, 1939 in Vilna," 14 November 1939, folder 186.

documentary reference to Eli Gumener that I was able to find. However, in a stunning accidental discovery during my research, I came upon a 26-minute silent film shot in Nowogrodek in 1931. I immediately recognized my Uncle Eli from our family photos. The film was made during a visit from America of the famous lexicographer Alexander Harkavy (1863–1939) to his city of birth. Gumener appears in two scenes: conducting a meeting at the Jewish orphanage and accompanying Harkavy from the town hall with dignitaries and citizens of Nowogrodek. This remarkable film was a "live" illustration of Gumener's continuing devotion to Jewish communal organizations. He carried on this work until the Nazis ended his life.

A Brief Historical Context

Ukraine became the battlefield for competing powers after the Russian Revolution. The Red Army invaded in January 1918 after Ukrainian nationalists proclaimed the establishment of the Ukrainian National Republic (UNM).[26] German and Austro-Hungarian troops pushed the Red Army out and occupied all of Ukraine from March to November 1919. Germany meddled in internal Ukrainian politics, installing a compliant and unpopular Ukrainian government that was eventually overthrown by a combination of Ukrainian nationalists and peasants. In August 1919, forces under General Anton Denikin from the White or Volunteer Army that had been founded by the anti-Bolshevik generals Mikhail Alekseev and Lavr Kornilov moved into Ukraine.[27] Complicating the matter was the attempt by Poland to absorb eastern Galicia, which formerly had been part of the Austro-Hungarian Empire but was also claimed by both the Bolsheviks and the Ukrainians. Polish troops were in Ukraine first as belligerents and then from May 1920 to July 1920 as allies of the Ukrainian National Republic against the Red Army until they were driven out by the conquering Soviet forces.[28] The Ukrainian peasants were also a complicating factor in this volatile period. They made up 91 percent of the population in Ukraine. Peasants constituted themselves into local militias or

---

[26] The first incursion into Ukraine occurred after the February Revolution. Known as the June Offensive (or Kerensky Offensive), its goal was to attack the Austro-Hungarian and German armies in Galicia. It failed miserably, and the German army pushed the Russians back through Galicia and Ukraine up to the Zbruch River.

[27] The Volunteer Army was the branch of the White Army that fought in South Russia during the Civil War. Denikin took command of the Volunteer Army in April 1918.

[28] Vasyl Kuchabsky, *Western Ukraine in Conflict with Poland and Bolshevism, 1918–1923* (Edmonton: Canadian Institute of Ukrainian Studies Press, 2009); Michael Palij, *The Ukrainian-Polish Defensive Alliance, 1919–1921: An Aspect of the Ukrainian Revolution* (Edmonton: Canadian Institute of Ukrainian Studies Press, 1995).

attached themselves to larger military forces, and frequently shifted their allegiance. Gumener sometimes employs the vague term "cossacks" to identify perpetrators of pogroms.[29]

The Russian Revolution of February 1917 did not initially engender a strong nationalist response in Ukraine. Ukrainian leaders envisioned Ukraine as part of a federation within a socialist Russia. The Bolshevik coup in October, however, awakened the Ukrainian leadership to a nationalist stance, and in January 1918 the Ukrainian parliament (the Central Rada) declared Ukraine an independent country: the Ukrainian National Republic (UNR, also known as the Ukrainian People's Republic).

The Directory was the executive council of the Ukrainian National Republic. Established on November 18, 1918, it was headed by Volodymyr Kyrylovych Vynnychenko (1880–1951). The Directory was created after Ukrainian nationalists overthrew the Hetmanate of "Hetman" Pavlo Skoropadsky (1873–1945), a regime sanctioned by Germany, which offered recognition and support in exchange for grain. The conservative and reactionary Hetmanate lasted from April to December 1918, sustained by the large number of German troops on Ukrainian territory. After the Allied defeat of Germany in October,

---

[29] In Ukraine the Cossacks had been a distinct semi-ethnic group in the regions between east and west of the Dnieper River until the late 18th century. They had their own settlements, culture, privileges, and economic structure. Due to wars, partitions, and annexations the Cossacks disappeared from Ukraine as a distinct social force. Thus, in the Civil War period there were no Ukrainian Cossacks in the proper sense of the term. All existing Cossack groups were located in Russia. Some fought in Denikin's Volunteer Army in Ukraine; others for the Bolsheviks. But for many Ukrainians, "Cossacks" conjured an ahistorical and folkloric image of fighters for a free Ukraine. Thus, the term was employed by the UNR military for its regular soldiers, and it was also used by peasant militias. In 1917 a movement of Free Cossacks emerged in Ukraine. These were rural vigilante groups whose purported goal was to protect their fellow peasants from local great landowners. The history of peasant involvement is complex. Although there were several anarchist insurgents (e.g., Nestor Mekhno [1888–1934]), most peasant groups—and there were hundreds—did not have a clear political orientation. Among the reasons that they were prone to change sides is that they resented the Red Army policies of requisitioning resources for the war effort and conscription, as well as the Bolshevik land reform goals. In addition, there was a strong rural-urban divide, in which peasants identified the city with Russians, Poles, and Jews, the latter whom they regarded as exploiters of the peasantry. They equally opposed the land policies of the Ukrainian National Republic and its peasant conscription. For an overview of peasants, anarchists, and Cossacks, see Peter Kenez, *The Defeat of the Whites: Civil War in South Russia, 1919–1920* (Berkeley: University of California Press, 1977). For an explanation of the various terms used for and by warlords during the Civil War, see Christopher Gilley, "Fighters for Ukrainian Independence? Imposture and Identity among Ukrainian Warlords 1917–22," *Historical Research* 90, 247 (2017): 172–90.

a combination of troops from the UNR and militias overthrew the Hetmanate and restored the Ukrainian National Republic.

Symon Petliura became the supreme commander of the Ukrainian Army and later president of the Directory of the Ukrainian National Republic.[30] Thus, when the Red Army launched its offensive against Ukraine with the goal of maintaining the integrity of the Russian imperial borders, it faced this opposing force as well as the anti-Bolshevik White Army, the peasants, and later the Poles.

Gumener does not share his sentiments regarding either the Russian Revolution or the Ukrainian national movement except as they pertain to the Jews. He states that the revolution created a leadership vacuum in Ukraine that was difficult to fill once the Civil War began. Without naming names, he condemns those Jewish leaders in Kiev who went to Moscow, Paris, or London, "abandoning the entire Jewish population in whose name they so liked to speak."[31]

A Ministry of Jewish Affairs was established within the Central Rada of the UNR, and later in the Directory. The fact that it was an administrative unit in the highest echelons of government reflects the initial vision of the Ukrainian nationalist movement. The major national minorities—Jews, Russians, and Poles—were promised "national personal autonomy" that was written into the constitution.[32] The events of the Civil War, however, quickly overwhelmed the nascent state, and the Jewish Ministry accomplished little in the area of national autonomy.[33]

---

[30] Petliura (1879–1926) was born in the province of Poltava. He studied for the priesthood in a Russian seminary but left before completing his studies. Petliura worked as an archivist and journalist and was engaged in nationalist activities. The Central Rada appointed him secretary for military affairs. He was selected head of the army after the overthrow of the Hetmanate regime. The troops that fought in Petliura's army perpetrated the largest number of pogroms. Petliura's responsibility for the pogroms, however, has been debated by historians. After the Civil War he emigrated to Paris, where he was assassinated in 1926 by Sholem Schwarzbard, a 39-year-old Jew from Balta, Podolia. After an eight-day trial, Schwarzbard was acquitted. For a history of the controversial trial, see David Engel, ed., *The Assassination of Symon Petliura and the Trial of Scholem Schwarzbard 1926–1927: A Selection of Documents* (Göttingen: Archive of Jewish History and Vandenhoeck & Ruprecht, 2016).

[31] Gumener, *A kapitl Ukraine*, 5.

[32] National Personal Autonomy (or National Cultural Autonomy) was an ideology that called for the right of minorities within states to craft and administer their own cultural and political activities.

[33] Henry Abramson analyzes the activities of the Ministry of Jewish Affairs during the Civil War. He notes that the attempt to establish national personal autonomy was "a grand failure" but agrees with Kurt Stillschweig that "the historical significance of

The various civil wars that followed the Russian Revolution represented a grievous period of violence. Under the fog of war and revolt, every side committed pogroms against the Jews. Murder, mass rapes, and unimaginable brutality and atrocities against the Jewish population were well documented by investigators such as Tcherikower, Heifetz, Shtif, Gumener, and others.[34] To gain a complete picture, we must add to these horrors rampant disease, plunder, destruction of homes and businesses, forced evacuations, and flight.[35] Approximately 1,200–1,500 pogroms were documented between 1917 and 1920. Estimates of the number of Jews killed range from 50,000 to more than 200,000.[36] Eighty percent of pogroms occurred in the three gubernias (admin-

---

Jewish Autonomy in the Ukraine does not lie so much in its practical realization and functioning, as in its first complete fulfillment of national Jewish demands." Henry Abramson, *A Prayer for the Government: Ukrainians and Jews in Revolutionary Times, 1917–1920* (Cambridge, MA: Harvard University Press, 1999), xvi; and Kurt Stillschweig, "Nationalism and Autonomy among Eastern European Jewry: Origin and Historical Development up to 1939," *Historia Judaica* 6 (1944): 59.

[34] Historians debate the meaning of pogrom. Were attacks state-sponsored, state-sanctioned, or spontaneous? Were attacks on Jews a subset of pogroms against other recognized social groups (e.g., landowners or Mennonites)? Were they expressions of anti-Jewish hatred, triggered by economic competition, or based on nationalistic fervor? The most current works on pogroms carefully parse the motives within the specific historical context of the event, making for a more nuanced understanding. On the theoretical problems associated with the term, see David Engel, "What's in a Pogrom? European Jews in the Age of Violence," in *Anti-Jewish Violence: Rethinking the Pogrom in East European History*, ed. Jonathan Dekel-Chen, David Gaunt, Natan M. Meir, and Israel Bartal (Bloomington: Indiana University Press, 2011), 19–37.

[35] Heifetz, *Slaughter of the Jews*; Alexander Prusin, *Nationalizing a Borderland: War, Ethnicity, and Anti-Jewish Violence in East Galicia, 1914–1920* (Tuscaloosa: University of Alabama Press, 2016); Irina Astashkevich, *Gendered Violence: Jewish Women in the Pogroms of 1917–1921* (Brookline, MA: Academic Studies Press, 2018); Elissa Bemporad, *A Legacy of Blood: Jews, Pogroms, and Ritual Murder in the Lands of the Soviets* (New York: Oxford University Press, 2019).

[36] An oft-used figure is from N. Gergel, who provides what is widely regarded as a conservative number at 60,000 deaths. Gergel, "The Pogroms in the Ukraine in 1918–21," *YIVO Annual of Jewish Social Studies* 6 (1951): 249. Nicolas Werth uses the number 100,000–150,000 in *Le Livre des pogroms: Antichambre d'un génocide, Ukraine, Russie, Biélorussie, 1917–1922* (Paris: Mémorial de la Shoah, 2010). Lidia Miliakova and Irina Ziuzina suggest 125,000 deaths in Ukraine; 25,000 in Belarus and Russia. See Lidia Miliakova and Irina Ziuzina, "Le travail d'enquête des organisations juives sur les pogroms d'Ukraine, de Biélorussie et de Russie soviétique pendant la guerre civile (1918–1922)" [The investigative work of Jewish organizations into the pogroms in Ukraine, Belarus and Soviet Russia during the Civil War (1918–1922)], in *Le Mouvement Social* 222 (2008): 61–80. Oleg Budnitskii cites Sergei Gusev-Orenburgsky's so-called "Crimson Book," *Kniga o evreiskikh pogromakh na Ukraine v 1919* (Petrograd, n.d.): 14, who uses

istrative regions of the Russian Empire) of Podolia, Volhynia, and Kiev.[37] The worst year was 1919. In terms of the responsibility of the perpetrators, the Directory troops accounted for approximately 40 percent of the attacks; the so-called insurgents or independent warlords 25 percent; Denikin's White or Volunteer Army 17 percent; the Red Army about 9 percent; the peasant bands of Nikifor Grigoriev nearly 4 percent, and the Polish army about 3 percent.[38]

In his report, *Pogrom geshikhte 1919–1920, Band 1: Di Ukrainishe shehite in 1919* (Pogrom History 1919–1920, Volume 1: The Ukrainian Slaughter in 1919), Elias Heifetz described the extent of the pogroms throughout Ukraine, bringing the testimony of witnesses and official investigators (including Gumener). Writing just two years after the events, he added a terrifying reminder:

> No account is taken in the above figures of the many victims who gave up their lives in places that could not be recorded because there has not been any connection with them so far and no investigations in those regions have yet been made…. Nor have those missing Jewish families been included who were exterminated in numerous villages and hamlets, or those who were killed during their flight from their ruined homes as they wandered from place to place, or those who were pulled out of railway trains and beaten to death, or those who were drowned by being thrown out of steamers, or those who were killed in the woods and the highways. There is no account taken of the great number of those who succumbed to their injuries and fell victims of contagious and other diseases which they contracted during their imprisonment in dark rooms without food, drink or clothing.[39]

The magnitude of death and destruction was unlike anything that had been previously recorded in Jewish history.

Every Jew who documented the pogroms regarded the creation of a historical record as a moral, even religious, obligation: to perpetuate Jewish collective memory.[40] Gumener was at the meeting in Kiev in May 1919 when

---

100,000, and the Soviet economist Iurii Larin, *Evrei i antisemitizm v SSSR* (Moscow: Gosudarstvennoe izdatel'stvo politicheskoi literatury, 1929), 55, who estimates 200,000. Oleg Budnitskii, *Russian Jews Between the Reds and the Whites, 1917–1920* (Philadelphia: University of Pennsylvania Press, 2012), 415 n. 2.

[37] Abramson, *A Prayer for the Government*, 109–40.

[38] Ibid., 115.

[39] Heifetz, *Slaughter of the Jews*, 179.

[40] On the imperative to leave a record of Jewish suffering in general, see Joshua M. Karlip, "Between Martyrology and Historiography: Elias Tcherikower and the Making

the Jewish National Secretariat in conjunction with the publishing house Folks-Farlag and the Central Committee [of Kiev] to Aid Pogrom Victims established the Editorial Board for Gathering and Researching Materials Regarding the Pogroms in Ukraine. The group would later change its name to the Historical Archive of Eastern Jewry. Its mission was to write a comprehensive history of the pogroms based on documentation and eyewitness accounts. A volume was published in 1923 in Berlin, where the editorial board resided, entitled *Anti-Semitism and Pogroms in the Ukraine in the Years 1917–1918: A History of Ukrainian-Jewish Relations.* It was not until 1965 that a second volume was published by the YIVO Institute for Jewish Research in New York. This book, entitled *The Pogroms in the Year 1919*, was based on the work of Elias Tcherikower. Although Gumener is not mentioned in the secondary literature in conjunction with the establishment of the Editorial Board, he certainly attended the first meeting: "I happened at that time to attend a conference of prominent Jewish activists in Kiev. We tried to agree on the question of collecting pogrom evidence and also to consider the question of guilt for the pogroms. Our mood during these deliberations was very gloomy. We do not even know, said one delegate, whether we will survive this year. Let us print the material about the pogroms so that at least something will be passed to the coming generations."[41]

Gumener was designated an "authorized investigator" for both the Russian Red Cross Society, which had a department to aid victims of the pogroms, and the Central Committee [of Kiev] to Aid Pogrom Victims created in January 1919.[42] The Central Committee coordinated the staff of various agencies involved in aid to document the pogroms. The documentation was gathered into several works, the most prominent Tcherikower's (also known as Cherik-

---

of a Pogrom Historian," *East European Jewish Affairs* 38, 3 (2008): 257–80; David Roskies, *Against the Apocalypse: Responses to Catastrophe in Modern Jewish Culture* (Cambridge, MA: Harvard University Press, 1984), 79–108; and Alexandra Garbarini, "Power in Truth Telling. Jewish Testimonial Strategies before the Shoah," in *Kinship, Community, and Self: Essays in Honor of David Warren Sabean*, ed. Jason Coy, Benjamin Marschke, Jared Poley, and Claudia Verhoeven (New York: Berghahn, 2015), 170–84.

[41] Gumener, *A kapitl Ukraine*, 82.

[42] The Russian Society of the Red Cross was founded in 1867 as a private aid organization. It was active in all the foreign conflicts that occurred during the tsarist state and continued to be engaged in aid work after the 1917 Revolution and during the Civil War. In August 1918 the Bolsheviks nationalized and reorganized it under the same name. Gumener does not tell us when he began to work for the Russian Red Cross. See Andrew J. Ringlee, "The Romanovs' Militant Charity: The Red Cross and Public Mobilization for War in Tsarist Russia, 1853–1914" (Ph.D. diss., University of North Carolina at Chapel Hill, 2016); and Miliakova and Ziuzina, "Le travail d'enquête," 61–80.

over) *Anti-Semitism and Pogroms in the Ukraine in the Years 1917–1918: The History of Ukrainian-Jewish Relations* and *The Pogroms in the Year 1919.*[43]

Gumener devotes some of his memoir to Jewish self-defense, and he includes a number of dramatic examples.[44] This topic at first glance seems strange: every warring party seemed to have its way with the civilian Jewish population. Jewish resistance, however, was a compelling topic after the 1903 Kishinev pogrom in Bessarabia in which 49 Jews were killed. Following on the heels of pogroms in 1881–83, Kishinev (now Chisinau, Moldova) captured the imagination of the Jewish world unlike other pogroms. In his widely published series of Hebrew poems entitled *In the City of Massacre*, Chaim Nachman Bialik (1873–1934) bitterly scolded and harangued Jews everywhere regarding Jewish passivity.[45]

Although Gumener was justifiably proud of Jewish resistance, pogroms continued throughout Ukraine, and would continue until the Red Army conquered the territory in 1921. Few communities were able to resist armed forces intent on plunder and murder. But Gumener's account of self-defense was motivated by the same historiographic imperative that compelled him to record the pogrom history: "A lot has been written and is still being written about the murdered Jews but very little, almost nothing, has been written how Jews fought heroically to protect their parents, brothers, and sisters. Jews will no longer die, as they did in Proskurov, like animals, like sheep to the slaughter."[46]

According to Gumener, two pogroms in Podolia in early 1919 caused Jews to lose faith in the Ukrainian National Republic: Proskurov and Felshtin. Proskurov (now called Khmelnytsky) was a town about 45 miles northeast of Komenetz-Podolsk. To form and strengthen his army, Petliura had incorporated peasant conscripts and Ukrainians who had served in the Russian army. One such battalion was led by Ivan Semesenko. Gumener draws a vivid picture of what happened in Proskurov in February 1919: "The slaughter took place over four hours. Armed soldiers from Semesenko's battalion accompa-

---

[43] E. Tcherikower [I. M. Cherikover], *Antisemitizm un pogromen in Ukraine, 1917–1918: Tsu der geshikhte fun ukrainish-yidishe batsiungen* [Antisemitism and pogroms in Ukraine, 1917–1918: A history of Ukrainian-Jewish relations] (Berlin: Yidisher literarisher farlag, 1923); and Tcherikower, *Di ukrainer pogromen in yor 1919* [The Ukrainian pogroms in 1919] (New York: YIVO, 1965). Much of the material gathered by the Editorial Board can be found in the Mizrakh Yidisher Historisher Arkhiv at YIVO in New York.

[44] Gumener, *A kapitl Ukraine*, 32–37.

[45] Steven Zipperstein, *Pogrom: Kishinev and the Tilt of History* (New York: W. W. Norton, 2019).

[46] Gumener, *A kapitl Ukraine*, 32.

nied by doctors and nurses encircled the neighborhoods where the poorest
Jews lived and began their bloody work.[47] Many Jews who lived in other
neighborhoods did not even know about the pogrom until early next morning
when the horrible cries of the relatives of the murdered people woke the entire
town. Almost 1,500 Jews were killed—children and elderly, men and women.
The pogromists did not show mercy towards anyone. The precise number of
murdered people is difficult to access because Semesenko did not allow the
dead to be buried in an orderly manner."[48]

The pogrom in Proskurov was immediately followed by one in the smaller
nearby town of Felshtin (Yiddish and Russian; Hvardiske in Ukrainian).
Troops again fighting in the name of the Ukrainian National Republic killed
approximately 600 Jews, a third of the entire Jewish population. These pogroms greatly weakened Jewish ties to the Ukrainian National Republic: "The
Proskurov and Felshtin pogroms brought about a complete break in the Jewish-Ukrainian relationship. The Jewish noncommunist groups that had been
positive towards the Ukrainian movement openly went over to the Bolshevik
side and helped them struggle against the Ukrainian regime."[49] As Gumener
will show, however, Jewish activists could not break entirely with either the
Ukrainian government or Ukrainian socialists, or for that matter, with the
Bolsheviks. The Jewish Ministry still had a voice in the UNR, and Jewish socialists tried repeatedly to collaborate with Ukrainian socialists. And in certain limited cases and for short periods of time, the ministry was able to ease
the burden of the Jewish communities under assault.

Gumener illustrates the muddle of battles and occupations in Podolia by
listing 16 governing powers from the February Revolution to January 1, 1921,
that captured the town of Proskurov and concludes: "As if in a motion picture,
the various powers alternated and with each power came new demands. And
with each power the professional bandits 'came a courting' and the Jewish
population soon felt their bite!"[50] Polly Zavadivker cites a letter from An-sky
to Chaim Zhitlowsky (October 11, 1920) where he too uses the metaphor of
a motion picture: "My book is also a kind of moving pictures [sic], with descriptions of 200 cities and shtetls in Poland, Galicia, and Bukovina, saying
what happened there and mentioning hundreds of local Jews."[51] Perhaps for

---

[47] Gumener explains the presence of medical personnel in his footnote: in case there
was resistance from the Jewish population, they could give aid to the wounded soldiers (ibid., 12).

[48] Ibid., 13.

[49] Ibid., 15.

[50] Ibid., 65.

[51] *1915 Diary of An-sky*, 33.

An-sky and Gumener, the camera image elicits the idea of countless fleeting images. The written narrative, however, fails in its attempt to deal with the indescribable experience of loss.

The Challenge of Providing Aid

Although there had been robust aid activities for Jewish communities in Galicia, Poland, and parts of Ukraine during World War I, the challenge in Podolia between 1918–20 was nearly insurmountable. Effective aid was hindered by four factors: the conflict between Bolsheviks and anti-Bolsheviks to control and shape Ukraine after the Russian Revolution, the fast-moving military events on the ground, the inability of outside organizations to bring aid to the war zones, and the discord between Jewish political parties. These factors kept communities fragile and weak, rendering the local Jewish population vulnerable and virtually paralyzing relief work in Podolia. Whether the pogroms could have been halted or not taken place at all is a hypothetical question.[52] For Gumener, in the spring and summer of 1919, they seemed unstoppable.

To gain a larger picture of the challenge he faced, it is instructive to compare what we know about Gumener's activities in early 1919 with those he describes in his memoir, which begins just two months later. Although there are very few documents attributed to Gumener besides his memoir, he reported on his activities in an article dated January–February 1919 in *Hilf*, a monthly journal published in Kiev by the Jewish Folks-Farlag. The focus of his activities then was on compensation for Jewish property damaged or lost due to unlawful military actions perpetrated by Russian troops during World War I.[53] Gumener was in Komenetz-Podolsk, working through a complicated bureaucratic system for documenting and assessing Jewish property losses: "In one Komenetz district alone 14,000 claims were collected. It is extremely difficult for the subcommittees.... Given that judges are overwhelmed with their daily work and are poorly paid and receive very little for administrative ex-

---

[52] Carole Fink offers the November 1918 pogrom in Lemberg in Galicia (L'vov in Russian; Lwow in Polish; Lviv in Ukrainian) as a case study of the inability or unwillingness of the Allied governments to mount a meaningful response to the well-documented atrocities. See Carole Fink, *Defending the Rights of Others: The Great Powers, the Jews, and International Minority Protection, 1878–1938* (Cambridge: Cambridge University Press, 2004), 110–21. For an analysis of how Polish politicians before World War II changed the pogrom's Jewish victims into provocateurs, see David Engel, "Lwów, 1918: The Transmutation of a Symbol and Its Legacy in the Holocaust," in *Contested Memories: Poles and Jews During the Holocaust and its Aftermath*, ed. Joshua Zimmerman (New Brunswick, NJ: Rutgers University Press, 2003), 32–44.

[53] E. Gumener, "Concerning Losses from the War," *Hilf*, no. 2-1 (Kiev: January–February 1919): 27–30.

penses, they cannot deal with the pressures of investigating claims. Further, both local people and representatives from the military are required to be on these committees.... Due to all these obstacles, we despaired of gaining even a little for losses; the despair was great even among the lawyers. Jews do not believe that anything will come from the entire situation."[54] In the *Hilf* article he recommends revising a compensation law promulgated by the Russian government in 1916 in the interest of "reconstructing the destroyed economy." Reading Gumener's suggestions for streamlining the process gives no hint of the challenges he would soon face in spring and summer 1919 when much of Podolia became a combat zone. Once the pogroms began in earnest, compensation and reconstruction was the least of the problems faced by aid workers. The more immediate and pressing need was safety, food, and shelter. When it comes to the delivery of aid in the field, relief organizations are stymied in the face of armies and militias perpetrating ongoing mass atrocities. Of course, Gumener could not have known then what he and other aid workers would encounter. It is through the memoir, which begins in February 1919, that we get a sense of the new obstacles they faced.

Joint Distribution Committee reports also reflect the challenges of providing aid "before" and "after," contrasting 1914 to 1918 with conditions in 1919 to 1920. Thus, a JDC summary report for the period October 1919 through April 1920 first describes the robust activities of the older aid organizations during World War I: "At the time of the World War a wide relief activity was developed in Wohlynia and Podolia.... The YEKOPO [EKOPO] had organized general dwelling places, cheap and free kitchens, consumers' cooperatives; the OZE had been running schools and free courses." The report goes on to describe the much narrower goals at the height of the pogroms: "In 1919, relief work in Wohlynia was conducted by the Committee for the Relief of Pogrom Sufferers with the Red Cross, and in Podolia by the Central Committee for the Relief of the Pogrom Sufferers with the Jewish Ministry.... The above named Jewish organizations, as YEKOPO and OZE, *had also at that time given all their energy to pogrom sufferers and abandoned the work among the war sufferers, who were not in such distress and did not require immediate relief to such an extent.*"[55] Gumener had also shifted the focus of his work from helping Jews who had lost property in the war to people who had suffered in the pogroms starting in spring 1919.

---

[54] Ibid., 30.

[55] JDC "Outline of the Report of the Activities of the J.D.C. in the Occupied Parts of Wohlynia and Podolia, October 1919–April 1920," folder 229.2. "Wohlynia" is sometimes used in English for Volhynia. My emphasis.

The lack of transportation, the poor communication, the unpredictable movement of armed forces, and the unstable centers of command meant that as the wars dragged on, administering aid became an increasingly local effort. In the face of shifting front lines, the Ukrainian National Republic and the Jewish Ministry were forced to repeatedly change locations, hampering logistical coordination. During the Civil War, the UNR was moved to temporary capitals in Vinnytsia, Zhmerynka, Proskuriv, Komenetz-Podolsk, and Rovne (in Yiddish; Rovno in Russian). Before the Joint Distribution Committee began its work in Ukraine, aid was primarily provided by the Petrograd EKOPO and the Russian Red Cross employing "travelling agents" such as Gumener. The Civil War, however, broke communication between the "center" (Petrograd) and the Kiev, Podolia, and Volhynia provinces. The towns of Kiev, Rostov, and Odessa then became the functioning logistics centers for relief work.

EKOPO depended heavily on JDC funds. Acquiring funds was no easy matter. Local activists, usually associated with political parties, requested funds from the JDC and passed the money on to EKOPO, which then distributed the resources to their local branches. Coordinating the transfer of funds was complex, as revealed in an April–December 1920 JDC internal report:

> Three hundred twenty thousand dollars which were advanced by the Russian Zionist organization called Merkaz to the Petrograd Relief Committee called EKOPO was refunded by the J.D.C. in June and July 1919. No communication with Russia until February 1920 when a special messenger brought a letter from Merkaz to Boris Goldberg, stating that in view of the terrible distress, the Merkaz again advanced to the EKOPO 133,000 in the hope that the J.D.C. will refund the money and asking that Goldberg authorize an additional advance to the EKOPO. Thereupon Goldberg cabled the J.D.C. offering to instruct a new advance of $250,000 to the EKOPO, if authorized by the J.D.C., which cable has remained unanswered. Simultaneously, Goldberg instructed the Merkaz to discontinue advances until an affirmative reply had been received from the J.D.C.[56]

In this example, multiple organizations were involved: a local Zionist organization in Ukraine (Merkaz) initiated the request to its representative Goldberg in London via a cable to Copenhagen (because there was no direct communication to Petersburg) who forwarded the request to JDC in New York. The approved funds were given to Merkaz (because banks were closed in Ukraine at this time), which sent it on to EKOPO in Petersburg. But for more than six

---

[56] JDC Archives, 1919–1921 New York Collection, Executive Staff, Administrative Committee Minutes, April–December 1920, folder 19.2.

months (June and July 1919 to February 1920) there was no communication from Russia.

On the local level, the critical example of transportation illustrates another of the many constraints Gumener and other aid workers faced in Podolia. The principal means for transporting troops and supplies in war was trains. In his 1915 diary about his work in Galicia, An-sky often mentions trains.[57] An-sky was utilizing the trains—generally troop carriers—to move from one area to another and to bring aid to Jewish victims. An-sky—despite real hardships— nevertheless had some ability to use the rail system. By contrast, Gumener writes that until the Civil War, Komenetz-Podolsk was not even connected to a railroad. Although there were trains by 1918, it is clear from his memoir that he was seldom able to use them. Once he traveled from Komenetz to Proskurov after the pogrom where, "at the Vinnitzer station [Ukrainian] soldiers broke into our car and taunted us with various anti-Semitic slurs."[58] For Jews, railroad stations were often sites of harassment, robbery, and even murder. In a second incident, he describes a frightening and dangerous journey fleeing Denikin's troops. Gumener's goal was to reach the Polish-occupied part of Volhynia, cross into Galicia, and from there travel to his hometown of Vilna. Ultimately, he was so frustrated by the danger and disfunction of the rail system that he abandoned the train and traveled to the border by renting a horse and wagon. A relief organization without access to adequate transport severely limited what the worker in the field could do.[59]

An incident in Komenetz-Podolsk in May 1919 shows another formidable crisis that required more from Gumener than material aid. He was called upon to assist the negotiations between contending political factions, to help organize a temporary militia, and to use his skill as a lawyer to release political prisoners. The events began on the eve of Passover. The Bolsheviks were approaching the town but were not expected for a few more days. The Di-

---

[57] January 17, 1915: "Trains carrying the wounded pass by one after another. I spent time in one of them. It was remarkably well equipped. Red Cross train no. 196 arrived from Kiev, on its way to Brody to pick up the wounded. We met the staff." January 20: "Telegrams about the location of the train cars have come in at last." January 22: "I spent the whole day dealing with the railway station director and commandant until I managed to retrieve the train cars from Ozerny. It took an equal amount of effort before I was able to get the cars hooked to a transport train leaving for Brody." The quotes are from *1915 Diary of S. An-sky*, 50, 54–55, 57–58, 60.

[58] Gumener, *A kapitl Ukraine*, 45.

[59] For a description of the transportation challenges, see JDC Archives, 1919–1921 New York Collection, Poland, Report: Polish Ukraine, Part 1, 1919–1920: "Outline of the Report of the Activities of the J.D.C. in the Occupied Parts of Wohlynia and Podolia, October 1919–April 1920," April 1, 1920, folder 229.2.

rectory was regrouping in Rovne. As usual, the vacuum created in the period between an outgoing and incoming power was fraught with danger. The remaining leadership in Komenetz decided to establish a committee whose responsibility was to maintain order until the Bolsheviks arrived. Gumener describes the fluid situation:

> After much friction, representatives of the right and left parties joined the committee. The new provincial commissar, Sichynskyi, was a very narrow-minded man who inhibited at every turn the committee's work. Alas, he was concerned that the committee, which had among its five members two moderate socialists (one a Ukrainian and the other a Jew) and the remainder rightists, would take power and delay the evacuation of the Ukrainians... At night the situation became more serious. Jews were preparing for [the Passover] seder and barricading the doors and gates. I was summoned by the city administration. All the members of the administration were present: Miranski, the chairman of the [city] Duma (a Russian Socialist Revolutionary and a Jew), Kylymnyk, the city mayor (a Ukrainian Social Democrat), and many others. The city hall was buzzing. Commissar Sichynskyi was restless. Representatives from various military units came to register at the municipality and announced that they would not abandon the territory of Ukraine and surrender to the Bolsheviks. As if out of nowhere, a large crowd of different types sprang up—shady and ordinary characters—and everyone loudly offered advice and imparted important news. Suddenly we heard that Jews were being beaten in the streets, which caused a panic. Luckily, it turned out, this was only partly true. A few Jews who went to shul to pray indeed received a few blows from the departing army. The city was calmer.... Mr. B and I went to a well-known leader for the first seder. It was quiet in the city. There were almost no Jews in the streets. Every door and gate were closed.... At the seder we met a large group of distinguished community leaders from Komenetz. The atmosphere was somber. Who knew what would happen in an hour from now? Or what will be in the morning?[60]

This passage shows some of the simultaneous factors facing a community under pressure: the wrangling among political factions over who would exercise power, the defiance of hot-headed anti-Bolshevik Ukrainians willing to fight a losing battle, the unruliness of the retreating Ukrainian People's Army, the challenges of organizing a local defense force, and the fear generated by ru-

---

[60] Gumener, *A kapitl Ukraine*, 26.

mors. Despite this chaos, Jews still attempted to create a bit of normalcy and celebrate a Jewish holiday.

As the hours passed the situation became more dire and uncertain. Sichynskyi slipped away in the middle of the night. The remaining leadership decided to form another committee consisting of Ukrainians and Jews. But another dangerous and unexpected situation emerged. The unattended prison outside the city held fifteen political prisoners and two hundred common criminals. The danger was twofold: insurgents who were still in the vicinity might release the common criminals who would join their militia. In addition, the political prisoners would likely be shot. Gumener was called upon in his capacity as a lawyer to extricate the political prisoners. Fortunately, in this particular case, the insurgents did not remain in the vicinity. But plunder or violence from passing insurgents was always a possibility. This particular incident in Komenetz provides an insider's view of the circumstances facing a city (and the aid worker) during the transition from one occupying power to another. Obtaining and distributing material goods for the needy was merely one of countless responsibilities that emerged from the exigencies of conflict zones.

Gumener's memoir also reveals another crucial challenge to aid work, namely, that the institutions in charge of relief changed frequently. Each change meant a new set of priorities—usually reflecting the ideology of the reigning authority—and new personnel. Consequently, a sustained approach to aid was nearly impossible.

One of the most vivid examples of this fluctuation occurred in November 1920 after the Bolsheviks had permanently retaken Komenetz-Podolsk from the Directory. Aid work would be reconfigured to reflect the Bolshevik's ideological policy, which meant that only Communists could have positions of responsibility. The Bolsheviks dissolved the existing local aid committees and insisted that aid be funneled through a Bolshevik agency, the "Division to Aid the Victims of Counter-Revolution" in the Kiev Department of Welfare. The Bolshevik policy was to liquidate the various Jewish communal organs and transfer their work to Soviet government institutions. These challenges were all exacerbated by parallel divisiveness within the leadership of the Jewish party elites, and Gumener devotes a great deal of space to describe this tragedy.

Party Divisiveness

The study of Jewish party divisions along ideological lines after the 1917 Revolution has been well documented in scholarship.[61] Before the revolution, the largest Jewish socialist parties were not oriented towards the Bolsheviks. As the Civil War dragged on and became more violent, the socialist parties engaged in internal debates over where to cast their lot: with the Ukrainian nationalists or with the Bolsheviks. The Bund in Ukraine eventually split over the question and formed the Bolshevik-oriented Kombund (Communist Bund) in February 1919.[62] Gumener's party Fareynikte was also torn between a pro- and anti-Bolshevik orientation. Like the Bund, the left Fareynikte faction became a communist party. We learn from Gumener's memoir that local parties did not always follow the lead of their main parties. In Komenetz, leaders of both the Bund and Fareynikte formed a new non-Bolshevik party in April 1919.[63]

Gumener's memoir treats an aspect of the subject which has been overlooked: namely, how in-fighting rooted in ideology affected aid policy at the local level. Since the creation of the Red Cross in 1864, neutrality, impartiality, and independence in providing aid have been basic principles in international relief work. Aid in contemporary times has developed into a complex network of bilateral and multilateral organizations that manage assistance to populations affected by war and natural disaster. In the late 19th and early 20th centuries, however, Jews concluded that their almost universal "outsider" status required their own aid organizations. In any case, until the mid-19th century, "poor relief" had traditionally been the responsibility not of governments or of international organizations, but of local religious communities. The American Jewish Joint Distribution Committee was created in 1914 in order to alleviate the suffering of Jews in Eastern Europe caught in the theater of war, as was

---

[61] For a close look at Jewish politics in Eastern Europe after the Russian Revolution, see Zvi Gitelman, *Jewish Nationality and Soviet Politics: The Jewish Sections of the CPSU, 1917–1930* (Princeton, NJ: Princeton University Press, 1972); and Baruch Gurevitz, *National Communism in the Soviet Union, 1918–1928* (Pittsburgh: University of Pittsburgh Press, 1980).

[62] Joshua Meyers, "A Portrait of Transition: From the Bund to Bolshevism in the Russian Revolution," *Jewish Social Studies: History, Culture, Society*, n.s., 24, 2 (2019): 107–34. On May 22, 1919, the Kombund (Communist Bund) and the Communist Fareynikte merged, forming the Komfarband (Jewish Communist Union).

[63] Gumener, *A kapitl Ukraine*, 41.

the Jewish Committee for Aid to War Victims (EKOPO).[64] Gumener worked for both organizations.

Unlike contemporary times in which refugee camps are generally the focal point of aid activities, during the Russian Civil War towns and cities in which the victims lived were the sites for aid. Even after campaigns of plunder, sacking, and burning, the pre-existing municipal institutions remained (e.g., hospitals and schools). Municipalities received and distributed aid. Towns also had political parties, and it was impossible to avoid the power relationships at work in these places.

Gumener spent much of the two years he chronicles in his memoir in Komenetz-Podolsk. In the 18th century the town had been under Polish rule but passed over to Russia with the 1793 partition of Poland. It was the capital of Podolia gubernia from 1793 to 1917. The town is approximately 50 miles from the Zbruch River, which formed the border between Austrian Galicia and imperial Russia and is 213 miles southwest of Kiev. According to the 1897 Russian census, there were 37,486 Jews, approximately 14 percent of the total population in town. During the Civil War, it was the route for armies as they retreated from Podolia to Galicia and advanced to Podolia from Galicia.

Gumener dates the first arrival of a foreign aid worker in Komenetz to January 1920 when an American whom he designates by the initials "B_R" arrived from Bucharest. This person was James Becker (1894–1970), who served in the US Army, then with the overseas division of the American Relief Administration before joining the JDC in 1920 as Acting European Director.[65]

A kapitl Ukraine provides the backstory about the aid brought by Becker that we do not find in the secondary literature. "In November 1919," he writes, "on the eve of the Ukrainian evacuation, a representative from the [aid] committee in Kishinev, S_N (Zionist) visited Komenetz-Podolsk."[66] Who was this unnamed representative? The answer comes from the memorial book *Yehudei*

---

[64] For premodern Jewish self-help, see Deborah Kaplan, *The Patrons and Their Poor: Jewish Community and Public Charity in Early Modern Europe* (Philadelphia: University of Pennsylvania Press, 2020); and Natan Meir, *Stepchildren of the Shtetl: The Destitute, Disabled, and Mad of Jewish Eastern Europe, 1800–1939* (Stanford, CA: Stanford University Press, 2020). For the history of Jewish international aid, see Granick, *International Jewish Humanitarianism*; Yehudah Bauer, *My Brother's Keeper: A History of the American Jewish Joint Distribution Society, 1929–1939* (Philadelphia: Jewish Publication Society, 1974); Michael R. Marrus, *The Unwanted: European Refugees in the Twentieth Century* (New York: Oxford University Press, 1985); and Beizer, *Relief in Time of Need*.

[65] Gumener, *A kapitl Ukraine*, 112. Becker was able to travel to Komenetz during the relatively short but calm period after Polish forces entered Podolia and Volhynia in November 1919.

[66] Ibid., 113.

Kishinev (translated as *The Jews of Kishinev [Chişinău, Moldova]*). After the news of the pogroms in Ukraine reached the Jews of Kishinev, an aid committee was established by the kehillah and authorized by the minister of Bessarabia on September 24, 1919. Two representatives from the committee were sent to Ukraine to investigate the situation and recommend how funds should be distributed. Only Shokhtman [S_N] was able to get through to Ukraine. "[He] visited a number of places that had pogroms and brought many details about the communities east of the Dniester that suffered from the pogroms and the need to send help. The committee immediately asked the Romanian government for permission to transfer money and goods to the victims in the Ukraine. With the help of Colonel Baker ["Becker" is mistakenly transliterated from the Yiddish into "Baker"] from the Joint in New York, 440,000 rubles were transferred in January 1920 to the Komenetz–Podolsk region.[67]

The discord between parties, however, constrained their ability to work together on relief at the local level. In the section "The Komenetz Jewish-American Aid Committee for the Pogrom Victims," Gumener provides an example of the in-fighting that plagued relief work and frustrated him so deeply.[68] This incident involved the relief funds brought by the JDC representative James Becker through the efforts of the Kishinev community.

When Becker arrived in Komenetz the existing social service facilities included a Jewish hospital, a home for the aged with 31 people, and two orphanages for 73 children. EKOPO and OZE ran soup kitchens and facilities for children (e.g., playgrounds and kindergartens). His report adds that in Komenetz there was "one cheap kitchen for 300 people," one Jewish hospital, one home for the aged with 31 people, two orphanages for 73 children, one kindergarten with 65 children, a "school for homeless children" with 120 pupils, and two other schools with 370 students.[69] All these institutions were severely underfunded. Positioning and jockeying began immediately upon Becker's arrival. "Feeling that they could get support from Kishinev, the Zionists, particularly the Tseire Tsiyon, demanded that the central aid committee be incorporated in the Komenetz kehillah. In addition, they held that the committee be composed in the same proportion as the National Assembly in Kiev (Ahdut 14 representatives, Zionists 24, Tseire Tsiyon 14, Folkspartey 4, Poale Tsiyon 11, Fareynikte

---

[67] See "The Report of the Ukraine Committee in Kishinev–Excerpts," in *Yehudei Kishinev (The Jews of Kishinev [Chişinău, Moldova]),* ed. Y. Koren (Tel Aviv, 1950), 225–26.

[68] Gumener, *A kapitl Ukraine,* 112–21.

[69] JDC Archives, 1919–1921 New York Collection, "Outline of the Report of the Activities of the J.D.C. in the Occupied Parts of Wohlynia and Podolia, October 1919–April 1920," 1 April 1920, folder 229.2.

12, Bund 23). The socialists, however, decided not to join a kehillah-run committee and established an independent committee."[70]

The situation was so chaotic that Becker refused to distribute any funds until the various factions found a way to work together. Gumener describes the compromise that was achieved: "The concern that the wealthy 'uncle' might leave without distributing the needed money was effective. A compromise committee was established in the following manner. Nine representatives in the committee come from the left … nine representatives come from the right … and three come from the kehillah." The compromise proved ineffective, and Gumener concludes: "And that was how in the worst way politics was introduced into the core of essential work in such areas as medical and social aid—needs that had nothing to do with political platforms."[71] The voices of local Jewish communal and party politics often spoke louder than those of policy makers in Petrograd, London, or New York.

The ideological subtleties between parties, however, are beyond this introduction.[72] Broadly speaking, the polar opposites were the Jewish secular socialist parties (in Gumener's memoir: Bund, Fareynikte, and Folkspartey) that believed that a Jewish future was possible in diaspora and the Zionists (in Gumener's memoir: Ahdut, Poale Tsiyon, and Tseire Tsiyon), who worked to prepare the ground for a future migration to Palestine. Gumener was solidly in the socialist, anti-Bolshevik camp. Tseire Tsiyon appears to be the *bête noire* in his memoir. This party consisted of younger Zionists and attracted intellectuals, artisans, and working-class people—the same constituency as the left-wing parties. The Jewish socialists placed Tseire Tsiyon in the right-wing camp along with mainstream Zionists and the religious party Ahdut, all of which tended to support the kehillah leadership.

According to Gumener, the Becker funds brought to Komenetz were distributed along ideological lines rather than by an objective assessment of needs: "The Zionists, and especially Tseire Tsiyon, who had a secure majority in the central aid committee, began to use the American money for necessities that had no relation to the pogrom victims. For example, a large sum was used to celebrate Lag B'Omer at the Maccabee sport center. Tseire Tsiyon also

---

[70] Gumener, *A kapitl Ukraine*, 112.

[71] Ibid., 114.

[72] For overviews of Jewish ideologies in the interwar period, see David Weinberg, *Between Tradition and Modernity: Haim Zhitlowski, Simon Dubnow, Ahad Ha-Am and the Shaping of Modern Jewish Identity* (New York: Holmes & Meier, 1996); Gitelman, *Emergence of Modern Jewish Politics*; Kalman Weiser, *Jewish People, Yiddish Nation: Noah Prylucki and the Folkist in Poland* (Toronto: University of Toronto Press, 2010); Joshua Karlip, *The Tragedy of a Generation: The Rise and Fall of Jewish Nationalism in Eastern Europe* (Cambridge, MA: Harvard University Press, 2013).

forcefully demanded subsidies for the musical group Kadimah that were rejected by the vote of the left and Ahdut. The committee's right-wing majority fiercely opposed every attempt by the left—which administered welfare—to make changes in the nutritional centers in the children's homes and to create an appropriate environment for the local activists. The end result was sad."[73]

Two areas that elicited some of the most passionate partisan arguments concerned education and language. The stage for this struggle was set well before the war and was rooted in fierce discussions over the shape of the Jewish collective future. The writings of Haim Zhitlowsky, Simon Dubnow, and Ahad Ha-Am, among many others in the Jewish intelligentsia, addressed the meaning of modernity in the Jewish context, the role of socialism, the proper language for Jewish self-emancipation (Yiddish or Hebrew), the proper "place" for the Jews (diaspora or the Land of Israel), and so forth.

Gumener does not hesitate to criticize what he perceives as the Zionists' attempt to control the community's educational and cultural organizations with their claim that the socialists collaborated with the Bolsheviks: "As soon as the Ukrainians arrived in Komenetz, Tarbut issued an announcement in Yiddish and Hebrew with a mogen dovid ["Jewish star"] and "tziyon" [Zion] at the top, which was posted in the streets of Komenetz.[74] The announcement said that the kindergarten had been seized by the Jewish socialists and by the Kultur Lige (the leaders of Narobraz) and was not under the control of Tarbut. In other circumstances, such behavior from the Komenetz Tseire Tsiyon would have surely spelled tragedy for the Jewish socialists. But the Ukrainians remained relatively calm and the issue passed without incident."[75] Gumener regarded this accusation as a dangerous attempt to undermine the socialists.

Gumener adds several appendixes to his memoir. They are translations of official documents from the Directory or Ministry of Jewish Affairs. The circular dated October 1920 was issued by the ministry, and warns local kehillahs that the exclusive use of Hebrew in official public life is illegal according to the National Personal Autonomy law promulgated on January 1, 1918, and reiterated in April 1919. The circular ends with the declaration: "The use of Hebrew instead of Yiddish for kehillah council business is completely illegal

---

[73] Gumener, *A kapitl Ukraine*, 116.

[74] Tarbut was a Hebrew primary school.

[75] Gumener, *A kapitl Ukraine*, 137. Narobraz was the Bolshevik agency for national and cultural education. The agency included a Jewish section. According to Gumener, the Zionists accused the Jewish socialists and activists in the Kultur Lige of being "leaders" in the Bolshevik educational agency—a dangerous claim when the Ukrainians were in power.

and forbidden."[76] The fact that this subject was still very much alive during the last gasps of the Jewish Ministry in the so-called Komenetz phase of the Directory that lasted from June to mid-November 1919 speaks powerfully to how seriously parties took their ideology.[77]

Gumener also criticizes what he sees as class favoritism: "For example, the Zionists received a million karbovantsi (Ukrainian currency) for a kindergarten, attended by many children from the wealthy classes, despite the fact that priority should have been to address the essential concerns of the victims who had not yet received any help. The left demanded funds for a model workers' school for children of the poor. When it was given the funds from the community ORT, the right demanded an even larger sum for the He-Halutz."[78] Class and ideology were inextricably bound up in the contentious struggle for power between parties.

Aid workers from abroad were cognizant of the role that politics played. A June 1920 report from JDC aid workers Elkanan Voorsanger and Dr. C. D. Spivak reveals that usually the first order of business when they arrived in a town was to consider the political landscape. On April 29, they left Warsaw by car for Rovne in the Volhynia district to distribute aid in Zhitomir. The Bolsheviks had retreated from Zhitomir and the Poles had just occupied the city. Upon arriving on May 1, the JDC representatives first assessed the organizational capacity of the community. Essentially this meant answering the question: can the various political factions work together? The following days were spent with local Jewish communal leaders hammering out which institutions should be funded. These heated discussions highlighted divisions along ideological lines. Nine days later, the JDC representatives drove back to Rovne and the next day to Warsaw.[79] In its reports, the JDC often gave a town by town assessment of the cooperation between "factions."

Jewish parties themselves were not stable. New coalitions were made and unmade. The leaders of both the Bund and Fareynikte decided that the political differences between them weakened the socialist presence in Komenetz-Podolsk. But rather than succumbing to the "inevitable" turn to the

---

[76] Ibid., 166.

[77] The Directory returned to Komenetz-Podolsk several times in its last year of existence (until November 1920).

[78] Founded in St. Petersburg in 1880, ORT's (Society for Trade and Agricultural Work) mission was to give poor Russian Jews practical skills for making a living. In 1921 it constituted itself into an international organization. He-Halutz was a local Zionist youth organization.

[79] JDC Archives, 1919–1921 New York Collection, Russia, General, 1920, "Report on Volhynia," June 7, 1920, folder 247.2.

Bolsheviks, they formed a new party in April 1919: "The local Bund and Fareynikte had to take an independent political orientation. In the midst of this crisis they saw how very harmful the disintegration of the socialist power was and demanded a unified position. Thus, the Fareynikte Bund [Unified Bund] was founded—first in Komenetz and then in the entire Podolia."[80] The Fareynikte Bund was active during the period that the Directory made its capital in Komenetz and participated in the Komenetz aid committee established in June 1919 by the Jewish Ministry. A memo dated March–April 1920 from JDC representatives Harry Fischer and Max Pine to Boris Bogen, director of the relief activities of the Joint Distribution Committee, notes: "This party is to be found only in Kamieniec Podolsk [sic] and is a combination of the Fareinigte [sic] and the Bund. Was at one time a stronger party having a large following among the workmen, but now it is asserted that its influence has completely weakened."[81] Indeed, Gumener laments the general weakening of the Jewish socialist parties by mid-1920.

The ideological divide colored how some Komenetz-Podolsk survivors of the pogrom era regarded Gumener, a socialist. Thus, in the yizkor book (memorial book) of Komenetz-Podolsk, published in Israel in 1964, Leon Blatman, a Zionist, recalls Gumener in a negative manner. Blatman notes that although the Jewish population of Komenetz was Zionist in the majority, the Ukrainian government preferred to work with the Jewish socialists. This observation is true because socialists dominated the Jewish governmental organs during the short-lived Ukrainian National Republic. But it was not the whole story.

In his account of the Bolsheviks' and Petliura's administration of Komenetz-Podolsk in June 1919, Blatman first treats Gumener as a lackey of the Bolsheviks and then accuses him of flipflopping to the Ukrainians:

> When the Petliura government under the pressure of the Red Army retreated all the way to Poland (Galicia), some local Jewish socialists conveniently forgot their allegiance to the Ukrainian government. In Komenetz-Podolsk [they] used the Bolsheviks to destroy the Kehillah and take over its functions. In [April] 1919, during the six weeks of the Bolsheviks' occupation, Messrs. Gumener, Bograd & Company were reigning supreme over the Jewish community. On the return from Poland in June 1919, the Petliura government settled for a few months in Komenetz-Podolsk, waiting for the liberation of Kiev. The Ministry of Jewish Affairs ... appointed as heads of the Ministry's departments the

---

[80] Gumener, *A kapitl Ukraine*, 41.

[81] JDC Archives, 1919–1921 New York Collection, Russia, General, 1920: "Letter from Joint Distribution Committee to Dr. Boris D. Bogen," April 1, 1920, folder 247.2.

same Jewish socialists who, only a few weeks before, had destroyed
the Kehillah and cooperated with the Bolsheviks. Again, Gumener,
Bograd & Co., held the power over the Kehillahs in Komenetz-Podolsk
and in all the cities and towns liberated from the Red Army.[82]

This observation is only partially accurate. Gumener was a member of the
anti-Bolshevik faction of the socialist party Fareynikte, which had split from
the pro-Bolshevik faction. Eventually the left Fareynikte and the Bund united
to become the Jewish Communist Union. This was not Gumener's ideological
home. But for pragmatic reasons, namely, the great needs of the decimated
Jewish community, Gumener felt that he had to cooperate with whatever occupying authority was present: "We, the Jewish socialists, held that the only
way to work for the Jewish masses was to live among them and to remain with
them. We thus refused every opportunity to leave Ukraine and go to Moscow
or Western Europe and from afar send various prescriptions as a way to heal
the very sick Jewish invalid. We had to stay in place and actively help the Jewish masses. Understandably, this required compromises and resulted in some
great mistakes."[83] Gumener, however, does not shy away from blaming units
of the Red Army for initiating violence against the Jews. Describing the May
1919 pogrom in Vinitza, he writes: "We assumed that if the peasants were to
enter Vinitza the Red Army would join the pogromists."[84] Gumener notes that
in Tchan, a town about 80 miles north of Komenetz, Jews and local peasants
even joined to repel rogue Red Army pogromists.[85] In fact, Red Army troops
sometimes fought against the local units of the Bolshevik security organiza-

[82] L. S. Blatman, ed., *Kamianets-Podilskyi Memorial Book* (New York: Sponsors of the
Kamenetz-Podolsk Memorial Book, 1966), 80. Bograd was a member of Fareynikte.
Blatman's dates are incorrect: Petliura retreated to Poland in 1920.

[83] Gumener, *A kapitl Ukraine,* 36. In his autobiographical sketch in M. Shalit's *Oyf di
hurves fun milhomes un mehumes,* Gumener notes that after 1920 he was not involved
with any political party. Although he does not mention it there, he remained ideologically in the camp of the "territorialists," a movement that advocated developing a
Jewish colony that did not have as its end goal the development of a state. The movement was represented by the Freeland League for Jewish Territorial Colonization. The
territorialists employed the term "internal autonomy" to mean the free development
of Jewish culture. See the entry in Yankl Salant, "Frayland-Lige," *YIVO Encyclopedia
of Jews in Eastern Europe,* https://yivoencyclopedia.org/article.aspx/Frayland-lige. Gumener's
death is noted in the English-language territorialist magazine *Freeland* 2, 4 (1946): 2,
where he is identified as the "president of the Novogrudaker Committee."

[84] Gumener, *A kapitl Ukraine,* 157. For scholarship on Bolshevik antisemitism in the
context of the Civil War, see Brendan McGeever, *Antisemitism and the Russian Revolution* (Cambridge: Cambridge University Press, 2019), 38–52, 88–111.

[85] Gumener, *A kapitl Ukraine,* 74.

tion Cheka, associating it with Jews. As Budnitskii notes, three-quarters of Jews who in the 1930s served in the NKVD, the notorious Soviet secret police agency, began their careers as Chekists during the Civil War—despite the fact that the Cheka itself had agents who were antisemitic.[86]

There were short periods of relative calm when attempts were made to stabilize communal institutions. The Polish-Soviet War, during which the Polish Army pushed the Red Army out of Volhynia and Podolia and captured Kiev and Komenetz created a breathing space for the JDC to bring aid to Podolia. This period coincided with the White Army's last attempt to start an offensive in summer 1919, which for a short while diverted the Red Army from Volhynia and Podolia. The JDC had established an office in Warsaw in June 1919. The battlefield, however, precluded entering Ukraine. The JDC had to wait for permission from the US State Department and for a "friendlier" occupying army before penetrating south Ukraine. Thus, it was not until the coalition of Ukrainians and Poles occupied parts of Podolia from November 1919 to July 1920, in the midst of the Polish-Soviet War, that the JDC deemed it safe for its aid workers to enter south Ukraine. The first American relief team arrived in Warsaw in February 1920 and established an office in Kiev in April 1920. "A great deal was accomplished through the significant amount of money and the large amount of clothes and product that was received. We opened distribution points for children. Orphans and the elderly were cared for. An entire array of centers was dedicated to medical aid. There was support for cooperatives, and help with credit was also organized, plus a variety of schools."[87]

Any positive development was exceptional and short-lived. Events overtook all efforts: by August the Volunteer Army controlled the regions west of the Dnieper River, including the Kiev and Podolia gubernias. The Red Army's counterattack began in October, and in November the Volunteer Army began a quick and disorderly retreat south. Its flight in the winter of 1919–20 was accompanied by anti-Jewish violence. The American presence disappeared, especially after the murder on July 5, 1920, of two American aid workers. Israel Friedlaender and Rabbi Bernard Cantor were on a fact-finding mission in

[86] Budnitskii, *Russian Jews Between the Reds and the Whites*, 112. The full name of the Cheka was the All-Russian Extraordinary Commission for Combating Counterrevolution and Sabotage. It was active from 1917–23 until it morphed into the OPGU (1923–34) and later the NKVD and KGB. For antisemitism within the Cheka during the Civil War period, see McGeever, *Antisemitism and the Russian Revolution*, 74–75.

[87] Gumener, *A kapitl Ukraine*, 115.

Podolia when they were killed by Red Army soldiers. (Gumener had met with
the American delegation in Komenetz shortly before the murders.)[88]

Once the Red Army controlled Ukraine the pogrom period was basically
over. But there emerged a new form of official persecution of Jews and others as the Soviets imposed their centralized, one-ideology rule. Gumener describes this period in the section "Bolsheviks in Komenetz-Podolsk (end of
1920 beginning 1921)."[89] All aid now was concentrated in the Jewish Public
Committee to Aid Jewish Pogrom Victims, known in Russian as the Evobkom
and as Yidgeskom in Yiddish.[90] In June 1920, the JDC had reluctantly signed
an agreement with the Soviets under which American aid would be funneled
through Yidgeskom. The agreement seemed the only way that the JDC could
operate in Ukraine. As part of the agreement, the JDC insisted that the noncommunist aid organizations that were still working in Ukraine participate,
namely, EKOPO, ORT, OZE, and Culture League.[91] For a while this arrange-
ment worked in Komenetz. The local Yidgeskom was staffed with both Jewish
communists and socialists, many of whom worked in the older Jewish aid
organizations. Yidgeskom was even engaged in emigration work with Jewish
organizations in Bessarabia. This collaboration, however, was only temporary. As Gumener notes: "The chairman of the Yidgeskom (E_N) arrived from
Kiev and suddenly issued an edict, ordering that the new commission could
only be composed of Communists. In vain the Komenetz Jewish Communists
showed E_N that his position greatly damaged aid activity but it did not help.
E_N was angry and wanted to take revenge on the Komenetz 'counterrevolutionaries.'"[92] This policy was part of the sovietization that took place as
the Bolsheviks purged local communal institutions of nonparty activists and
professionals.

Interestingly, whenever leaders and members of the Jewish community
were arrested, politics was set aside in an effort to save the accused. Gumener
describes the anguish of the Komenetz Jewish community when the Cheka
brought 16 Zionists from Mohilev to Komenetz for trial. They were accused of
being supporters of the Whites. Komenetz had suffered a similar show trial
when the UNR's secret police arrested Alexander Khomski and accused him

---

[88] Ibid., 135; Beizer, *Relief in Time of Need*, 86–87.

[89] Gumener, *A kapitl Ukraine*, 127–36.

[90] Jewish Public Committee to Aid Jewish Pogrom Victims (Evobkom or Evobshchest-
kom (Rus.), Yidgeskom (Yid.) was conceived as an umbrella organization overseen
by the Soviet government consisting of the established organizations (EKOPO, ORT,
OZE, and the Kultur Lige) and the Jewish socialist parties.

[91] Granick, "First American Organization in Soviet Russia," 61–93.

[92] Gumener, *A kapitl Ukraine*, 135.

of being a counterrevolutionary, that is, a supporter of the Bolsheviks. "The Jewish socialists took vigorous steps to defend the Mohilev Zionists. Unable to speak directly with the authorities in whose hands the fate of the men lay, we quickly appealed to the Jewish communists. We argued that it was simply ridiculous to accuse as counterrevolutionaries men whom we knew were loyal and who had even saved many Jewish Communists from death. Ukrainian pogromists turned all Jews into Bolsheviks and based on this accusation committed great atrocities. Now Russian Bolsheviks want to transform all Jews into counterrevolutionaries, and antisemitism again found favorable soil. Fortunately, the local Jewish communists took an interest in the situation and did everything to save the arrestees."[93] In the Khomski trial the Jewish Ministry—despite its very weakened state—was able to intervene and save the accused from the death penalty; the defendants in the latter trial received various sentences but none were shot. The Jewish activists were powerless and the Jewish population in despair, as Gumener states:

> In truth, the strong socialist organizations that we had in Podolia in the years 1917–19 no longer existed. During the pogrom violence the Bolsheviks had undermined the existence of the Jewish socialist parties. Their ranks were increasingly thinned and their impact on the surrounding life weakened. The Fareynikte Bund did not resonate with the Jewish workers. Dejected, persecuted, and exhausted, the Jewish workers were indifferent to political and social issues. Some individuals remained with the socialist parties, and some joined the Bolsheviks. The masses however, remained without a direction.[94]

Gumener's Last Period in Podolia

In this last period of Gumener's work in Podolia, the Cheka was very active. Both Jews and Christians suffered. The closing and sovietization of businesses led to corruption and unemployment. The situation in Komenetz-Podolsk was unbearable: "Every day new arrests and searches with no ends. I met a known communist, a former Bundist, who came for a few days to Komenetz. He wondered how we could live in such a situation. Komenetz, he said, resembles an insane asylum."[95] Gumener decided to leave Ukraine permanently. Fearing imminent arrest, he and some other activists fled Komenetz-Podolsk in the

---

[93] Ibid., 131.

[94] Ibid., 133.

[95] Ibid., 145.

middle of the night for Galicia and from there continued to Poland "without saying goodbye to friends and relatives."[96]

How then did Gumener assess his experiences in Podolia? At the end of his memoir, he speaks as both an aid worker and a socialist. And as a socialist, he takes responsibility for the decisions made under the harshest conditions imaginable. But he insists that living among the masses, and being engaged in Jewish political and communal life, was still more honorable than fleeing from the challenge. As noted, he admits that working in conditions of continuous crisis required compromises: "We lived in a period in Ukraine when every word, every step from various Jewish groups could cost tens, hundreds, and even thousands of Jewish lives."[97] A careful reading of Gumener's memoir reveals some of those dangerous and delicate moments that required political adroitness. This reality was not always understood or appreciated, as seen in Leon Blatman's post-war claim that Gumener flip-floped between Petliura's and the Bolshevik's regime in Komenetz-Poldosk.

At the end there is also a bitter statement condemning the relative inaction of Polish Jews towards their Ukrainian Jewish brethren. He writes: "In the years 1914–15 aid workers saw the warm reception given by the Ukrainian Jews to the homeless Jews of Galicia and Poland who had suffered in the war. Now they could not help themselves from asking what would happen if the Ukrainian Jews were homeless and needed help from Galician and Polish Jews—how would the latter treat them? The bitter answer was provided by life itself. It was simply difficult to comprehend and to believe that the Polish Jews who in their time received such material and moral support from the Ukrainian Jews would forget so soon."[98] These are the Jews from Galicia and Bukovina who were expelled by the Russian Army to the Pale of Settlement in August–November 1914 and deported in larger numbers during the Russian army's retreat in the face of German forces, from March to September 1915.[99] Of course, Polish Jews in 1920 were not in great shape. The Jewish population faced broad pauperization, national boycotts from the right, and accusations of Bolshevism, and was desperately engaged in diplomacy at the League of Nations to defend the minority rights that had been promised in Article 7 of

---

[96] Ibid., 154.

[97] Ibid., 157.

[98] Ibid., 155.

[99] Eric Lohr, "The Russian Army and the Jews: Mass Deportation, Hostages, and Violence during World War I," *Russian Review* 60 (2001): 404–19; and Mark von Hagen, *War in a European Borderland: Occupations and Occupation Plans in Galicia and Ukraine, 1914–1918* (Seattle: University of Washington Press, 2007).

Poland's Minority Treaty signed at Versailles in 1919.[100] Gumener returned to Vilna in 1921 and in 1925 moved to Nowogrodek, where he continued to work in refugee resettlement, especially in the protection of Jewish orphans displaced by World War I and the Russian Civil War.

What broad conclusions can we cull from Gumener's experiences? Was it simply that the Jewish groups could not overcome their "petty" disagreements? This is not a fair assessment. Despite the circumstances, each group, rightly or wrongly, sincerely believed that their own visions would shape the very future of the Jewish people. In other words, they trusted that there would be a Jewish future. These were not simply petty differences, as much as they may seem to us today. The array of forces, however, that Jewish communities faced was overwhelming, and the community had neither the power nor the allies to deal with the challenges. Even if the Jewish factions had been united in their response to the terrors, there was no power that could stop the pogroms.

In the memoir's final sentence written in 1921, Gumener already shares his concern for the unknown worrying future: "Now, as we are forced to leave, perhaps for a long time, Ukraine in general and specifically Podolia, we can no longer give advice to our comrades and friends who remain there. We can only send them our deepest brotherly love and compassion."[101]

---

[100] Fink, *Defending the Rights of Others*, 285–94.

[101] Gumener, *A kapitl Ukraine*, 158.

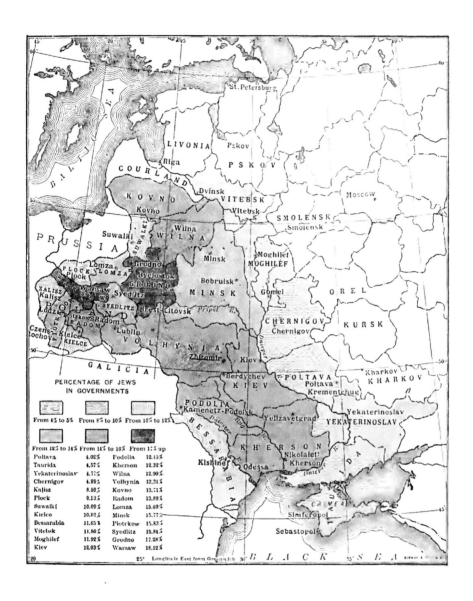

Figure 4. Map of Western Russia showing the Jewish Pale of Settlement. Isidore Singer, ed., *The Jewish Encyclopedia* (New York: Funk and Wagnalls, 1901), 10: 531. *Source:* Wikimedia Commons.

Figure 5. Pale of Settlement (1791–1917). In Judith Reesa Baskin and Kenneth Seeskin, *The Cambridge Guide to Jewish History, Religion, and Culture* (Cambridge: University Press, 2010), 186. Reproduced with permission of the Licensor through PLSclear.

Brief Chronology

Dates and events are roughly correlated with the sections in *A Ukrainian Chapter* (the book's sections are in bold)

February 1917	The Russian Revolution.
October 1917	The Bolshevik victory in the Russian Revolution.
January 1918	The Ukrainian National Republic (UNR) proclaims its independence. Ukraine is invaded by the Red Army.
February 1918	The UNR evacuates Kiev.
March 1918	The Treaty of Brest-Litovsk.
April–December 1918	Germany occupies Ukraine. The Red Army retreats. The period of the Hetmanate regime. The end of World War I.
November 1918	The creation of Western Ukrainian National Republic (ZUNR) in eastern Galicia.
December 1918	The Hetmanate is overthrown, and the period of the Directory of the UNR begins.
January–March 1919	The second Red Army offensive in Ukraine. The Directory evacuates Kiev and relocates to Vinnytsia, Zhmerynka, Proskurov, and Rovno. The act of union between the West Ukrainian National Republic and the UNR.
	Gumener's memoir begins

February 1919

February 15, 1919. The pogroms in Proskurov and Felshin.

Pogrom Terror in Komenetz and the Region. Pogroms are perpetrated by all sides: Directory troops, peasant militias, Denikin's White forces, and the Red Army. Gumener describes the formation of the Okhrany Committee.

Spring–Fall 1919

Bolsheviks in Podolia (Spring 1919). The establishment of Komenetz Jewish socialist council. The formation of the Fareynikte Bund.

Petliura's Army Attacks Podolia (Summer 1919). The height of the pogrom period. Gumener's flight from Komenetz. The pogrom in Komenetz (June 3–6). Ukrainians initiate the Khomski show trial in Komenetz.

The Ukrainian Movement and the Jewish Pogroms (Summer 1919). Gumener's review of Jewish attitudes towards the Ukrainian national movement.

Aid Activity for the Victims. The Central Committee to Aid Pogrom Victims is registered in Kiev in February 1919. The Red Army occupies Kiev and Komenetz. The Central Committee is closed in May. Gumener describes the competition between the Soviet aid committee based in the Evsektsiia and the committee of the Red Cross.

The Mood of the Jewish Population under the Soviet regime (Summer 1919). Gumener attends the first meeting of the Editorial Board for Gathering and Researching Materials Regarding the Pogroms in Ukraine. The

White Army advances into southern Ukraine and the Red Army retreats.

The Situation of the Jews in the Komenetz Period of the Ukrainian National Republic. The Directory resides intermittently in Komenetz from June to mid-November. A new aid committee is established. The persecutions from the Directory's counter-intelligence agents. The White Army offensive (August/September to December).

The Jewish Ministry in August–November 1919 (Komenetz Period). Gumener describes aid activity in Komenetz, as well as the relationship between the Jewish Ministry and the kehillot.

November–December 1919   **The Second Death Throes of the Ukrainian National Republic.** The ZUNR army retreats. Polish forces are in Podolia and Volhynia, making their headquarters in Komenetz. Gumener travels to Vilna. Pressured by the Poles, the White Army, and the Red Army, Petliura retreats to Volhynia and then to Warsaw, seeking an alliance with Poland. The Red Army counteroffensive against Denikin's White Army begins.

April 1920–July 1920   **Under the Polish Occupation (end of 1919–July 1920).** Polish forces control Kiev (to June) and Komenetz (to July). Denikin's White Army instigates pogroms in Podolia.

The Komenetz Jewish-American Relief Committee for the Pogrom Victims. Aid is funneled through the JDC by the Jewish community in Kishinev. In January 1920, JDC representative James Becker arrives in Komenetz with funds. Gumener describes the interparty conflicts over control of the aid. Additional JDC missions to Komenetz take place in February, March, and July 1920.

The Polish Assault on Kiev (April–June 1920). The alliance of Polish and UNR armies. The Directory is headquartered in Vinitza. Gumener describes the relationship between Jewish parties and the Jewish Ministry in Vinitza. The Red Army counter offensive against Polish-Ukrainian forces begins. The death of JDC representatives Friedlaender and Cantor. The Red Army captures Kiev in June and Komenetz in July.

Bolsheviks in Podolia again (Summer 1920). The Bolsheviks in Komenetz, and the activity of the Cheka. The Bolsheviks initiate the show trial of the Mohilev Zionists in Komenetz. The Jewish Public Committee to Aid Jewish Pogrom Victims (Yidgeskom) begins working in Kiev in July.

September 1920

The Ukrainians retake Komenetz-Podolsk and the region (September 1920). The Directory regains control of Komenetz. Gumener describes Jewish party politics under the Directory.

November 1920

Bolsheviks in Komenetz-Podolsk (end of 1920, beginning of 1921). The Red Army is victorious in Ukraine. Petliura's army is defeated. The White Army is driven out of Ukraine. Gumener describes the sovietization of aid work in Komemetz, and the Cheka persecution of aid workers in Yidgeskom.

Our Wandering in Galicia and Poland. Gumener describes his final flight from Ukraine.

Conclusion.

A Ukrainian Chapter:
An Aid Worker's Memoir of Sorrow (Podolia, 1918–20)

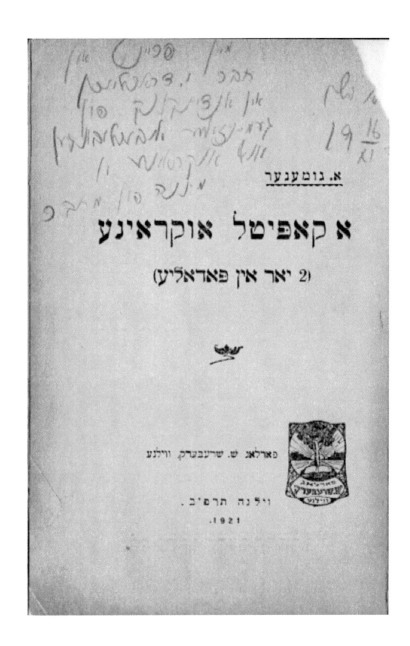

א. גומענער

א קאפיטל אוקראינע

(יאר אין פאדאליע (2

פארלאג ש. שרעבערק, ווילנע

ווילנה תרפ״ב

1921.

Title page from the 1921 edition of *A kapitl Ukraine: Tsvey yor in Podolye,*
with Eli Gumener's inscription

Introduction

Tens of thousands of Jewish families were slaughtered, and thousands of communities were destroyed in horrible pogroms throughout Ukraine. The general story has been well documented. But the blood-soaked events in Podolia, which for the last two years was isolated from the entire world in a unique environment, have hardly been spoken about. The horrible and unprecedented events that occurred there are altogether ignored in Yiddish literature.

For this reason, I consider it my obligation to record everything that I experienced in the past two years. My active participation in Jewish communal and political life in Podolia, as well as in local government, gave me the opportunity to see and to hear everything that I have written. Unfortunately, except for a few items, my large archive was lost, and I have had to reconstruct the facts from memory. I am especially thankful to Mr. M. Fuchs for helping me.

I do not have political or party goals. I simply record what I know for future historians who will want to write the bloody tragedy of a powerless people put to the sword, and of the heroic moments that make up the thorny wreath of martyrdom in Podolia.

The author
May 1921, Vilne–Komenetz-Podolsk

Komenetz and Podolia

Podolia has always been a remote and isolated corner of Russia.[1] Industry was barely developed there. The only industry was sugar production, whose factories were located for the most part near small towns and villages. Jews worked in these factories solely as managers, bookkeepers, and brokers. They were mostly involved in commerce and trades connected to local use. The branches of Jewish industrial production we encounter in Lithuania and Poland that emphasized exports were not found in Podolia.

Even worse, in hindsight, was the situation in the provincial center, Komenetz-Podolsk.[2] Until the war it was without a railway. The Jewish population made its livelihood by providing services to landowners and minor government officials. Political and cultural life in Podolia was meagre and mediocre.

The Society for Aid to the Jewish Poor provided social services, and the Talmud Torah was the cultural center. The half-assimilated, secularly trained intelligentsia, both from the upper and middle class, played the central role in all organizations. The war and then the revolution, however, caused a great upheaval. The older, wealthier classes and the communal activists left and were replaced by so-called speculators and war profiteers.

The workers' movement was also very weak in Podolia. Even after the Russian Revolution, one could not find suitable people to take positions in local self-government. And the few Jewish activists who were fit to take up responsible positions were attacked from all sides of the political spectrum.

The cultural and intellectual poverty played no small part in the events that occurred in Podolia. Although there were activists that spoke in the name of the 500,000 Podolian Jews, rarely was the general Jewish population consulted. In Kiev these "benefactors" sat and squabbled among themselves for

---

[1] Podolia was an administrative unit (*gubernia*) in the Russian Empire. It is located in the southwestern part of present-day Ukraine. The 1897 Russian census estimated the population of Podolia at 3 million, with Jews comprising about 12 percent of the population (369,000). Stephen Rudnitsky uses the figure 3.7 million in 1910, with about 448,000 Jews (12 percent of the population). See Stephen Rudnitsky, *Ukraine: The Land and Its People. An Introduction to Its Geography* (New York: Rand McNally, 1918), 132–35.—Trans.

[2] Komenetz-Podolsk (Yid.), Kamyanets-Podilskyy (Ukr.), Kamenets Podolskiy (Rus.) is located in southwest Podolia on the Smotrych River (a tributary of the Dniester) near the borders of Galicia and Bessarabia. On the eve of World War I, there were approximately 23,000 Jews in the town, almost half of the total population. See Benyamin Lukin, "Kam'ianets'-Podil's'kyi," in *The YIVO Encyclopedia of Jews in Eastern Europe*, https://yivoencyclopedia.org/article.aspx/Kamianets-Podilskyi.—Trans.

positions in the Nationality Council.[3] Very rarely was the province privileged to see a representative from Kiev. The Jews of Podolia were left helpless during their most terrible moments and could not even count on moral support from Kiev.

The dilapidated and disorganized conditions in the province also had a negative effect upon Jewish political leaders in Ukraine. They did not feel responsible for anyone, and left the entire Jewish population in the dust. As the situation worsened, the Jewish political leaders in Kiev deserted the Jews of Podolia. Some went to Moscow and others to Paris or London, abandoning the entire Jewish population in whose name they so liked to speak.

February 15, 1919 (Proskurov Pogrom)

The pogrom in Proskurov marked the beginning of a new bloody history for both Podolia and Ukraine.[4] There had already been pogroms in Barditchev, Zhitomir, Ovrutch, and other places.[5] But the Jews hoped that these were random and isolated events. The Proskurov pogrom, however, showed the Jews what to expect in the near future from their Ukrainian rulers.[6]

---

[3] On January 25, 1918, the Ukrainian parliament, the Central Rada, established the Ukrainian National Republic (UNR). The UNR committed itself to the idea of national autonomy for minority groups. A cabinet-level position, the vice-secretary for Jewish affairs (later the minister of Jewish affairs), was established. The Nationality Council was formed by the vice-secretary for Jewish affairs, whose representation was supposed to come from the various Jewish parties. Popular elections, however, were never held, leading to ongoing intraparty fights over representation in the government.—Trans.

[4] Proskurov (today Khmelnytskyy) is located 45 miles northeast of Komenetz-Podolsk. A 1909 census records approximately 17,000 Jews, nearly half of the total population.—Trans.

[5] Barditchev (Yid.), Berdichev (Rus.), Berdychiv (Ukr.) is 198 miles northeast of Komenetz-Podolsk. Ovrutch (Yid.), Ovruch (Rus., Ukr.) is 335 miles northeast of Komenetz-Podolsk.—Trans.

[6] There were pogroms on December 28, 1918 and January 16, 1919 in Ovrutch (Volhynia gubernia). Approximately 50 people were murdered there. In Barditchev the pogroms began on January 15, 1919 and continued for three days. The shops and the houses were looted. Tens of Jews were killed. In Zhitomir the first pogrom began on January 7, 1919, and continued for five days. The result of that pogrom was 80 murdered, countless wounded, and many women raped. The damage amounted to tens of millions [rubles].

On shabbes, February 15, 1919, a pitiless and horrific pogrom was per-petrated in Proskurov, and several days later in Felshtin.[7] Although inno-cent Jewish blood was spilled in virtually every Jewish town in Ukraine, Proskurov and Felshtin surpassed all previous incidents in their shocking gruesomeness, horror, and cruelty. Officially initiated and organized by the representatives of the Ukrainian regime, they were conducted with wild cold-blooded abandon, and with a nightmarish cynical sadism.

There have already been investigations regarding the pogroms (for ex-ample, the lawyer Hillerson from Kiev) and there will probably be further in-quiries.[8] Here I simply want to relate my own impressions. I knew Proskurov and Felshtin very well. I often visited these towns as a representative of the Petersburg and the Kiev Committees (EKOPO and KOPE).[9]

Proskurov is the most interesting town in Podolia. It lies near the railroad between Kiev and Volotchisk on one side and Shepetovka and Komenetz on the other.[10] Proskurov had always engaged in robust commerce. There were several factories and mills. Jewish communal life was more developed there than in other towns in Podolia. Interesting intellectuals and activists of vari-ous political shades lived in Proskurov.

I was in Proskurov a month before the pogrom for private business and spent a few days in relative quiet. There were no hints that dark clouds were gathering over the unfortunate town. But in reality Ukraine already smelled of gunpowder.

The Directory under Vynnychenko, that future Communist, was in-creasingly losing ground. No positive alternative authority emerged after the Ukrainian peasants had ousted the Hetman.[11] For the Jewish population ter-

---

[7] Felshtin (today Hvardiske) is located 93 miles northwest of Komenetz-Podolsk. Ac-cording to the 1897 census, its Jewish population stood at 1,885.—Trans.

[8] A. I. Hillerson [Gillerson] was a representative of the Central Committee (Kiev) to Aid Pogrom Victims.—Trans.

[9] KOPE, the Kiev Society for Aid to Jewish War Veterans, was the sister organization of EKOPO.—Trans.

[10] Volotchisk (Yid.), Volochisk (Rus.), Volochysk (Ukr.) is in Volhynia gubernia and is 61 miles north of Komenetz. Shepetovka (Yid. and Rus.), Shepetivka (Ukr.) is in Vol-hynia gubernia and is 105 miles north of Komenetz. —Trans.

[11] The Directory was the executive council of the UNR, created after Ukrainians over-threw the Hetmanate of Pavlo Skoropadsky, the conservative and reactionary regime that ruled from April to December 1918. Volodymyr Kyrylovych Vynnychenko (1880–1951) was prime minister in the Directory but stepped down because he did not agree with its Entente-oriented policy. He moved to Vienna, where he tried to convince Le-nin to support an independent Ukrainian republic. Vynnychenko is also known as one of the fathers of modern Ukrainian literature.—Trans.

rible days began, namely, the events in Ovrutch, Zhitomir, Barditchev, and other places.

On January 12, 1919, the proclamations of the Directory were issued after various Jewish groups began to raise a tumult about the pogroms.[12] On the one hand, the Directory in its proclamations claimed that the pogroms were entirely the result of counterrevolutionary activity that defamed the Ukrainian People's Army. On the other hand, the Directory called on the Jewish population to combat "anarchistic Bolshevik elements" and in effect officially emphasized the presence of Communists among the Jewish population.

In order to placate both the military and the Jewish population in such a tense moment, the Directory extracted a promise from the Jewish democrats (?) [sic] (read: right socialists, Folkspartey, Zionists, and Ahdut) to reproach the Jewish Communists, and suggested that perhaps (?!) [sic] the Jewish community should establish an espionage agency ("counterrevolutionary") that would uncover (!) [sic] Jewish Communists and turn them over to the wild Ukrainian military that already regarded every young Jew as a Bolshevik.[13] One could see that the Ukrainians had taken the position that all Jews were answerable for Jewish Communists.

In the meantime, the situation of the UNR became increasingly difficult as the Bolsheviks became more popular. In order to salvage their position, the Ukrainian activists thought up the following scheme: the Bolsheviks always claim that power has to belong to the working class. Well and good. In Ukraine, however, there are two categories of workers: peasants and industrial workers. So, the government will convene a workers' congress to decide the fate of Ukraine. The idea was that the peasants, who are the majority in

---

[12] See Appendix No. 1, 98.—Trans.

[13] In 1920, Vynnychenko returned to Ukraine from abroad and denounced Semesenko. He also denounced an independent/autonomous Ukrainian Communist Party and was particularly sharp against Petliura. He would take an important role in the government of the UNR. [*Democrats* was a term generally employed for socialist parties. In this instance, where the parties mentioned are not socialists, Gumener is using the term ironically. Founded in 1906 by the renowned historian Simon Dubnow and Yisroel Efroikin, the Folkspartey (People's Party, known as Folkists) advocated nonterritorial autonomy and called for the right of Jews to administer their own education, culture, and communal welfare. It accepted the need to work with other national (non-Jewish) parties. One of its leaders, Wolf (Yaakov Zeev) Latzky-Bertholdi, briefly served as minister for Jewish affairs in the UNR. Ahdut (Unity) was a religious party founded in 1918 in Russia by Rabbi Yisrael Meir ha-Kohen (the Hafets Hayim). Although it was critical of Zionist ideology, it generally allied with the Zionist parties against the socialists during the period of the UNR.—Trans.]

the country, would dominate the congress and thus weaken the Bolshevik movement. But this plan came to naught.[14]

Pressure from the Bolshevik army forced the administration of the UNR to evacuate Kiev and relocate to Vinitza at the beginning of February 1919.[15] The ministry's cabinet turned to the right and effective power was ultimately transferred to the "atamanchiks."[16] In February 1919 a petty ataman named Semesenko found himself in Proskurov.[17]

The local Ukrainian Bolsheviks were also active. They agitated extensively for the Soviet regime, and were preparing to establish workers' councils [soviets], including in Proskurov.

The chasm between Ukrainian and Jewish political groups widened all the more. When the Directory was still in Kiev it made an effort to forge an agreement between Ukrainian and non-Ukrainian socialist groups (among the Jews, the Bund and Fareynikte), but the negotiations failed. The Jewish socialist press led a fierce campaign (in *Naye tsayt*—Fareynikte—and in *Folk-*

---

[14] This "Workers' Congress" met in Kiev on January 22, 1919. The UNR hoped to shore up its support among the peasants. But as the Red Army continued its drive towards Kiev, many peasant and worker delegates either simply went back to their homes or defected to the Ukrainian Bolsheviks.—Trans.

[15] This was the time that Vynnychenko resigned from the Directory and went abroad. [The Red Army entered Ukraine on January 3, 1919. By January 26, it occupied Kiev and the Directory was forced to relocate to Vinitza (Yid.), Vinnitsa (Rus.), Vinnytsya (Ukr.), which is approximately 69 miles from Komenetz. Symon Petliura was commander of the Ukrainian army and president of the Directory. In Vinitza he established a new right-wing, anti-Bolshevik ruling council and tried unsuccessfully to gain Entente support. This government failed and another council was established in April 1919 and again in August 1919.—Trans.]

[16] Conspicuous among the Ukrainian peasant masses were the Cossacks, who very often were bandits, and who because of the war, were unaccustomed to normal work. These peasant-Cossacks formed insurgent divisions; ordinary criminals would often join them. At the head of these divisions were usually former officers, very often monarchists, and Ukrainian chauvinist intellectuals who all bore the title *ataman*. The ataman was fully independent and often transferred his loyalties from the Ukrainians back to the Bolsheviks and vice versa (e.g., Gregoriev in 1919 and Volokh in Lubar in Volhynia gubernia in 1919). [*Ataman* (*otaman* in Ukrainian) was a Russian title for Cossack leaders but was also utilized to designate various non-Cossack commanders. For Ukrainian insurgents the term elicited the romantic image of the warrior who fought for freedom against repressive governments.—Trans.]

[17] Ataman Ivan Semesenko (1894–1920) was commander of the Petliura brigade of the Zaporozhian Cossacks, Third Haidamak Regiment. He was responsible for the February 1919 pogroms in Proskurov and Felshtin, among other pogroms. It is believed that he was executed by the Ukrainian authorities in 1920.—Trans.

spartey tsaytung—the Bund) against Poale Tsiyon, which participated in the Ukrainian Ministry (Revutsky, Goldelman).[18]

At the [Ukrainian] Workers' Congress, M. Rafes, the leader of the Ukrainian Bund, came out as an ally of the Russian Soviet authority. Consequently, the Fareynikte split into right- and left-wing factions. As usual, the Jewish bourgeois parties did not take a side.[19] The factionalization between Jews and Ukrainians was also reflected in the province, where it took on a more radical character. There were some progressive-leaning Ukrainian activists who were against violent excesses, but regrettably, they were few and weak.

The situation became even more serious. In the face of the Red Army assault, the territory of the UNR shrank. Proskurov, as I have already written, occupied a very important geographic position, and it was rumored that a communist uprising was being prepared in the town. The atmosphere was tense. On February 6, Ataman Semesenko published the following order:

---

[18] Abraham Revutsky, *In di shvere teg oif Ukraine: Zikhroines fun a yidishn ministr* [In the terrible days in Ukraine: Recollections from a Jewish minister] (Berlin: Yidisher literarisher farlag, 1924); Goldelman, *Jewish National Autonomy in Ukraine*. The Bund and Fareynikte did not want the Zionist parties to have influence in the government. Abraham Revutsky (1889–1946) was a member of Poale Tsiyon and served as the third minister of Jewish affairs in the Directory. Solomon Goldelman (1885–1974) was also a member of Poale Tsiyon. In December 1918, he was appointed acting minister of labor and acting secretary for national minorities in the government of the Directory. In 1919 he also served as deputy to Serhiy Ostapenko, the minister of trade and industry, and in 1920 he was deputy minister of labor in Prime Minister Mazepa's cabinet. His books *Jewish National Autonomy in Ukraine, 1917–1920* and *Letters from a Jewish Social Democrat about Ukraine* were published in Vienna in 1921.—Trans.

[19] Moshe Rafes (1883–1942) was born in Vilna and was head of the Bund in Kiev. After the UNR declared its independence, Rafes urged peace with Soviet Russia and the establishment of a Ukrainian Socialist Republic. Although Rafes gave ideological reasons for turning to communism, historian Brendan McGeever has argued convincingly that antisemitism and the pogroms also served as a powerful catalyst for the decision of Rafes and many other socialist Jews to support the Bolsheviks. After the Civil War, Rafes lived in Moscow. He was arrested in May 1938 and died in a Gulag camp in 1942. See McGeever, *Antisemitism and the Russian Revolution*, 148. Gumener states in several passages that the Proskurov and Felshtin pogroms triggered an exodus to the Bolshevik camp. The impression is that this shift was not always ideologically motivated but was the lesser of the two evils when faced with the choice of the Red Army or the UNR forces.—Trans.

Order

> To Petliura's Zaporozhian Cossack Brigade from the Ukrainian Peo-
> ple's Army.

> Proskurov, February 6, 1919, Garrison Division. No. 6.

> I am ordering the population to stop its anarchistic demonstration. I
> have enough force to deal with you. More than anything I want to
> make the Jews aware. You are a despised nation and yet you create
> such turmoil between Christians! Is life not precious to you? Have you
> not mercy on your own people? We don't bother you—so be silent. You
> are such a miserable people and still you agitate against the impover-
> ished masses!

> Signed: Commander of the Zaporozhian Cossack Brigade, Ataman
> Semesenko

> From the original copied by Brigade Sergeant Yatsenko.

In the air one felt the lust for Jewish blood. Travel was impossible because
Jews were killed on the trains and on the roads.

The Communists, both Jewish and Christian, decided to resist the authority of the UNR and to support the Soviet regime. The Jewish socialists,
however, asked them not to take such a step because it would end catastrophically for the Jewish population. P. Krupnik, who was the chairman of the
Proskurov Kultur Lige and a leader in Fareynikte, argued that an uprising
would accomplish nothing, except that rivers of Jewish blood would flow in
the streets. Unfortunately, his prophecy was fulfilled: he was among the thousands of Jews killed the next day.[20]

There were some who believed that there was no uprising in Proskurov
and that the Ukrainians invented it in order to justify their actions. This is
incorrect; there was an attempted uprising. Ukrainian soldiers who ostensibly joined the "revolutionaries" possibly had instructions from Semesenko to
participate, giving him the excuse to perpetrate a bloodbath.

On shabbes morning, February 15, 1919, a rumor spread in Proskurov that
the leaders of the Ukrainian authority had been arrested and that the city
council had been taken over by local Bolsheviks. The Jewish population quietly went about its business. Occasionally, one could hear shooting.

---

[20] Perets Krupnik was a teacher and communal activist in Proskurov.—Trans.

The Jewish socialist parties met in the Bund meeting hall to decide what to do in this emerging situation. Suddenly there was an explosion from a bomb in the hall and the participants fled. The "uprising" was suppressed, and it was tense in the city. Everyone was ordered to go home. And then it began....

The slaughter took place over four hours. Armed soldiers from Semesenko's battalion accompanied by doctors and nurses encircled the neighborhoods where the poorest Jews lived and began their bloody work.[21] Many Jews who lived in other neighborhoods did not even know about the pogrom until early the next morning when the horrible cries of the relatives of the murdered people woke the entire town.

Approximately 1,500 Jews were killed: children and elderly, men and women. The pogromists did not show mercy towards anyone. The precise number of murdered people is difficult to access because Semesenko did not allow the dead to be buried in an orderly manner.

The Jewish population was completely devastated. The feeling of terror was great. There was no help in sight, and the wild animal Semesenko threatened that he would slaughter the entire town and warned that the Jews would do best to believe him.

Stories about the Proskurov pogrom made one's hair stand on end. In one account a Ukrainian doctor sent his servant to participate in the slaughter. The servant returned and told the doctor that he had encountered a Jewish girl who was so beautiful he was unable to lift a hand against her. The doctor left and murdered the girl himself. We heard that the Bolsheviks shot this doctor in Odessa.[22] In other accounts we heard that some soldiers' humane feelings arose and that they merely broke windows and did not murder.

From that day on, the Jews of Proskurov no longer tried to hide. They say that if all 20,000 Jews would have gone out in the street and fought the murderers the victims would not have been so helpless.

After the pogrom, Proskurov seemed a dead town. Though people went out, conducted business, and worked, February 15 always hovered before their eyes. When one met a Proskurov Jew and spoke with him about the events of February 15, his demeanor would change. His eyes would flash and one could see in them a great rage that sought revenge. After the pogrom the majority of socialist Jews aligned with the Bolsheviks, and the wealthy class fled.

Felshtin is a small Jewish town near Proskurov. It had a small-town cultural life and Jewish political parties. There were no Bolsheviks, and under-

---

[21] In case there was resistance from the Jewish population, they could give aid to the wounded Cossacks.

[22] Elias Heifetz utilizes the report of A. I. Hillerson and identifies the doctor as a Dr. Skornik (*Slaughter of the Jews*, 213).—Trans.

standably after Proskurov, the Felshtin Jews, even the most extreme leftists, would not have considered an uprising. Yet the pogrom did not miss them either.

Thanks to an act of treachery by a Felshtin official whom the Bolsheviks later shot in Proskurov, an enraged squad from Semesenko's army attacked the town and perpetrated a terrible pogrom.[23] One-third of the Jewish population was killed. Six to seven hundred innocent Jews fell at the hands of the wild Ukrainian Cossacks, the butchers of "Cossackistan." Memento mori (a memory of death) was worn on the heads of the Jewish population.

No help was possible. Cut off from the entire world the Jewish population in Podolia waited for yom ha-din [the Day of Judgement] to arrive. Political parties at this moment were irrelevant: no more Zionists, socialists, Bolsheviks, and Ahdut. Only Jews for slaughter.

The Proskurov and Felshtin pogroms brought about a complete break in the Jewish-Ukrainian relationship. The Jewish noncommunist groups that had been positive towards the Ukrainian movement openly went over to the Bolshevik side and helped it struggle against the Ukrainian regime. And for a long time the gulf between the Jewish masses and the Ukrainian national movement increased.

Pogrom Terror in Komenetz and in the District

Komenetz-Podolsk is known as the official Ukrainian city. The relationship between the Jewish and Ukrainian populations was always friendly. When the municipal government was created after the revolution in 1917, Ukrainians and Jewish socialists had even forged a political bloc.[24]

And yet discord between Ukrainians and Jews arose in this transition period. For example, in January 1918 the Russian military withdrew from the Galician front, occupied Komenetz, and introduced Soviet rule. A month later the Ukrainians chased the Bolsheviks out with German help. But the discord between the Ukrainians and the Jewish socialists that had been experienced in Kiev continued in Komenetz. The Ukrainians even boycotted the first cel-

---

[23] Heifetz explains the "act of treachery." After the pogrom in Proskurov, Semesenko had promised that he would not attack Felshtin and would order his troops out of the town. The order was supposed to have been sent by telegram, but a postal telegraph worker hid it. The troops in Felshtin were already in a mood to attack Jews, and on February 18, three days after the assault on Proskurov, Felshtin experienced a pogrom. See Heifetz, *Slaughter of the Jews*, 232.—Trans.

[24] In his short autobiographical statement in Shalit, *Oyf di hurves fun milhomes un mehumes*, 829–34, Gumener wrote that in 1917 he was a deputy mayor in Komenetz—a position he held until the Hetmanate regime took power.—Trans.

ebratory gathering in honor of Taras Shevchenko in the Komenetz duma.[25] They did not want to commemorate his memory together with Jews. Despite the boycott, a resolution to rename Romanov Street and a school "Taras Shevchenko" was introduced by the Jewish socialists and passed almost entirely with Jewish votes.

This is how the politics of the narrow-minded Ukrainian leaders played itself out in Komenetz before the Brest Peace. With the Treaty of Brest they thought that German bayonets would give them a glowing future.[26] But as the situation of the Ukrainians worsened [under the Hetman], the relationship between the Ukrainian and the Jewish socialists improved. They energetically protested together against the Hetman and helped the Directory in its revolt against his regime.[27]

The Jewish activists who served in the Komenetz city administration helped establish a Ukrainian university in the city.[28] But even after these events, the representatives of the newborn "sovereign" nation[29] looked with great suspicion at the Jewish, Russian, and Polish minorities. At every opportunity the Ukrainians emphasized that the deciding word regarding political questions belonged to them alone.

Following the celebratory days after the Directory's revolt [against the Hetman], discord between Ukrainian and Jewish socialists immediately began over the mayoral elections in Komenetz-Podolsk. Every attempt to create an organization that would unite the democratic forces of Ukrainians and non-Ukrainians failed. The relationship between Jews and Ukrainians became colder and then ended. Elections for a Workers' Congress occurred in January 1919, with only a small interruption. It was, however, quiet in the city.

All of a sudden Proskurov!

---

[25] A famous Ukrainian poet and fighter for national and social freedom.

[26] At the beginning of 1918, the Ukrainians negotiated a separate peace with the Germans in Brest. [On March 3, 1918, the Bolshevik government in Moscow and the Central Powers signed the Treaty of Brest-Litovsk, ending their military conflict, and forcing the Bolsheviks to recognize the UNR. Ukrainian nationalists negotiated an agreement with Germany by which Ukraine would supply grain and stock in return for protection against the Bolsheviks. Germany occupied Kiev on March 1, 1918.—Trans.]

[27] The Germans dissolved the Ukrainian Central Rada and installed the Hetman on April 30, 1918.

[28] The University was opened in October 1918. The theologian Ivan Ohienko (1882–1972) was its first rector. He also served as minister of higher education for the UNR.—Trans.

[29] "Ruling" nation.

Proskurov was so unexpected and cruel that nobody wanted to believe it. Mr. "D" reported that on shabbes February 15 he was in Proskurov and as he arrived at the station in Hrechana [?], he heard shooting. Wagon drivers related to him that there was "upheaval" in Proskurov.[30]

In the Komenetz newspaper *Life in Podolia* an order from the gubernial administrator (who was later caught stealing and fled) to the Proskurov district commander appeared about excesses against Jews: "Don't kill women and children." This meant that women and children were actually killed in Proskurov and that Jewish men should be killed immediately.

The Jewish population was up in arms. A rumor spread that the villain Semesenko was assembling troops in Komenetz. There was a terrible panic in the city, and anxiety rose to the highest pitch. The rumor was enough to make Jews want to flee, and they were already beginning to shut their shops and shutter their windows. To this day, I can still hear the clanging of closing windows and gates echoing in my ears. But what could anyone do? Travel was too dangerous: Jews were killed on the trains and the roads. On one side was the Romanian border and on the other was the Galician-Polish front.

The Komenetz kehillah sent delegations to the Ukrainian authorities: appealing, begging, insisting on its innocence, and pleading. It went to the rector of the university, I. Ohienko, who promised to do everything he could.

Altman (Zionist) and I were with H. Kyrylenko, the provincial commissioner for aid, who had just arrived from Proskurov.[31] The conversation with him made a terrible impression on us: "Jews revolted and, naturally, there were innocent casualties." We then went to the provincial commissioner, Mr. Stepura, a good Christian, a local lawyer. He promised that he would take every measure to rescue Komenetz but that Jews needed to remain peaceful. "In Proskurov, you need to understand, twelve Jews revolted, arrested the commandant, took over the post office, and, naturally, there were innocent casualties." During talks with the Ukrainian activists everyone agreed that there will be slaughter if there is an insurrection. What could be done?

The community worked tirelessly to avoid a disaster. It sent a delegation, which I already mentioned. It sent telegrams to the Jewish ministers in Vinitza, to the Ukrainian government, and to the Vinitza Jewish community.[32] But that community had already lost its governing authority. Hardly any plenary

---

[30] The identity of this place is unclear: it may be the small village of Hrechana or the village Hrechyntsi, both about one hour from Proskurov.—Trans.

[31] Sholem Altman (1864–?) was a Zionist leader in Komenetz. He was born in Bessarabia, emigrated to Palestine, and returned to Ukraine before the Civil War to establish a Hebrew school in Zhvanets, Podolia. He returned to Palestine in 1921.—Trans.

[32] Vinitza became the capital of Podolia in 1917.—Trans.

meetings were taking place at that time. The police had even dispersed a kehillah meeting. Fearing violence, meetings were almost never called.

The mood was fearful. Everyone went around as if their verdict had been read, and they had been sentenced and were only waiting for yom ha-din to arrive.

The Jewish socialists were also in a terrible situation. On the one hand, they were close to the Ukrainian parties (i.e., Ukrainian Social Democrats, Ukrainian Socialist Revolutionaries) and had more influence over them.[33] Thus, a greater responsibility lay upon their shoulders. On the other hand, they were terrorized by the Ukrainian authorities who suspected all Jews of being Bolsheviks.

The aforementioned Commissar Stepura sent for the lawyer K (Folkspartey) and B (a Menshevik), distinguished activists from Komenetz-Podolsk, and announced that he had information that a revolt was being prepared. He warned us that despite the fact that the Jewish socialists (Mr. B and I) were against an uprising, we would be held responsible if the events of Proskurov reoccurred.

The Jewish socialists did everything they could. In Komenetz there was a Workers' Club where around two hundred workers used to gather every evening.[34] Many Jews feared that the workers in the club, which was dominated by Jewish socialists, [might provoke the Ukrainians]. The Jewish socialists agreed to close the Workers' Club in order not to give the slightest chance for the kind of provocation that occurred in Proskurov.

Soon after the decision to close the Workers' Club the Komenetz rabbi [Israel] Gutman sent a representative in the name of the bes din [rabbinical court] and asked me to make every effort that the club remain temporarily closed. All gatherings came to a halt. The Jewish socialists negotiated with the Jewish Bolsheviks and persuaded them, if at all possible, not to allow an uprising in Komenetz. This request was not difficult to fulfill because Komenetz did not play an important strategic role for the Bolsheviks. An uprising could

---

[33] These two parties were at the forefront of Ukrainian nation-building activities during World War I. The Ukrainian Social Democratic Party (USDP) was ideologically Marxist, though the Bolsheviks rejected it as a petty bourgeoise nationalist party. Several of its members had high-ranking positions in the UNR government. The Ukrainian Socialist Revolutionary Party (UPSR) also argued for territorial autonomy for Ukrainians. Its support among the peasantry and ex-soldiers was wider than that of the USPD. In 1918, it had the largest caucus in the Central Rada, though the SR had greater representation in later ministries because its base consisted of more intellectuals and professionals.—Trans.

[34] The general number of members of the club was 600–700 Jews and Christians, made up of Tseire Tsiyon, anarchists, and Bolsheviks.

only end catastrophically for the Jewish population. The Jewish Bolsheviks kept their word and did not allow an uprising.

The situation in the town and in the region became more dangerous every day. The demoralized Ukrainian army retreated from the Zbruch and projected its anger on the innocent Jewish population.[35] Units of the retreating Ukrainian army began to appear in and around Komenetz. Everyday representatives from small Jewish towns in the region came to Komenetz to ask for help. But what could the Jewish authorities do? They barely could do anything for themselves to preserve the life of the Komenetz community. How much less so for the towns.

At the end of March [1919] the municipality sent an urgent request for a meeting to the leaders of the professional unions, the Workers' Club, the Jewish socialist party (except for Poale Tsiyon), and even the Jewish Bolsheviks. What was happening? The Ukrainian government had fallen.[36] On March 22 a committee was established in Komenetz-Podolsk to protect the Republic.[37] It included representatives from Ukrainian socialist parties, district peasant collectives, and the military authority in Komenetz. The chairman of the committee was [Volodymyr] Chekhivsky, a Ukrainian Social Democrat and former prime minister after the uprising against the Hetmanate. (Among the members of the committee were [Serhiy] Ostapenko, [Isaak] Mazepa, [Mykhailo] Tkachenko, and other known Ukrainian political leaders.)[38]

---

[35] The Zbruch River marks the former border between Austria (Galicia) and Russia (Podolia).

[36] The Red Army forced the Directory out of Kiev; the Directory retreated to Vinitza, Zhmerynka, Proskurov, Komenetz, and Rovne.—Trans.

[37] The official name of the committee was the Committee for the Defense of the Republic. *Okhrany* is Ukrainian for "protection."—Trans.

[38] The Okhrany Committee was established in Komenetz in March 1919 by a number of prominent Ukrainian leaders after the Directory fled Kiev. They wanted to move the Ukrainian national movement in a more leftward direction and to negotiate with the Bolsheviks to end the war. Volodymyr Musiyovych Chekhivsky (1876–1937) served as prime minister of the UNR from December 26, 1918 to February 11, 1919. He advocated cooperation with the Bolsheviks. In February 1919, he resigned from the government. Serhiy Ostapenko (1881–1937) was a member of the Ukrainian Socialist Revolutionary Party. In July 1919 he became a member of the faculty at the newly established university in Komenetz. Isaak Mazepa (1884–1952) was a member of the Ukrainian Social Democratic Workers Party. In April 1919 he became minister of internal affairs for the UNR and served as prime minister from August 1919 to May 1920. Mykhailo Tkachenko (1879–1920) was a member of the Ukrainian Social Democratic Workers Party and served in the Central Rada. He was minister of justice and minister of the interior in the UNR. For an account of the Okhrany Committee, see Pavlo Khrystiuk, *Zamitky i materiialy do istoriï ukraïns'koï revoliutsiï, 1917–1920* [Notes

The committee delayed the evacuation of the remaining ministries to Rovne as had been ordered by the Directory.[39] The committee's goal was to end the Directory's fluctuations, and above all, to stop its antagonistic orientation to the Bolsheviks and make peace [with Soviet Russia]. Towards this goal the committee sent two delegations: one to the Directory and the other to the Bolsheviks.

The committee invited us, the Jewish socialists, as well as remaining representatives from other worker organizations, to join. They let it be known that they considered it very important that non-Ukrainian parties take a role in the delegations, especially the one to the Bolsheviks.

Since everyone, from the right socialists to the Jewish Bolsheviks, were worried about the pogrom threat hovering over the Jewish population, the first question we introduced in the session of the so-called Okhrany Committee was what it was going to do to protect the Jewish population.[40] We were assured that everything would be done to preserve Jewish lives. But naturally, they could only be saved if "order" prevailed. Our situation turned desperate: to join the Okhrany Committee would mean taking a big political risk. If the committee failed, we might provoke a lot of trouble for the Jewish population. But to decline to join a left-leaning Ukrainian committee might be interpreted on the part of the Ukrainians that we opposed their policies.[41] We decided to wait and see what would happen. That same day we received news of the arrival of suspicious types who were searching for "kikes" in the committee. It was therefore very easy to understand why the most distinguished Ukrainian leaders among us spoke out against the Directory.[42] A few days later, Mr. Chekhivsky acknowleged our wait-and-see policy and claimed that the one thing that the committee had accomplished was to save the Jewish population from a pogrom. In reality nothing was accomplished by the Okhrany Committee. A delegation was not even sent to the Bolsheviks, and

---

and materials on the Ukrainian revolution, 1917–1920] (Ukraïns′kyi sotsiologichnyi instytut, 1921–22; repr., New York: Vyd-vo Chartoryĭs′kykh, 1969), 4: 110–15.—Trans.

[39] From April to May 1919 Rovne (Yid.), Rivne (Ukr.), Rovno (Rus.) served as the temporary capital of the UNR. It is approximately 180 miles north of Komenetz.—Trans.

[40] This was what the committee was called.

[41] The Jewish leaders also worried that Petliura and the Directory would oppose this committee, which would bring serious negative consequences for the Jews. On the other hand, not joining the committee would be regarded unfavorably by the Komenetz Ukrainian leadership. Upon hearing that the war front had stabilized, however, the committee dissolved itself on March 28.—Trans.

[42] The Directory saw in the Okhrany a "disguised Bolshevik."

the Directory itself did not want to negotiate with the delegation. The delegation was even arrested.

Meanwhile, a minor ataman named Khomadenko arrived in Komenetz and arrested the top Ukrainian leaders, including [V.A.] Golubovich (former premier), [Henryk] Jozewski, [Isaak] Mazepa, and A. Stepanenko [Arkadi Stepanenko]; however, they were released the same day.[43] The ataman wondered why the Yids ["Zhyds"] had not taken a part in the "marriage." "Aha," he said. "We taught them well in Proskurov."[44]

Relentless, the ataman wanted to inspect the houses, ostensibly to look for weapons. We understood that this was just a prelude [to a pogrom]. The situation in the city became tense. Fortunately for the Jewish population, this ataman ruffled distinguished Ukrainian government officials and a special Galician division was brought to Komenetz to arrest him and disarm his Cossacks. The town was calm. The Galician division brought complete order and remained until the arrival of the Bolsheviks. They also helped stop the "junkers."[45]

In the province the situation was much more dangerous than in Komenetz. In town one could at least speak to the authorities and to community

---

[43] "Khomadenko" was probably Khomadovskyi, a young man who was acting on the orders of a right-wing member of the Directory. He did not have a mandate from the Directory to arrest these Komenetz leaders; in fact, Petliura ordered their release. Vsevolod Golubovich [Holubovych] (1885–1939) was a member of the Ukrainian Socialist Revolutionary Party. He was the second prime minister of the Central Rada and a delegate at the Brest-Litovsk peace talks. Golubovich edited an anti-Bolshevik newspaper. In August 1920 the Bolsheviks arrested him in Komenetz. He was tried in 1921 and sentenced to five years in a labor camp but released the same year. He was arrested again in 1932 and died in 1939. Born in Kiev, Henryk Jozewski (1892–1981) was a Pole who advocated for a Polish-Ukrainian alliance. In 1920, he served in the UNR government as deputy minister of the interior under Petliura. Arkadi Stepanenko was a member of the Ukrainian Socialist Revolutionary Party and participated in the Central Rada. An anti-Bolshevik, he was imprisoned and executed in Kiev in 1938.—Trans.

[44] The word *zhyd* was used in western Ukraine to refer to Jews. It was not regarded as derogatory. The same is true of the related Polish word *żyd*. By contrast, the Russian word *zhid* is pejorative. It is impossible to know from the Yiddish in what sense Gumener is employing the word. The context strongly suggests that the ataman was referring to Jews in a derogatory manner; I have used the word "Yids" to convey the sentiment. The ataman wondered why the Jews did not join the Okhrany Committee. For the term *zhyd*, see Paul Robert Magocsi and Yohanan Petrovsky-Shtern, *Jews and Ukrainians: A Millennium of Co-Existence* (Toronto: University of Toronto Press, 2016), 7. For a fuller account of the Okhrany Committee, see Reshetar, *Ukrainian Revolution*, 265–67.—Trans.

[45] The term *junker* in Russian can refer to army volunteers or to students in officer candidate schools.—Trans.

leaders; in the smaller towns, however, a few armed soldiers or bandits could attack and wreak the greatest havoc.

The Ukrainian leadership [i.e., the Directory] took an entirely passive attitude towards the pogroms in order to marginalize the Okhrany Committee. It could not get through its peasant head that the pogroms not only destroyed the Jews but were also destroying the UNR. Even the Ukrainian circles upon which the UNR depended were not hopeful about the future.

After the Proskurov pogrom I participated in meetings between the Komenetz city council and Ukrainian intellectuals from the zemstvos assembly of Podolia.[46] Many members did not try to hide their negative attitude towards the authority of the UNR. And when news arrived that Petliura had taken Zhitomir, the assembly made a motion to send him a telegram of greeting. The tone was very cold, and in it the assembly demanded that Petliura restrain his army and not allow excesses (a Zionist councilman and I, plus six or eight Ukrainians were against sending the telegram).[47]

In this period we did not receive any news from the Jewish Ministry. We heard that Mr. Revutsky, the Jewish minister (Poale Tsiyon), fled after the Proskurov pogrom and had given the ministry to Mr. [Pinchas] Krasny (Folkspartey).[48] Two or three lower-level officials who said they represented

---

[46] Gubernia People's Assembly [Ukrainian]. [The exact name and dates for this assembly are unclear. The organization is most likely a Congress of the Zemstvos of Podolia gubernia. Zemstvos were local government institutions that were introduced in imperial Russia in 1864 to give the land-owning gentry a greater voice in local governance. Within a few years a nongentry professional class dominated the zemstvos. Although the Bolsheviks dissolved them in 1918, some zemstvos in Ukraine continued in places where the Bolsheviks had not firmly embedded themselves. For a history of the zemstvos, see Dorothy Atkinson, "The Zemstvo and the Peasantry," in *The Zemstvo in Russia: An Experiment in Local Self-Government*, ed. Terence Emmons and Wayne S. Vucinich (Cambridge: Cambridge University Press, 1982), 79–132. For the name and dates, see Isaak Mazepa, *Ukraïna v ohni i buri revoliutsiï, 1917–1921* [Ukraine in the fire and storm of revolution, 1917–1921] (Prague, 1942), 1: 140, who refers to it as "[Kam"ianets'] District Peasants' Congress" and dates it March 20–22, 1919, and Pavlo Khrystiuk, who calls it "Kam"ianets Labor Congress," and dates it March 21–22, 1919.—Trans.]

[47] The tone of the telegram reflected the assembly's displeasure that troops acting in the name of Petliura perpetrated pogroms in various towns, including in Zhitomir on March 22.—Trans.

[48] Revutsky resigned when Petliura fled Kiev in the wake of the Red Army's assault. Pinchas Krasny (1881–1939) was a member of Poale Tsiyon. He worked in the Jewish Ministry under Revutsky. When Revutsky resigned, he put Krasny in charge. Krasny would be the last minister of Jewish affairs in the UNR. In 1939, he was executed in Kiev by the Soviets.—Trans.

the Ministry for Jewish Affairs came to Komenetz with some ministers. Mr. Krasny went to Odessa and we waited for him.

One fine morning Mr. Krasny arrived with a delegation from the Komenetz community to discuss the pogroms. I met with him in the name of the Kultur Lige to speak about the state of the communal institutions. Mr. Krasny left on the same day, however, and we never saw him again! Then the Ukrainian regime left for Rivne. The Jewish Ministry had made the worst impression on us. The leadership of Poale Tsiyon was embarrassed and the Fareynikte and the Bundists smirked.

I have to add that when the Jewish Ministry was in Vinitza we had intentionally sent a Christian student [to relate our concerns] but he returned empty handed.[49] The days and perhaps the hours of the UNR were numbered. The entire Jewish population and the majority of the Ukrainians waited impatiently for it to become extinct.

Bolsheviks in Podolia (Spring 1919)

Erev pesach in 1919 was unsettling for the Jews in Komenetz. The Bolsheviks had taken Yarmolintz.[50] The coachmen from the nearby town of Dinovitz did not come as usual that day, a sure sign that a new power would be arriving soon. The municipal authorities formed a committee that would be responsible for maintaining order. After much friction, representatives of the right and left parties joined the committee. Sichynskyi, the new provincial commissar, was a very narrow-minded man who inhibited at every turn the committee's work. Alas, he was concerned that the committee, which had among its five members two moderate socialists (one a Ukrainian and the other a Jew) and the remainder rightists, would take power and delay the evacuation of the Ukrainians. Luckily, Mikhalapov, a Russian Menshevik (and later a Bolshevik) who was an administrator with the town police, was on the side of the committee.

At night the situation became more serious. Jews were preparing for [the Passover] seder and also barricading doors and gates.

I was summoned by the city administration. All the members of the administration were present: the chairman of the [city] Duma, Miranski (a Russian Socialist [Social] Revolutionary and a Jew), the mayor, Kylymnyk (a Ukrainian Social Democrat), and many others.

---

[49] Jews could not travel because of the danger on the trains and the roads.

[50] Yarmolintz (Yid.), Yarmolyntsi (Ukr.) is 36 miles north of Komenetz. Dinovitz (Yid.), Dunayevtsy (Rus.), Dunayivtsi (Ukr.) is 18 miles northeast of Komenetz.—Trans.

The city hall was buzzing. Commissar Sichynskyi was restless. Representatives from various military units came to register at the municipality and announced that they would not abandon the territory of Ukraine and surrender to the Bolsheviks. As if out of nowhere, a large crowd of different types sprang up—shady and ordinary characters—and everyone loudly offered advice and imparted important news.

Suddenly we heard that Jews were being beaten in the streets, which caused a panic. It turned out that this was only partly true. A few Jews who went to shul to pray indeed received a few blows from the departing army. The city was calmer. In the municipal building a member of the committee remained awake all night. Mr. B and I went to a well-known leader for the first seder. It was quiet in the city. There were almost no Jews in the streets. Every door and gate was closed. A Galician military division passed quietly through the city. We entered the administration of the municipal police. The municipal militia included police personnel and armed soldiers who had decided to remain in Komenetz and not evacuate to Galicia. Their commanders assured us that the city would not fall into disorder. This made our souls a little lighter, and we went to the seder. At the seder we met a large group of distinguished community leaders from Komenetz. The atmosphere was somber. Who knew what would happen an hour from now? Or what will be in the morning?

At four o'clock in the morning there was a knock on the door. Mr. Mikhalapov, the commander of the militia, arrived and informed us that the "hero," Mr. Sichynskyi, had slipped away at night and deserted the entire population. The city was left without an authority.

We immediately got dressed and went to the city hall. Jews in festive dress gathered in small groups in the street. The atmosphere was tense. Mr. Miranski, the chairman of the Duma,[51] Kylymnyk, the mayor, and others arrived at the city hall. A new "Committee to Uphold Order" was quickly formed, which was composed only of socialists, both Ukrainian and Jewish. We assumed that the Bolsheviks would have more trust in such a committee than in an expressly rightist group, but you can also decide that for yourself.

We quickly made a plan. We decided to release a statement announcing that until a legal authority emerged, power would be in the hands of the city administration; in addition, no violence would be tolerated. We had enough arms to put down troublemaking elements.[52] And in reality, there were 200 police personnel with two machine guns and a military squad under the jurisdiction of the city administration. The majority of this force consisted of

---

[51] City administration.

[52] Within a few hours an announcement came from Mr. Sichynskyi that he had transferred authority to the city administration.

Jews who had been soldiers, under the direction of former Jewish noncommissioned officers. We also had 500–600 regular military troops who pledged themselves to the city administration. We registered the remaining military units and secured the storehouses of merchandise and ammunition.

Then from the prison came alarming news. Since I am an attorney, I went there with the prosecutor and the prison warden, and released the political prisoners, per the instruction of the committee. Our presence reassured the prisoners. We released 15 people, among them 12 peasants who were being held illegally.

Unexpectedly, some haidamaks appeared.[53] They were withdrawing towards Galicia and got lost near the Komenetz prison, which was located two versts from town. My heart sank. If the haidamaks found out that I, a Jew, even with the presence of the prosecutor, released political prisoners, they would surely kill me. It would be fair to say that with 15 freed political prisoners we saved the town, because in the prison there were 200 common criminals. I could have hidden myself in the prison, but I didn't trust the prison administration. I remained incredibly calm. Fortunately, the haidamaks were in a hurry and did not stop near the prison.

Within 20 minutes we heard fire from artillery, machine guns, and rifles. The sounds came from a battle between retreating Ukrainian troops, haidamaks, and the military that had decided to remain in the city.

After a while it was calm. The prosecutor and I were given horses and we rode to town. The quiet streets were covered with announcements from the city administration. The population became calm. Former soldiers (Jews and non-Jews) patrolled the streets. A Polish lawyer by the name of Wyrzykowski, assisted by a Jewish officer named Shkolnik, brought the situation under control.

We felt more secure, meaning that Komenetz had avoided a slaughter! But why had calamity struck Proskurov? What was the reason that Komenetz, finding itself in the same situation, was spared a pogrom and Proskurov was not? Perhaps Komenetz had a sympathetic Ukrainian intelligentsia that protected the Jewish population? Perhaps in Komenetz the Jewish socialist intelligentsia was more aggressive? Perhaps Proskurov panicked everyone and that had an effect? Perhaps???

The atmosphere in Komenetz was now hopeful. Jews in holiday finery walked the streets in good spirits. The city was divided into 28 districts and every district established its own guards. Here and there one could see a patrol—a group of armed young Jewish men—under the command of a Jewish

---

[53] *Haidamak* designates members of particular units and divisions of the Directory's army as well as members of Ukrainian peasant insurgent or irregular militias. One cannot always tell which participant is meant in the memoir.—Trans.

officer—who maintained order. The city was completely calm. Even the number of petty thieveries decreased.

We didn't know precisely what would happen and what the new rulers, the Bolsheviks, would bring, but one thing was good: we were free of the pogromists.

Suddenly, however, we heard reports that in Orinin[54] retreating Ukrainian military troops instigated a massacre. There were many casualties. We wanted to run, to do something, to beg someone, but there wasn't anyone to whom we could go. There was no Ukrainian governing authority.

People were stirred up. Many wanted to go to Orinin, but in the end I was the one to go in a carriage with four militiamen. It was already quiet when we arrived. There were two victims and the haidamaks were still not far from the town. We spent a few hours there and were able to bring calm to the town before we left. But what else would happen?

A few days later a small number of battered Bolshevik military troops finally entered Komenetz. The entire city greeted them with great fanfare, especially the Jewish population. Young and old, poor and rich—everyone was in the street. Without a doubt we were glad. "Let the Bolsheviks take everything that we have but at least they will let us live," proclaimed the wealthy.

But we still worried what would happen if the marauders, the haidamaks, were able to break into the city. They would take everything and kill many innocent Jews.

At night armed soldiers—Bolsheviks with cannons and machine guns— were posted at the Komenetz administrative building. I approached and saw the Oriner rabbi and other Jews among the soldiers.

"What's happening? How did you get here?" I asked. "It's bad. The haidamaks returned to Orinin and did terrible things. The Bolsheviks are the only messiah," they answered.

Two Komenetz Jews approached me—the wealthy merchant A. Sh_ and an intellectual member of Tseire Tsiyon: "It's rumored that the haidamaks are on the march." Their faces were filled with despair. The only hope for the wealthy merchant Jew was that the Bolsheviks remain, even if they were to throw him out of his house. But wouldn't they kill him?

---

[54] A town 15 versts from Komenetz and 16 versts from the former Austrian border. It lay between Komenetz and the border. [Orinin (Rus., Yid.), Orynyn (Ukr.) is 10 miles northwest of Komenetz. The town experienced pogroms in March, May, and June of 1919. A Jewish self-defense force was organized in Orinin by Iosif Donovich Grinberg (1895–1935), who had been a soldier in the Russian Imperial Army during World War I. His self-defense group cooperated with the Red Army and fought against pogromists associated with Petliura's army as well as against local peasant bands.—Trans.]

Historians in the future will discover much material about how the Jewish population and the Jewish worker fought heroically against various Ukrainian groups who had, in their battles against the Bolsheviks, slaughtered the Jewish population. A lot has been written and is still being written about the murdered Jews, but very little, almost nothing, has been written about how Jews fought valiantly to protect their parents, brothers, and sisters. Jews will no longer die like animals, like sheep to the slaughter as they did in Proskurov. Here I will present a few stories of Jewish self-defense.

Orinin

Orinin is a small Jewish town situated between Komenetz and the border (Zbruch). Driven out of Podolia by the Bolsheviks, the haidamaks were on the other side of the Zbruch. For political reasons (namely, the war in Galicia between the Poles and Galician Ukrainians), the Bolsheviks did not cross the Zbruch and were not attentive to the border of Podolia.[55] For a long time the border was protected by local peasants together with the Jewish youth of Orinin and small units of the Red Army.

On a Friday night at the end of May, Baron, the chairman from the Komenetz revkom, summoned the head of the Jewish socialists (Fareynikte Bund), H_B, and told him that a band of haidamaks had entered Orinin and murdered Jews.[56] The Komenetz revkom did not have adequate forces to face the haidamaks. He warned that if the Jewish population did not join in the defense, not only Orinin but also the Jews of Komenetz would be in great danger.

There was no time to delay. A battalion of Jewish workers had already been sent to the battle front, but unfortunately they were few and ineffective. We had to organize more Jewish units. We gathered members from different parties, former soldiers, and even men who had never held a gun in their hands, let alone been in battle. They were going to Orinin. There was no other choice.

They left Komenetz at night. The Jewish population slept quietly. In the group there were 60 to 70 Red Army troops, a few officers, one artillery piece, and 60 Jewish fighters.

The defenders had gone eight versts (there was still seven versts to Orinin) when suddenly the order was given to lie down. They encountered fierce

---

[55] Battles were fought in eastern Galicia during the Polish-Ukrainian War of 1918 and also in 1919 between Poland and the West Ukrainian People's Republic based in Galicia, which was allied with the UNR.—Trans.

[56] The revkoms served as local administrations for the Bolsheviks. From June 1919, they were under the authority of the Soviet government. See McGeever, *Antisemitism and the Russian Revolution*, 115–16.—Trans.

firing from artillery and machine guns coming from the Ukrainian side. Jews who had been in war immediately realized that the shooting clearly was not from a band of [peasant] pogromists but from the regular military troops who had entered Orinin, and, as usual, initiated a pogrom.

We learned later that the revkom knew about this situation but had kept silent because it was not sure that Jewish youth would be willing to fight regular Ukrainian troops. A Poale Tsiyon member who was a Communist and a member of revkom wanted to reveal the secret but was strictly forbidden from doing so. We learned all this later. But what about this current predicament?

A strong enemy stood before us, and behind us the Bolsheviks were positioned with swords and revolvers and did not permit anyone to retreat. In any case, it was already too late to retreat. Komenetz was eight versts away and the entire detachment would have been killed if it had tried to go back.

And then there was a miracle. The anger and hatred towards the murderers, and the concern for the danger to oneself and dear ones stirred up fierce emotions. Dragging Red Army soldiers with them into battle, the Jewish volunteers threw themselves on the haidamaks. The haidamaks could not hold out. They trembled and began to flee and abandon their weapons. They fell on their knees and asked for mercy.

The men were enraged. These same Jewish youth, who in their entire lives would not even hurt a fly on the wall, went out of their minds and without mercy beat the haidamaks right and left. One young haidamak was on his knees and begged for his life. "How many Jews did you kill?" he was asked. One? A deadly blow was the answer.

Sixty Jewish volunteers aided by a few Red Army soldiers defeated 600 haidamaks. Sixty haidamaks were killed; 2 Jews were killed (one a Tseire Tsiyon). The Bolshevik paper *Kiev News* reported that the assault on Komenetz was repelled and "sixty were killed on the battlefield." The Jews made it clear to the atamans that they would not allow another Proskurov. After the battle the Red Army did not want to let the Jewish volunteers go and kept them to be mobilized. Only with a great effort were they able to free themselves. The Jewish population of Orinin was saved at the cost of "only" 15 victims from the town. The entire town from young to old was then evacuated by foot to Komenetz.

While the events in Orinin were unfolding, the Jewish population in Komenetz was greatly unsettled. The leadership had gone to Orinin, and we did not know what was happening or what would happen to Komenetz itself. There was great joy when we saw the returning heroes. A warm welcome was also given to the local Jews who had fled from Orinin.

Immediately after the battle, the leaders of the Jewish Communists came by coach to Orinin. The story of Orinin emanated like a ray of light from the sun between the dark clouds of the terrible pogroms in Podolia.

Vinitza

Litin is a small Jewish town not far from Vinitza.[57] This town suffered greatly from different pogrom groups led by the bandit Shepel.[58]

The Bolsheviks had a simple remedy for the insurgents in this particular region. They would send troops—Cheka divisions—against the village that had helped the bandits, shell the village with artillery, and return at night to town (Vinitza). The peasants, however, would not turn over the insurgents. And despite these and similar measures, the peasants were incensed at the Soviet regime, or as the insurgents put it: "at the Communists and the Yids [zhydes]."

In May 1919 two to three thousand peasants from the surrounding villages decided to march on Vinitza. (The month of May, which included Grigoriev's uprising, was in general very unfortunate for the Jews of Ukraine.)[59] Most were armed with axes, pitchforks, and similar weapons.[60]

The situation of the Jews in Vinitza was grave. The detachments of the Red Army that were in Vinitza at the time were inclined to be anti-Bolshevik and battled the Cheka. As usual, in such cases, antisemitic agitation was heard. The Jewish population was in great danger and the Red Army was

---

[57] Litin (Yid., Rus.), Lityn (Ukr.) is 50 miles northwest of Komenetz. Pogroms were perpetrated in Vinitza and Litin in May 1919.—Trans.

[58] Iakiv Matviiovych Shepel (1894–1921?) was born to a peasant family near Litin. In 1919 he led insurgent peasant bands in the area.—Trans.

[59] Nikifor Grigoriev (1885–1919) was born Nychypir Servetnyk in a small village in Podolia. He was a paramilitary leader who switched back and forth from the Ukrainian cause to the Bolsheviks during the Civil War. Immediately after the October Revolution, he supported the UNR and served in its army. During the revolt against the Hetman, however, he formed his own army. Defying Petliura's order in January 1919 to engage the White Army in the south, Grigoriev joined Red Army forces to attack Petliura's troops, forcing them to retreat to Podolia. He resisted the authority of the Bolsheviks and in May led a movement against both the Bolsheviks and the Directory. Pressed by the Red Army, Grigoriev sought a partnership with Nestor Makhno, who led his own independent army. Grigoriev and Makhno parted ways when the latter negotiated for an alliance with the White Army. In July, he was killed in a shootout with either Makhno or one of his officers.—Trans.

[60] They had already plundered Litin. The first pogrom in Litin occurred on May 15. One hundred ten Jews were killed.

altogether passive. Quite the contrary, we assumed that if the peasants were to enter Vinitza, the Red Army would join the pogromists.

Jews sought hiding places. There was terrible panic in the town. News arrived that the insurgents were already a few versts from the town. But the story of what had happened in Proskurov saved the Jews. We could no longer make peace with the thought of young people hiding in the attics and cellars and letting themselves be slaughtered like sheep.

Jewish workers and young men quickly established armed divisions. They fired at the insurgents from an armored train. The Jewish Communist, Heidelman, commanded the division from the train station that advanced against the peasant bands. The unorganized peasant masses, faced with a proper defense, fled in great panic. The Jews of Vinitza were saved! In the battle, however, the hero Heidelman fell at the front line.

Proskurov

The Proskurov pogrom was a major psychological blow to the Jewish workers in town. Some became passive and indifferent to political life. The majority, however, allied themselves to the Bolsheviks.

The Bolsheviks knew how to take advantage of the strained situation. As soon as they entered Proskurov—after the February pogrom—they worked strenuously to enlist the Jewish worker into the ranks of the Red Army, especially those who fought bravely against the Petliurists. When the Ukrainians attacked Podolia in June 1919, the Bolsheviks built regiments from Jewish and non-Jewish workers.

The demoralized Red Army soon withdrew, however, and for a long time only the workers defended the city of Proskurov. The Ukrainian military leaders later acknowledged that the Jewish workers had fought bravely.

Khmelnik

Khmelnik is a city with 10,000 Jewish inhabitants that lies in a very isolated area.[61] For the Bolsheviks, the town was insignificant from a strategic point of view, and for this reason they seldom defended it. The city was expendable, and the insurgents would often attack. The Jewish population decided to establish self-defense. Seven companies of 100 men—a full military battalion—were created. As they usually did with every self-defense group, the

---

[61] Khmelnik (Yid.), Khmel'nik (Rus.), Khmil'nyk (Ukr.) is 53 miles north of Komenetz.—Trans.

Bolsheviks tried several times to seize their weapons. But they encountered resistance and finally left the Khmelnik Jews alone.

The fight with the insurgents was fierce. They attacked Khmelnik several times, and each time they were pushed back. A Jew was found who was disloyal to the Jewish population; he was arrested and sentenced to death.

The insurgents found another means of getting to the Jews. They would attack trains that had come from Khmelnik in isolated areas. Then they removed and killed some Khmelnik Jews. They sent the others back as a warning to surrender. Khmelnik was like a besieged fortress. As a representative from the Red Cross, I was required to visit Khmelnik but could not reach it.

In August or September 1919, the Khmelnik Jews found out that a regular [Ukrainian] army from Galicia that had not perpetrated pogroms was on its way to Komenetz. Representatives from the Khmelnik community went to Komenetz to make sure that the Ukrainians knew they were not fighting against the UNR but only against the pogromists. Because they took this precaution, the Galician military forces arrived in Khmelnik without incident, and it was saved from the pogromists. It is interesting to note that in Khmelnik relations between Jews and peasants were good.

I could present more cases where Jews heroically defended themselves; however, these four stories, for which there is ample factual material, clearly reveal that under the storm of events the Jews actively resisted the murderers who plundered and slaughtered the Jewish population.

The Bolsheviks had brilliantly exploited the pogroms perpetrated by the Ukrainians. When they entered Komenetz the Bolsheviks represented themselves not only as fighters against class oppression, but also as defenders and liberators of the Jews. They claimed that they had found a secret order from Petliura in which he ordered the Proskurov and Felshtin pogroms. And the Jewish population believed this claim: how else could there have been such slaughter and nobody punished?!

In this period the Bolsheviks were generally tolerant towards the Jewish population. They cautiously implemented their experimental economic policy towards the merchant class. The Bolsheviks were also positively inclined towards the Jewish socialists, applying all sorts of methods to draw them to their cause. And after all the traumatic events, the Jewish socialists were generally sympathetic towards the Bolsheviks. Although they did not accept any administrative positions they fully supported the Soviet regime. And despite the fact that the Bolshevik authorities in Kiev had instructed the Komenetz revkom not to recognize any nationalistic demands, the local revkom recognized a Jewish socialist council that had been established in Komenetz.

The Jewish socialist parties, whose position was national autonomy, would not be reassured until an autonomous governing structure was in place that would support the Jewish working masses and work for Jewish culture. That was why they decided to establish a temporary Jewish socialist council. This council included the Bund, Fareynikte, Poale Tsiyon, the Communist Bund, United Communist, and the Communist Poale Tsiyon.

The Jewish socialist council took over every school in the community. Hebrew schools were turned into Yiddish schools. The council also determined the fate of the Komenetz kehillah, concluding that its existence was superfluous after the council transferred to itself the kehillah's cultural work, as well as its remaining functions (aid, registries) and other municipal institutions. The council informed the Jewish population about these changes, and revkom dissolved the kehillah. The local population recognized the revkom and the Jewish socialist council.

The Zionists, however, submitted an interesting memorandum to revkom. They explained that they accepted the principles of the Bolshevik workers' school. But they wanted to make the revkom aware that the Jewish socialists who were the major players in the council wished to take advantage of it only to push their party agenda regarding "German jargon [Yiddish]."[62]

The newly created organization in Komenetz, the Fareynikte Bund, played a large role in establishing the Jewish socialist council and spreading it throughout Podolia.[63]

The province already opposed the ministry's Central Committee [of Kiev to Aid Pogrom Victims], which sat isolated in Kiev and yet directed policies. This sentiment was especially felt in Komenetz. The central committee [of the Bund and Fareynikte] discussed the question of uniting. The main factors that had divided the two parties in the past increasingly lost their distinctiveness. The Russian Revolution had so deepened and complicated every question of principle that both movements had to revise their positions.

It was superfluous to speak about the kehillah's competence when the left and the right factions could not work together. The Jewish socialists promoted the liquidation of the Jewish kehillahs. Even those [socialists] who were not oriented to the Communists were under the influence of the idea of the "dic-

---

[62] The material about the Jewish socialist council was available until February 1921. I have, however, no information about its fate. [In the "culture wars" between Zionists and Bundists, the question of what constitutes the national language of the Jewish masses was a central issue. The Zionists championed Hebrew; the Bundists insisted that Yiddish should be the prevailing language in schools, publications, and administration.—Trans.]

[63] The Fareynikte Bund was active April through June 1919, when the Bolsheviks administered Komenetz. It was also active after the Directory made its capital in Komenetz (June to mid-November), participating in the aid committee established in June by the Jewish Ministry.—Trans.

tatorship of the proletariat." They envisioned an autonomy plan that would be established through Jewish workers' councils. The right-wing majorities, who in fact held the power in most democratic kehillahs, also advocated such a position.

The main political positions that had separated the Bund and Fareynikte weakened. Events, especially the pogrom waves and the frequent change of power, tore apart the ties of the province to Kiev. Moreover, Kiev was engaged with other political issues, and its positions were often not appropriate for the circumstances in the province.

The local Bund and Fareynikte were forced to take an independent political orientation. They saw how very harmful the disintegration of the socialist power was and now wanted a cohesive position. Thus, a united party was founded—first in Komenetz and then in the entire Podolia. The united organization—Bund and Fareynikte—took the name Fareynikte Bund. As an independent party the Fareynikte Bund would play a very important role.[64]

From April to June 1919 the Jewish population lived more or less peacefully until the Ukrainian army attacked [Podolia]. We were certain about the present but did not know what tomorrow would bring. We feared the Ukrainians, who were perpetrating the violent pogroms, but we also did not trust the Bolsheviks.

Petliura's Army Attacks Podolia (Summer 1919)[65]

In the beginning of May I served as a delegate to a Kultur Lige conference in Kiev. I visited the center with some other colleagues. We had been cut off for eight months, and were full of hope that we would receive answers to the many questions that remained following the recent nightmarish events. On the way to Kiev we had learned of Grigoriev's famous revolt against the Soviet regime.[66] Within a short time came the unsettling news about the peasant uprising in Podolia.

---

[64] See Appendix No. 3.

[65] In August 1919, Petliura's forces launched successful attacks on Kiev and Odessa. But they suffered severe casualties as they fought on several fronts against the Polish army, Denikin's White (Volunteer) Army, and the Bolsheviks.—Trans.

[66] Grigoriev—a former Ukrainian ataman—had crossed over to the Bolsheviks. In May 1919 he organized an uprising against the Soviet authority. Terrible pogroms took place in the region of Grigoriev's uprising. In Kiev province: Olysk, Bohslov, Bielozorka, Cherkoss (1,000 Jews killed), Smela (80 victims), Rakhmestrivke (30 Jews killed), Tsibulev (20 victims). Poltava province: Veselyi Podil [?], Zolotonosha (20 Jews killed), Kobiliak, Kremenchug (50 victims), Yelisavetgrod (3,000 victims), Radomishel (1,000 victims). All this information came from the book *Di Yidishe avtonomye un der*

The Jewish socialist circles in Kiev were very tense. Their situation in general was difficult because the Jewish Communists did not trust them. The same atmosphere was also felt in the Kultur Lige conference.

Mr. Rafes, and after him Mr. Levitan, came to greet the conference and behaved so brusque and even crude that the Presidium found it necessary to stop them in the middle of their address.[67] I was also interested in, and attended, the conference of the Communist Bund that was established at that time. The question about uniting with the left Fareynikte was addressed at the conference. Levitan announced that the left Fareynikte was ready to join the Communist Bund and renounce its nationalistic demands. The new party would be called Komfarbund.[68]

Pogroms continued to flood every corner of Ukraine. Ukraine was drowning in Jewish blood—pogroms without bounds and without measure. From every location Jews came and told terrible stories about the flow of Jewish blood. But the Central Committee [of Kiev to Aid Pogrom Victims], the only relief organization that helped Jews who had suffered from the pogroms, was liquidating itself: the Communist Bund had sent a memorandum to the highest Bolshevik circles [claiming that] the Jewish socialists had left the aid committee and all that remained were the right-wing Jewish parties.

The authorities in Kiev thoroughly disappointed us. They decided to liquidate the Central Committee. The liquidation of the old Jewish workers' party, the lack of direction, and the powerlessness of the remaining leaders from the Jewish socialist parties, plus the tragedies from the terrible pogroms, completely crushed us.

We also received unsettling news about Komenetz and left Kiev to return home. Our hearts were burdened. We secured a seat on a train with great dif-

---

natsyonaler sekretaryat in Ukraine: Materyaln un dokumentn [Jewish autonomy and the national secretariat in Ukraine: Materials and documents] (Kiev: Idisher folks-farlag, 1920).

[67] Rafes was a leader in the Ukrainian Bund and later in the Communist Bund and the Kombund. He also was a member of the Jewish Yevsektsye in the Communist Party. Levitan was a former Fareynikter, later a member of Kombund, and also a member of Yevsektsye. See *Di Yidishe avtonomye un der natsyonaler sekretaryat in Ukraine*, 292. [Mikhail Levitan (1882–1937) was a member of Fareynikte until he joined the Communist Party in May 1919. He helped create a communist-oriented Yiddish culture among Ukrainian and Russian Jews. In 1937 the Bolsheviks accused him of being a Trotskyist and he was executed.—Trans.]

[68] The Komfarbund was initially rejected by the Ukrainian Communist Party for being nationalist; however, the Central Committee of the Russian Communist Party accepted the new party, and the Central Executive Committee of the Ukrainian Soviet Government included Komfarbund members.—Trans.

ficulty. At the Vinitza station soldiers broke into our car and taunted us with various antisemitic slurs but did not become violent.

We arrived at the Proskurov train station. Apprehension was in the air. The haidamaks were sighted not far from the border. I met some students from Komenetz and they related that it was not calm in the city.

I arrived in Komenetz. The mood was very grave. We heard that haidamaks had entered Orinin again. We met at the offices of the revkom. We sensed that its power was ending. The Red Army soldier guarding the door was allowing anyone to enter. The authority of the revkom was at an end because the haidamaks were only eight versts from Komenetz.

One felt the antisemitic mood everywhere. Ukrainians who were members of the Bolshevik military were demoralized. Among them were former Ukrainian officers engaged in antisemitic agitation. In a village not far from Komenetz two Ukrainian teachers distributed proclamations among the peasants, calling upon them to resist the "Communists and the Yids." The teachers and several officer-provocateurs were shot by Red soldiers.

These events enraged the Bolsheviks and they applied repressive measures against the Ukrainian leaders. In turn, this response created an acute antisemitic atmosphere. The Jewish population was completely at a loss. The mood was very tense. Everyone was expecting a pogrom.

I went to the Workers' Club, where many workers were walking around armed with rifles. A dreadful silence permeated the town. The "house committee"—the town militia—kept good watch to ensure order. The Jewish population slept that night, but what would be tomorrow?

In the morning the entire community woke to terrible artillery shelling. The student S knocked at my door. He was a bit of a leftist, a little petty bourgeois-like, who opposed every authority and always warned when a power was nearing the end. I got dressed, took a small pack, and decided to leave Komenetz in case the Bolsheviks withdrew. A group of Jewish socialists also decided to go into "goles."[69]

The town was in chaos. Jews went through the streets nervously. We suddenly heard shooting from machine guns—a battle was occurring near the city....

We went to the revkom and heard the catastrophic news: the haidamaks were expected to arrive in Komenetz today. We left the city without even saying farewell to our close ones and friends. We said goodbye to a friend, Kylymnyk, the city mayor. We told him that we were leaving Komenetz by foot and asked that he take every measure within his power to save the Jewish population. He pressed our hands firmly and his eyes filled with tears.

---

[69] The Hebrew and Yiddish word for "exile."—Trans.

On our way out we ran into a prominent Bolshevik—S—and told him that we intend to leave Komenetz by foot. We thought that he would allow us to evacuate by train with the rest of the Bolshevik administrators. "Nu, go," he answered curtly. He did not offer a place for us on the train. This was understandable because we were not Bolsheviks and technically we should not be evacuated. But in the eyes of the haidamaks we were Bolsheviks, and they wanted to kill us. So we left. We learned later that the haidamaks diligently searched for us in the first days, and particularly for me, a committed socialist.

We departed Komenetz by foot. Many of us left behind parents, brothers, and sisters. The sound of the haidamak artillery barrage grew stronger. This sound was the duel between the Bolsheviks and the Ukrainians.

We went to Kitaigorod.[70] The entire way was flooded with groups of Jews: young people, workers, merchants, intellectuals, rich and poor—everyone fled. Whole families went—wives with small children. A 72-year-old Jewish woman was with us too. A small number rode, the others walked. We went, not knowing where. For the frightened, nervous Jews, the word *haidamak* was enough to make them get up and run. We could not imagine what the future would be like, even what the next morning would bring. Many fled, simply as they were, without a kopeck in their pocket, abandoning their homes and all their possessions. There was only one thought on everyone's mind: flee and save yourself. If the attack from the Ukrainians had not come so unexpectedly, it might have been possible for the entire Jewish population to have prepared and to have left Komenetz.

A rich Jewish baker with his wife and small children hauled sacks on his back filled with household items. It was hot and difficult for him to carry his possessions. Recently he had paid a "tax" to the Bolsheviks. (It goes without saying that he was not their biggest friend.) He could have stayed. So why did he flee with the Bolsheviks? Because he was more terrified of the haidamaks. He was an old acquaintance of ours, and he cried bitterly: "See what you've done!"

We arrived in Kitaigorod. It was market day. The peasants gathered and were surprised and looked on as we Jews hurried by. They began to murmur. Already we heard hateful rabble-rousing cries. A dread fell on the town.

We entered a Jewish home—an inn—and requested a samovar with tea. The owner was frightened and asked that we leave immediately. He said that peasant bandits were wandering around the town searching for young people from Komenetz. The peasants, sensing that there was no longer any authority in the area, and influenced by antisemitism and criminal elements,

---

[70] A small Jewish town, fourteen versts from Komenetz, it lies between large mountains. [Kitaigorod (Yid.), Kitay Gorod (Rus.), Kytaihorod (Ukr.) is 11 miles east of Komenetz.—Trans.]

preyed upon the Jews in order to rob and to kill them. The pogrom fear that the Komenetz Jews brought with them infected the Kitaigorod Jews as well. It soon became apparent that indeed the Kitaigorod Jews had something to fear.[71]

We left the inn and went to a family with whom we were acquainted. They took us in immediately in a friendly manner. But shortly the hostess ran in and asked us to have mercy on them and leave her house. She was told that the peasants were searching for Jews from Komenetz and she was worried about her family. We saw that our presence made the hostess very anxious and sensed that in general the mood in Kitaigorod was tense. We decided to leave the town despite the danger to ourselves. We feared that we would run into peasants who were leaving in all directions after the market was over.

We began wandering through gardens and climbing over fences, until we made it out of the town. Then we journeyed across the high mountains that surround the town and slowly made our way to a road.

But here we faced a question: where do we go next? We had lost one of our companions in the tumult. We did not know what had become of him. However, in our group were new refugees: two gymnasium students and some ordinary Jews.

We met a peasant and asked him for directions to the nearest town. He answered: "Yes, yes, guys. What did you do? You'll come to a bad end. They are already waiting for you," and he pointed the way. We decided, however, to go in another direction.

We went very quickly. We were in the middle of a field. No Jewish homes were around. We had decided that it would be better to leave the villages early before the peasants returned from the Kitaigorod market. Everything we encountered frightened us. We were extremely anxious. When we saw a peasant in the distance we were convinced that he was spying on us. We continued on more quickly. Then we saw a gentile boy mounting a horse and we thought that he was riding to the village to inform on us. In the distance we saw figures hiding themselves from us and our hearts nearly fell out of our chests from fear. But it turned out that they too were Jews who had run away from Komenetz and so we fled together.

We ran into a Jew we knew. He said he would arrange a wagon to transport us but not everyone could fit in it. We did not want the group to be separated, so we continued to march all together by foot.

From a distance we saw the Soviyar paper factory and decided to rest there. We had already gone 30 versts [about 20 miles] without rest or food.

---

[71] See the pogrom in Kitaigorod. [Ukrainian troops perpetrated pogroms in the town for five days after the Red Army retreated from Kitaigorod on the eve of the Jewish holiday Shavuot (June 3, 1919).—Trans.]

But as we approached the factory, we sensed hostility from the workers and decided to push on.

We walked a few more versts and saw Red Army soldiers with a commander whom we knew standing near a tavern. We decided that we would ask to go with them. But the Red soldiers were carrying some valuable articles and were also afraid of the peasants. They asked us to leave. We continued alone.

We were so frightened that we could not allow ourselves to rest even for ten minutes. I went four nights without sleep, the entire day with nothing to eat, and felt my feet giving way. I begged that we should rest a bit but the group did not listen. There was only one need—to get as far away from Kitaigorod as possible.

In the villages people looked at us suspiciously. "What's that shooting we hear? And what is happening in Komenetz?" the peasants asked. "The Romanians were attacking."[72] Only in one village did a peasant give us water, and even a few potatoes. We devised ways to avoid the villages as much as possible because we didn't trust the peasants.

"When will we finally see a Jewish town with an ordinary Jew?" exclaimed the former Menshevik B, now a Jewish socialist. We did not know where we were going. We estimated from information given to us by passing peasants that only ten versts away there was a Jewish town called Zvantchik.[73] Just ten versts more and we would be saved!

We continued by sheer force of will. But we had no more strength! Darkness came and we still did not see a town. Various thoughts crept into our minds. It seemed as if the village was fleeing from us! We will not live to see a Jewish town.… But finally Zvantchik appeared.

We rested a bit before entering the town. But the atmosphere there was also strained. The peasants told us that insurgents were in a village not far from here. Our hearts were gloomy. We could not go on. We had no more strength. We would stay overnight and then decide what to do.

We entered the town. It was the evening of the holiday of Shvues [Shavuot, June 3, 1919]. Jews were going to shul in holiday dress. We entered a Jewish guesthouse. The innkeeper, however, was not very happy with our presence.

"I don't have anything. The military even drank up the water today," she said. She softened up when we showed her a coin. She set up a samovar, served eggs, bread, and even challah. The group ate and went straight to bed.

---

[72] In May 1919, Romanian forces occupied a portion of Pokuttya, a region in southwestern Ukraine that had been part of Galicia in the Hapsburg Empire. The Romanian army handed eastern Pokuttya over to Poland in August 1919.—Trans.

[73] Zvantchik (Yid.), Velikiy Zhvanchik (Rus.), Velikiy Zhvanchik (Ukr.) is 20 miles east of Komenetz.—Trans.

We could no longer feel our feet; they were like pieces of wood. We discovered that our lost friend was here in Zvantchik. In the tumult he was able to escape in a Jewish wagon.

The next day I set out to find a wagon so that we could continue to travel right after the holiday. I found a Jew, a wagon driver, and began to speak to him about a wagon, but he did not want to respond. It is a holiday, he answered piously, and on holidays he did not want to talk about wagons. Only after I explained to him that I am a representative of the Central Committee to Aid Pogrom Victims and began to reproach him a bit did he become more amiable.[74] He said that he would arrange a wagon early the next morning. And indeed, at dawn he provided us with a wagon.

We went to Ushitza.[75] We entered the town and I sent for the local community leaders, old acquaintances, from our joint work in EKOPO. They came but I did not see much joy in their faces. The opposite: they would be happier if the "homeless refugees" would avoid Ushitza. If the Romanians, they said, saw a group gathering here, it would end badly. They would shell the town from the other side of the Dniester.[76] Even so they provided us with lodgings and food. Meanwhile, more people who were fleeing arrived, all acquaintances, and all from Komenetz. They joined our group.

What was happening meanwhile in Komenetz no one knew. We decide to go to the county seat and get the news there.

We arrived at Nei-Ushitz and became more despondent upon hearing the news.[77] The Komenetz revkom had already evacuated all the way to Zhmerin-ka.[78] We learned, incidentally, that a tattered military unit from the Red Army had robbed the Jewish population of Dinovitz and Minkovitz when they were withdrawing.[79] Again we felt dejected. We continued further—towards Kiev.

During this time Komenetz-Podolsk and its vicinity experienced great difficulties. On the day we left Komenetz (June 3, Erev Shvues) Ukrainian mili-

---

[74] Gumener uses the word *musar*, which connotes reproach and is also a traditional world for ethics.—Trans.

[75] This town lies on the Dniester (now on the Romanian border, 50 versts from Komenetz). [Ushitza (Yid.), Staraya Ushitsa (Rus.), Stara Ushytsya (Ukr.) is 26 miles east of Komenetz.—Trans.]

[76] A few days after we left, the Romanians did indeed shell the town.

[77] Nei-Ushitz (Yid.), Novaya Ushitsa (Rus.), Nova Ushytsya (Ukr.) is 35 miles east of Komenetz.—Trans.

[78] Zhmerinka, a well-known station between Kiev and Orom, 130 versts from Komenetz. [Zhmerinka (Yid., Rus.), Zhmerynka (Ukr.) is 57 miles north of Komenetz.—Trans.]

[79] Minkovitz (Yid.), Minkovtsy (Rus.), Mynkivtsi (Ukr.) is 27 miles northeast of Komenetz.—Trans.

tary units under the leadership of General Udovichenko took the city.[80] Greeting the military were several prominent persons, including Kylymnyk, the city mayor and a Ukrainian Social Democrat, Bednev, professor at Komenetz University, [Leib] Kleiderman, chairman of the Jewish kehillah (and member of Ahdut), Miranski, chairman of the Duma, and some others. The pogrom mood among the Ukrainian military was strong. When Mr. Kleiderman appeared—an old Jew with a big grey beard—the Cossacks immediately wanted to pounce on him and only with great effort was it possible to hold them back. The delegation strongly begged the military leaders to prevent a pogrom in Komenetz, but the impression left by the talks was discouraging.

A deadly silence reigned in the city. Jews hid in cellars and attics. There could not be any talk of organizing resistance against regular military troops. Jews were nowhere to be seen. A few young people who risked going into the street were detained by military intelligence units and driven by horsemen to headquarters far outside the city. The majority of these young people were killed. A few saved themselves after suffering many physical and demoralizing hardships.

This was the signal for the pogrom, which lasted three days [June 3–6]. Both military units and the local population participated. It occurred without any interference from the military authority, which was responsible for maintaining order in the city. Acting as if they had received prior orders, the pogromists killed only men. Children and women were spared.

Jews of different [political] views and classes were killed. The town was completely plundered. There were cases when they even took furniture from the houses. Christian servants who for some reason or another were unhappy with the Jewish families for whom they worked would denounce them as Bolsheviks. Murders were committed with exceptional barbarity and brutality.

Some Ukrainians, such as the town mayor Kylymnyk, Professor Bednev, and others, energetically defended the Jews and saved quite a few. Kylymnyk informed the Ukrainian authority that he was resigning from his post because it was shameful to be called a mayor of a Ukrainian town where such barbarous events occurred—where innocent people were killed right in the street. His protests, however, did not make any difference.

The pogrom wound down only after the wild rabble had rampaged for three days. The pogrom atmosphere, however, remained for a long time afterward. Terror engulfed the town. Pillagers would brutally kill or wound peo-

---

[80] Oleksandr Ivanovich (Oleksander) Udovychenko (1887–1975) was head of the Sixteenth Infantry Brigade of the Ukrainian Galician Army, formed out of the Ukrainian National Army. This unit became the Third Special Riflemen Division that fought against the Red Army in Podolia. At the end of 1919 he was taken prisoner by the Volunteer Army.—Trans.

ple who were beginning to return after fleeing to nearby towns. Two young brothers, both students, from the Makhnovski family were killed in front of their parents. Altogether 52 Jews were killed in Komenetz or on the road to town.[81]

Finally, the Ukrainian civil administration arrived and imposed some order using the political secret police. Naturally they first searched for Communists, which included those who had fled in terror with the Bolsheviks out of concern that Ukrainians would target them had they stayed. They searched mainly for young people who had taken part in the Orinin battle.

The secret police wanted to use the events at Orinin for a sensational political trial that would make clear that the Jews were conducting a war against the Ukrainians.

To give this trial a special "local flavor," they arrested Alexander Khomski, a young Jewish man, the son of a bourgeois half-assimilated Jewish family.

Khomski had no political ties whatsoever. He had been in Orinin, as had tens of other Jewish young people, to save the Jews from being slaughtered. The reactionary Ukrainian military circles wanted to show with the Khomski trial that even Jews from bourgeois families followed the Bolsheviks and led an open war against the Ukrainians. You can understand that these claims gave more than a little fuel for antisemitic pogrom agitation.

Khomski's trial drew great attention in Jewish communal circles; they sensed in it a great danger. The military resisted any attempt by Jewish communal leaders and the Jewish Ministry to avoid a public trial.

The trial was conducted very tendentiously, and all the evidence rested on the word of an agent of the secret police. Khomski was accused of being a Communist who worked on behalf of the Soviet authorities against the interests of the UNR. Distinguished Ukrainian leaders came and served as witnesses on behalf of Khomski to no avail. The court sentenced him to death. Thanks to the energetic members of the Jewish Ministry, however, he was spared the death sentence.

The Jews of Komenetz experienced many other troubles. The civilian authorities finally established some order in town. The province, however, was entirely in the hands of the atamans. A terrible pogrom like Proskurov occurred in Kitaigorod.[82] It started when the army—with a commander at its head—entered and for a few days terrorized the Jewish population. The commander demanded "contributions" in amounts that could not be raised by a

---

[81] It was widely held among Jews in Ukraine that Komenetz was considered the luckiest city in the region because it had suffered the least.

[82] We have already written about Kitaigorod. This is a small Jewish town four versts from Komenetz.

small town.[83] Then posters were pasted in the streets calling for a pogrom. And finally, it ended with the slaughter of Jews. In one night 78 men and women were butchered.[84] The pogromists committed brutal acts. Pogroms on a smaller scale took place in many small towns in the region.

We should note that the Romanians saved some Jewish towns that lay by the Dniester: Studenitsa (the Kitaigorod murderers wanted to repeat the pogrom there), Ushitza, and Kalyus.[85] The Romanians, at the request of the local Jewish population, demanded that the pogromists clear out of these towns.

The Ukrainian Movement and the Jewish Pogroms (Summer 1919)

Throughout the summer of 1919 I traveled to towns and shtetls in Ukraine as a representative of the Russian Red Cross in order to help Jewish pogrom victims. There was unease everywhere. Attacks from the Ukrainians and from the retreating Red Army, as well as pogroms against the Jews were the topics of the day.

Much has been written and discussed in different political and communal circles about the causes of the pogroms in Ukraine. I do not wish to review the question in its entire breadth and depth, that is, in a manner that it deserves. I only want to note some specific events and describe them in greater detail.

The strained relationship in Russia between urban and rural that had deepened during the war, and especially after the revolution in 1917, took an extreme form in Ukraine due to nationalist feelings. In Ukrainian cities the majority of the population was made up of Jews, Russians, former administrative bureaucrats, and a small percent of Ukrainians and Poles. Podolia, which is about the size of Switzerland, had a population of five million people. The Jews made up 12 percent of the inhabitants. Among the urban population, however, Jews made up 50–60 percent.[86]

The miserable ignorant Ukrainian peasant class woke up from its long sleep. The chauvinistic petty bourgeois Ukrainian intelligentsia established itself at the head of the peasant movement. They were the ideological leaders of the peasants, the fighters for the peasant's social and national liberation. The urban population, however, was not sympathetic towards the Ukrainian

---

[83] "Contributions" meant monetary extortions.—Trans.

[84] The Kitaigorod orphans are currently housed in the orphanage OZE with the Kultur Lige in Komenetz-Podolsk.

[85] Studenitsa (Yid., Rus., Ukr.) is 17 miles east of Komenetz. Kalis (Yid.), Kalyus (Rus., Ukr.) is 34 miles east of Komenetz. These small towns are just east of the Dniester River. The Romanian army occupied the territory just west of the river.—Trans.

[86] See n. 1.—Trans.

movement, which was supported by the peasants. Thus, it was a challenge to create an effective government.

The Ukrainian Social Democrat Mazepa, a distinguished Ukrainian prime minister, wrote: "According to the census of 1879 [sic. 1897], Ukraine had a majority peasant population. The Russian and Jewish population, which comprised 22 percent, took a negative stance towards the idea [of an independent] Ukraine."[87] Furthermore, he wrote: "The revolution in Ukraine was vulnerable. On the one hand, the cities that had a Ukrainian minority could not lead the revolution to victory without the help of the countryside; on the other hand, the Ukrainian countryside could not realize the goals of the revolution without a leading role from the cities with a non-Ukrainian minority."[88] And he concluded: "The cultural centers, in all Ukrainian towns and villages, were in the hands of the Russians and the Jews. The best proof were the results of the municipal elections that were held in accord with Kerensky's law.[89] Ukrainians in these elections made few gains; the majority were Russians and Jews, who often were even antagonistic to the [Rada's] general secretary and to the idea of Ukrainian sovereignty itself. Mr. Vynnychenko writes, for example, that the Kiev municipality for a long time did not want to give a residence to the General Secretary who was forced to rent a dirty hotel with poor services."[90] This is Mazepa's description of the urban population's relationship to the Ukrainian peasant movement.[91]

---

[87] See *Vil'na Ukraïna* [Free Ukraine] (L'viv, 1921), 15.

[88] *Vil'na Ukraïna*, 16.

[89] Alexander Kerensky (1881–1970) served as prime minister of Russia's Provisional Government after the February 1917 revolution. He initially opposed Ukrainian independence but in June and July 1917 negotiated with the Central Rada and recognized Ukrainian autonomy. Elections for a Ukrainian Constituent Assembly were held between November 12 and December 5, 1917. The beginning of the Civil War, however, precluded the establishment of the Assembly. Scholars have concluded that Ukrainian nationalists did very well in the elections, especially in the villages. Still, there was a significant divide between urban and rural populations. Russians and Jews comprised a large percentage of the cities, and were not enthusiastic about Ukrainian sovereignty, preferring a federated system within Russia. See Steven Guthier, "The Popular Base of Ukrainian Nationalism in 1917," *Slavic Review* 38, 1 (1979): 41.—Trans.

[90] *Vil'na Ukraïna*, 23.

[91] The historian Geoff Eley frames the issue succinctly: "Winning the consent of the peasantry was absolutely fundamental to the democratic legitimacy of the competing political leaderships between 1917 and 1920, as well as to their actual political survival. This was pre-eminently true of the Ukrainian nationalists, for the Russified nature of the cities deprived them of an alternative social base and the failure to bid strongly enough for the peasants' support proved fatal to both the Hetmanate and the Directory." See Eley, "Remapping the Nation," 234.—Trans.

In reality, Jews of various classes had differing attitudes [to the Russian revolution and the Ukrainian national movement]. The large Jewish bourgeoisie (the "Brodskys" and the "Halperins") was sympathetic to the Russian Revolution in so far that [the revolution] freed it from the shameful restrictions that the old tsarist feudal system had established. The social side of the Russian Revolution, however, was foreign and even scared them. Noting that workers and peasants were a majority in the Ukrainian Central Rada, they took an openly antagonistic position towards the Ukrainian peasant movement (Dobry, Gutnik).[92]

The Jewish middle and petty bourgeoisie took another position. They sympathized with the nationalist character of the Ukrainian movement. The Zionists always emphasized the same position relative to the Ukrainian movement. At the Central Rada's People's Convention in 1919 in Kiev, they emphasized their loyalty to the national movement. Zionists were at the head of the Jewish delegation that went to meet the Directory in Kiev in 1919 (Vynnychenko and Petliura were in the Directory). In Komenetz-Podolsk [Sholem] Altman (a Zionist delegate in the National Assembly) emphasized the Zionists' positive position towards the Ukrainian movement when he was in the delegation that greeted Petliura.[93]

Despite their efforts, the Zionists and Ukrainian parties did not establish a relationship. The right-wing Ukrainian parties were antisemitic and could not forge a dialogue with the left. The positive position of the Zionist parties towards the Ukrainian movement, which had the sympathy of both the [Jewish] middle and petty bourgeois, simply remained no more than official pronouncements.

In reality these social classes [the middle and petty bourgeois] had an entirely different relationship to the new Ukrainian movement. The Jewish merchant, broker, and lease holder had long associated themselves with the

---

[92] Gutnik, a leader from the Odessa Jewish bourgeoisie, was minister during the Hetman government in Ukraine. He voted to rescind National Personal Autonomy. [Gumener is using the names of haute bourgeoisie families in 19th-century Russia generically. The Brodsky and Halperin families were sugar producers and exporters. Gumener explains that on the one hand the upper Jewish bourgeoisie was glad that it no longer would be hampered by a monarchy that held on to its prerogatives by limiting the capitalist activities of Jews to the Pale of Settlement. On the other hand, the upper bourgeoisie feared that the Revolution would lead to the re-distribution of wealth and resources to the peasant class. Abram Dobry (1867–1936) was a Jewish banker and sugar industrialist who served in the financial sector of the UNR. He emigrated to France in 1920. Sergei Gutnik (Israel Mikhelov) was a member of the Kadet party and an industrialist who served in Skoropadsky's government.—Trans.]

[93] A delegation greeted Petliura on July 17, 1919 when he entered Komenetz. The Jewish members expressed the Jewish community's support for the UNR.—Trans.

powerful actors who had played dominant roles in Ukraine, namely, the no-
bleman, the manager, the civil servant, etc. They found it very difficult to
suddenly fit into the new political situation. This [discomfort] was felt very
strongly in the time of the Hetman, when the Germans occupied Ukraine and
the former landed aristocracy began to play the dominant role again.

The groups from the Jewish population that could have allied with the
peasants were the artisans. And indeed, the relationships between them and
the peasants were relatively good, in contrast to other classes. The peasants
considered the merchants to be speculators who drove up prices. They therefore treated them with disdain. And according to the limited understanding
of the peasant, they believed that Jewish merchants were guilty of causing
high prices. They had an entirely different attitude towards the artisans. Having lost their position in the city, the artisans went to the villages, where they
very often received produce instead of money for their work. Thus, in many
places in Podolia artisans and peasants established amicable relationships.
The Jewish artisans, however, were not organized politically and they mostly
followed the lead of other parties. Recently, the artisans came out with independent political platforms.[94]

The Jewish intelligentsia did not look favorably upon the Ukrainian
movement. Nurtured in Russian gymnasiums and in Russian universities,
raised in the Russian spirit and culture, it was very hard for them to accept
the Ukrainian movement.

The Jewish worker, however, took another position. The Jewish socialists
committed themselves to the [nationalists'] side from the very beginning of
the Ukrainian movement. In 1917 Rafes (Bundist) went to Petrograd to defend
the interests of the Ukrainians before the Provisional Government of Kerensky. He spoke out sharply against Greater Russian Bolshevism (1917, 1918).[95]

Zolotarev (Bund) was general secretary in the Ukrainian Secretariat
(Ministry), Silberfarb (Fareynikte), was the first minister for Jewish affairs in
Ukraine, and [Yehuda] Novakovski (Fareynikte, and later a prominent Com-
munist) was very popular among the Ukrainians and played an important
role in the Central Rada.[96] At a Fareynikte conference in Kiev in April 1918,
Rafes passionately defended the Ukrainian movement, and insisted that

[94] See Appendix 2.

[95] The majority of the Bund had an internationalist outlook, that is, it argued for minority rights in societies that are culturally diverse but not suited for federal solutions.
By contrast, Rafes advocated that Ukraine become part of a federated Russia.—Trans.

[96] Aleksandr Zolotarev (1879–1938) was a Bundist who became a member of the
Central Council of Ukraine, a member of the Kiev Duma, and state controller for the
General Secretariat of Ukraine. He was executed in the Stalinist purges. Yehuda No-
vakovski (1879–1933) was a member of Fareynikte. When the party split into a left

Ukraine could be a "Ukrainian Judea." Poale Tsiyon always sympathized with the Ukrainians. But the Ukrainians, with their deeply held chauvinistic politics, very quickly rejected the Jewish socialists.

For the Jewish worker the question was with whom to stand: the Bolshevik Greater Russian movement or the Ukrainian petty bourgeois. He chose the former. "He who always was part of the vanguard of the revolution does not want and cannot remain behind," claimed the new Jewish Communists.[97] But soon after, and to the great misfortune of the Jewish population, various upheavals began in Ukraine that resulted in the bloody massacres of the Jews. This was the nature of the Jewish-Ukrainian relationship in the years 1917 and 1918 of the revolution.

The following list illustrates the number of different regimes that occupied Proskurov alone from the February Revolution to January 1, 1921: Kerensky's regime, Ukrainian authorities, Bolsheviks, Germans with the Central Rada, Hetman, Directory, Bolsheviks, Directory, Bolsheviks, the Directory with Galician troops, Denikin, Poles, Ukrainians and Poles, Bolsheviks, Ukrainians, and Bolsheviks. As if in a motion picture, the various powers alternated, and with each power came new demands. And with each power the professional bandits "came a courting" and the Jewish population soon felt their bite!

These [occupiers] were groups of people who "educated themselves" in the activities of war. Their professions were robbery, killing, and slaughter, and it was easiest to apply these activities on the defenseless Jewish population. In the places where the Jewish population had an organized active resistance the robbers withdrew.

In general, two moments tended to be the worst for the Jewish population, namely, when a new regime entered a town and when it exited. In these situations, the ragged hungry soldiers would very often fling themselves upon the town to search for food and clothing and this often would end in a pogrom.

Worst of all was the specifically cultivated hatred towards the Jews, which was used in the Ukrainian movement as a means, a well-known means, from the time of the tsar, to temper the disgruntled peasants and Cossacks. The antisemitism that had struck deep roots in Ukraine now blossomed widely. No salt, no products, no boots, no underwear and clothes to be found: the Yids hid them. The Bolsheviks attacked Ukraine; times are bad: the dirty Russians and Yids are guilty. Slowly, the idea grew that the Yids are always at fault. The wildest instincts from the darkest masses were awakened and provoked …

---

and right wing, Novakovski joined the former, which advocated an alliance with the Soviets. He held various positions in the Soviet government.—Trans.

[97] M. Rafes, *Two Years of Revolution in Ukraine or the Crisis of the Bund* (Moscow, 1920).

and that's how they wanted to win their sympathy. "The Yids seized power," was the slogan of the insurgents.

In fact, this was absolutely wrong. Although Jews took a large role in the Soviet institutions and in revkom, they constituted only a small percent compared to non-Jews. But the Christian population was not accustomed to see Jewish officials at government offices and regarded them as a thorn in their eyes. Taking into consideration the antisemitic mood of the non-Jewish population, the Bolsheviks stopped sending Jewish instructors to Ukraine and Podolia in 1920.

The greatest culpability for the pogroms rested with the leadership of the Ukrainian movement. It committed an unspeakable grave crime against the Jews and bore guilt with regard to the Ukrainian population. The Ukrainian intelligentsia was almost completely criminally silent regarding the pogroms, or in the best case, paid little attention to the fight against the pogromists.[98]

It is interesting to quote parts of [Solomon] Goldelman's book (past minister of labor), *Letters from a Jewish Social Democrat Regarding Ukraine*. "I must regretfully state," he wrote in June 1919, "that the majority of the local ministers, Social Revolutionaries and their leaders, were either dominated by the ideology that equated the pogroms with the battle against the Bolsheviks, or they were so blinded by their chauvinism, that they were ready to utilize the pogrom mood of the peasants for the sake of the Ukrainian movement." Further on he added: "I had to start educating, building positive relationships with the Social Democrats before they too became infected by the antisemitic madness—the possibility of its development needed to be energetically stopped. I had to lobby the Ukrainian ministry and the leaders of the Revolutionary Socialism."

After the terrible pogroms in 1919, "investigative commissions" were established but they did not accomplish anything. The most important organizers of the Jewish pogroms ([Mykola] Palienko, Semesenko, and others) were not punished.[99] The investigative commissions were ineffective, and the Jewish population did not have faith in them and were cold towards them. The lack of punishment and the tolerance towards the murderers created an atmosphere among the Christian population that killing Jews was permissible. True, there were exhortations about the pogroms, but no tangible action. The pogroms erased from the earth entire Jewish towns and villages, exterminated tens of thousands of Jews, and destroyed the great Jewish community

[98] See *Di Yidishe avtonomye un der natsyonaler sekretaryat in Ukraine*, 99 and onward.

[99] Mykola Palienko ("Polkovnyk") (1896–1944) was captain of artillery in the Directory army. He commanded the battalion known as Kuren Smerti (The Clan of Death). From 1934 to 1939 he served in the Polish army. Later, he joined the SS division "Galicia" and died in battle against the Red Army in 1944.—Trans.

in Ukraine. They also destroyed Ukrainian towns, demoralized the Ukrainian army, and compromised the Ukrainian movement.[100]

The pogroms even pushed the Jewish bourgeois groups into the ranks of the Bolsheviks. In 1919, Jewish workers led an active campaign against the Ukrainian insurgents because wherever they appeared, they simply mowed down all Jews. A real war was waged: on one side stood a regular army and armed peasants, and on the other side unarmed Jewish towns. "After we finish the war with the Jewish people" … wrote an insurgent in Litin in one of his proclamations.

"We lived quietly in our small town. There was no party politics," wrote a Jew from a small town to the Komenetz Committee to Aid the Pogrom Victims. But in his quiet little town in Podolia bandits slaughtered, raped women, robbed, and pillaged. The young men fled. They asked for weapons from the Bolsheviks in order to establish self-defense, but the Bolsheviks refused: "Either you are with us and will join the Red Army or you are against us and cannot be trusted with weapons." And how did the Jewish Communists behave at the time? In a time of social revolution, they wrote in their newspapers: "The only path for the Jewish masses is to stand with the Soviet authority; if not, they are in danger of being exterminated."

A special Jewish military battalion with a central bureau called Yevsektsye was established in Kiev. It recruited men from Jewish towns that had suffered from pogroms.[101] I happened to be in a small Jewish village, B, that had had a pogrom two days before. We were waiting for Petliura's troops to retake the town. In the meantime, I observed the work of an instructor from the Yevsektsye. I already wrote what happened in Kitaigorod. There were two options for Jewish youth: either stay in town and be killed with their parents, brothers, and sisters, or join the Red Army to fight the pogromists. The young people asked the instructor questions, deliberated, and finally dejectedly said farewell to their relatives and went to Kiev. Many young Jews would learn military tactics and then join the Jewish section of the International Bolshevik Regiment.[102] In reality, the Soviets used them only against pogrom bands and would send the untrained and inexperienced troops to the front.

The entire summer of 1919 the Jewish population of Podolia that bordered on Galicia suffered from pogroms. The borderlands of Podolia that in

---

[100] For the politics around pogrom investigations, see Christopher Gilley, "Beyond Petliura: The Ukrainian National Movement and the 1919 Pogroms," *East European Jewish Affairs* 47, 1 (2017): 45–61.—Trans.

[101] Yevsektsye (Evreiskaia Voennaia Sektsiia/Jewish Military Section) was a special recruitment section of the Red Army to enlist Jewish youth.—Trans.

[102] A multiethnic division that included Jewish self-defense units.—Trans.

general were not so affected during the [peasant] uprisings experienced mil-
itary-sponsored pogroms from the regular forces of the UNR. The rest of Podolia suffered more from the pogroms that were organized by the [peasant]
insurgents. The largest pogroms took place in the months of May through
August. During its offensive against the Bolsheviks in May, June, and August
1919, the UNR's military left a bloody path in many Jewish towns and villages.

In May and June there were pogroms in Orinin and 28 people were killed.
Pogroms perpetrated by the military took place in the following towns and
villages: Shatova, Dinovitz, Minkovitz, Yolteshkey, Maravna-Krilovitz, Verbo-
vitz, Bar, Zhmerinka, Bralov (28 young people killed), Kopaigorod, Volkovinitza, Derazhnia, Slobkovitz (very many victims), Yarmolintz, Yarishov, Zhvanchik, and Proskurov; the counties: Kamanetz, Proskurov, Mohilever, and
Nei-Ushitz.[103]

As terrible as were the pogroms by the military units, the cruelty of the
peasant bands was worse. The entire summer wild peasant bands went on a
rampage: they murdered, robbed, and raped. They established a permanent
pogrom.

The people of Litin suffered greatly, as did the Jewish population in the
Haysin and Broslev districts.[104] Haysin, a county seat with a dynamic cultural
life (there was even a Jewish gymnasium), was completely destroyed and hundreds of Jews fell victims. (All the information is taken from *Jewish Autonomy
and the National Secretariat in Ukraine.*)

Several months earlier in the district of Haysin there were pogroms in
the following places: Granov, which was organized by Petliura's troops. The
town was burned down and 5 Jews were killed. Kublish, which was initiated

---

[103] All of these towns are either in Podolia or Volhynia. Shatova (Yid.), Shatava (Rus.,
Ukr.) is 10 miles northeast of Komenetz. Yolteshkev (Yid.), Yaltushkov (Rus.), Yaltush-
kiv (Ukr.) is 38 miles southwest of Komenetz. Maravna-Krilovitz (Yid.), Murovanye
Kurilovtsy (Rus.), Murovani Kurylivtsi (Ukr.) is 55 miles southeast of Komenetz. Ver-
bovitz (Yid.), Verbovets (Rus., Ukr.) is 112 miles southwest of Komenetz. Bar (Yid., Rus.,
Ukr.) is 39 miles southeast of Komenetz. Bralov, Brailov (Rus.), Brailiv (Ukr.) is 77 miles
northeast of Komenetz. Kopaigorod (Yid.), Kopaygorod (Rus.), Kopaihorod (Ukr.) is 54
miles southeast of Komenetz. Volkovinitza (Yid.), Volkovintsy (Rus., Ukr.) is 60 miles
southeast of Komemetz. Derazhna (Yid.), Derazhnaya (Rus.), Derazhne (Ukr.) is 153
miles northeast of Komenetz. Slobkovitz (Yid.), Solobkovtsy (Rus.), Solobkivtsi (Ukr.)
is 33 miles south of Komenetz. Yarishov (Yid.), Yaryshev (Rus.), Yaryshiv (Ukr.) is 69
miles southeast of Komenetz.—Trans.

[104] Haysin (Yid.), Gaysin (Rus.), Haysyn (Ukr.) is 128 miles east of Komenetz.—Trans.

by Petliura's troops and where 30 Jews were killed. Teplik, where Petliura's troops plundered the entire town and hundreds of victims fell.[105]

From May 9 to 11 Broslev experienced its first pogroms organized by Ataman [Ananii] Volynetz.[106] Up to 200 Jews were killed. As in Haysin, pogroms in Broslev continued for the entire summer.[107] The Broslev district suffered greatly. There were pogroms in Nemirov, Tultchin, Shpikov, and Potchera (30 girls were raped there and contracted venereal disease).[108]

A terrible pogrom occurred in Trostinits.[109] The garrison in Trostinits consisted of 100 Red Army soldiers, about half Jewish and the rest Christian. During the peasant uprising, the [non-Jewish] soldiers from the Red Army joined the insurgents. On May 14 they gathered the Jewish population—those 12 years and older—to the site of the revkom and killed nearly 250 souls (men only), leaving 900 orphans and widows.

In Yampol district the following places suffered pogroms: Yampol, Popovtsy, Kopaigorod, Yarishov, Litshenitz, Azarenits, Sharigrod, and Krasnoya.[110] In Olgopol district the following towns suffered: Bershad, Chitchilnik, Lishtin. The Balte region also suffered greatly: Balte, Pistchanka, and Ribnitza.[111] At the beginning of February 1919 Balte was lost to the Bolsheviks

---

[105] Granov (Yid., Rus.), Hraniv (Ukr.) is 123 miles southeast of Komenetz. Kublich (Yid., Rus., Ukr.) is 131 miles southeast of Komenetz. Teplik (Yid., Rus., Ukr.) is 136 miles southeast of Komenetz.—Trans.

[106] Ananii Volynets (1894–1941) was born in Karbovka, near Haysin. He commanded troops in the Haysin region of Podolia. Volynets participated in the 1919 uprising against the Hetman government and also fought against the Bolsheviks. The Soviets arrested him in 1939 and he was executed in 1941.—Trans.

[107] Broslev (Yid.), Bratslav (Rus., Ukr.) is 108 miles east of Komenetz.—Trans.

[108] For a study on gender-based violence during the pogrom period, see Astashkevich, *Gendered Violence*. Nemirov (Yid., Rus.), Nemyriv (Ukr.) is 105 miles northeast of Komenetz. Tultchin (Yid.), Tulchin (Rus., Ukr.) is 104 miles southeast of Komenetz. Shpikov (Yid., Rus.), Shpykiv (Ukr.) is 90 miles east of Komenetz. Potchera (Yid.), Pechora (Rus., Ukr.) is 98 miles northeast of Komenetz.—Trans.

[109] Trostinits (Yid.), Trostyanets (Rus.), Trostianets (Ukr.) is 365 miles northeast of Komenetz.—Trans.

[110] These towns are all in Podolia. Yampol (Yid., Rus.), Yampil (Ukr.) is 90 miles north of Komenetz. Popovtsy (Yid., Rus., Ukr.) is 68 miles north of Komenetz. Litshenitz (Yid.), Luchinets (Rus.), Luchynets (Ukr.) is 57 miles east of Komenetz. Azarenits (Yid.), Ozarintsy (Rus.), Ozaryntsi (Ukr.) is 57 miles southeast of Komenetz. Sharigrod (Yid.), Shargorod (Rus., Ukr.) is 68 miles east of Komenetz. Krasnoya (Yid.), Krasnoye (Rus.), Krasne (Ukr.) is 132 miles northwest of Komenetz.—Trans.

[111] We had very little information about the vicinity of Olgopol and Balta. [Bershad (Yid., Rus., Ukr.) is 136 miles east of Komenetz. Chitchilnik (Yid.), Chechelnik (Rus.),

and was back in the hands of Petliura's army. Ukrainian soldiers immediately started to rob and torture. Most Jewish homes and stores were plundered. Twenty-seven Jews were shot, many were wounded, and many women were raped.

A month later a second pogrom occurred. Cruel and horrible events took place. Elderly people and women were killed, children were speared and put on pikes, and gold rings were removed together with fingers. The corpses of the murdered lay on the ground for an entire week and were not allowed to be taken for burial. Later there was another pogrom in Balte and a large part of the town was burned down.

In the region of Vinitza pogroms occurred in the following towns: Yanov, Kolenivka, Pikov, Bralov, and Zhmerinka. The town of Vinitza itself was not touched.[112]

In the district of Litin, the town of Litin suffered terribly. The first pogrom occurred on May 15. One hundred ten victims fell, and Litin suffered the entire summer from a permanent pogrom. The number of victims from these various pogroms was limited, but the town was completely devastated. Many homes and the market shops were burned down. The bandits harnessed together two old Jews to a wagon, forced them into the woods, and hanged them there. The Jewish residents fled to Vinitza. These pogroms were led by Shepel.

In Litin district Nay-Kosntin, Alt-Sinyove, and Pilava suffered greatly.[113] In the district of Letichev relatively fewer Jews were touched by the pogroms; more people suffered in Derazhnia, Mikhalpol, and Volkovinitza.[114] Many Jews were also killed on the road, especially around the villages. There were many small Jewish communities in Podolia and all of them were destroyed.

Chechelnyk (Ukr.) is 131 miles southeast of Komenetz. Lishtin (Yid.), Leschchin (Rus.), Lishchyn (Ukr.) is 195 miles northeast of Komenetz. It is in the province of Volhynia. Balte (Yid.), Balta (Rus., Ukr.) is 149 miles southeast of Komenetz. Pistchanka (Yid.), Peschanka (Rus.), Pishchanka (Ukr.) is 110 miles southeast of Komenetz. Ribnitza (Yid.), Rybnitsa (Rus.), Ribnitsa (Ukr.) is 128 miles southeast of Komenetz in present-day Moldova.—Trans.]

[112] Yanov (Yid.), Ivanovo (Rus.), Ivanava (Bel.) is 242 miles northeast of Komenetz. Kolenivka (Yid.), Kalinovka (Rus.), Kalynivka (Ukr.) is 103 miles northeast of Komenetz. Pikov (Yid., Rus.), Novyy Pikov (Ukr.) is 99 miles northeast of Komenetz.—Trans.

[113] Nay-Kosntin (Yid.), Novy Konstantinov (Rus.), Novokostyantyniv (Ukr.) is 274 miles northeast of Komenetz. Alt-Sinyove (Yid.), Staraya Sinyava (Rus., Ukr.) is 79 miles northeast of Komenetz. Pilava (Yid.), Pilyava (Rus.), Pylyava (Ukr.) is 75 miles northeast of Komenetz.—Trans.

[114] Mikhalpol is 28 miles south of Komenetz.—Trans.

Some pogroms were perpetrated by Bolshevik military units called the "Turkestan Division" and the "Bessarabian Division."[115] The Red Army conducted pogroms in the following places: Minkovitz and Yolteshkev (according to the testimony of Dr. Sh, a Jewish Communist), and in the area of Vapnyerko, Proskurov district (two Jews were killed), and in Mikhalpol.[116] In July through August the town of Slobkovitz found itself on the front between the Bolsheviks and the Ukrainians. It was not uncommon for troops from both armies that were on opposite ends of the town to rob and kill Jews. Some Jews from Slobkovitz lost their minds from fear.

Jews and [local] peasants attacked the Red Army in Tchan, a town in Volhynia province not far from Proskurov. After the Red Army suppressed the uprising a pogrom took place. The town was sacked and approximately 50 people were killed.[117] In Litin a Bolshevik division terrorized and devastated the Jewish population for two weeks after the May 15 pogrom. In general, most Red Army pogroms resulted in plunder. Only in a few cases were Jews killed.

Yet everything that I have been describing here is only a drop from the sea of suffering that the Jewish population experienced in the summer of 1919. There were cases in which the murderers tortured their victims with such abandon that one's hair stood on end. The fragmented news reports only give a superficial pale picture of the reality of blood-drenched Podolia. No wonder the Jewish population was totally bewildered and consumed by the fear of death.

Some Jews joined the Bolsheviks and entered the Red Army. A large number, however, left their homes with their last little rags and wandered aimlessly with the hope of finding a safe haven. Entire groups of Jews wandered through the land not knowing where they were going. Jews from small towns tried to go to larger towns such as Komenetz, Vinitza, Kiev, Odessa, and other places. They also tried to get to the Dniester River, hoping to cross over to Bessarabia (Romania).

A community of half a million Jews was destroyed within a short period of time. The surviving population was exhausted, terrorized, and remained in terrible need of aid.

---

[115] The Turkestan Division (Turkestan Red Army) was formed in March 1919. It fought insurgent forces and the White Army and was disbanded in June 1919. The Bessarabian Division (Romanian Volunteer Corps or Volunteer Corps of Transylvanians-Bukovinians) was established in February 1917 from ethnic Romanian prisoners of war held by Russia at the time of the Russian Civil War. In 1920 its units were repatriated to Romania.—Trans.

[116] Vapnyarka (Yid., Rus., Ukr.) is 99 miles from Komenetz.—Trans.

[117] Tchan (Yid.), Teofipol (Rus., Ukr.) is 80 miles north of Komenetz.—Trans.

Jews whom the pogromists had not murdered were killed by the typhoid epidemic, which took thousands of Jewish lives.[118] The pogrom victims who were robbed down to their shoelaces and even their underwear lived in filth that contributed to the spread of the epidemic. Entire communities were starving. There were cases where barefoot and tattered Jews—both young and old—went to work for the peasants in the fields in order to earn a living.

Aid Activity for the Victims

The pogroms left a horrible legacy: thousands of orphans, hundreds of widows, women who had been raped, and devastated towns and villages. Had there been a greater effort on the part of the activists among the Jewish population, the victims could have been cared for, and their terrible trauma somewhat lightened.

In January 1919, after pogroms in Barditchev and Zhitomir and much discord between parties, [the Ministry of Jewish Affairs in Kiev under Abraham Revutsky] established a relief committee named the "Central Committee to Aid Pogrom Victims."[119] Of the promised five million rubles that the Directory had targeted for the victims, the Committee received only one and a half million from the Jewish Ministry. In addition, 400,000 rubles were raised from private sources.[120] Despite this small amount, we applied ourselves to aid work. The united effort, however, did not last long.

Conflict immediately arose and the representatives from the left parties exited the Committee. The Committee found itself in a difficult situation. Dominated by members of right-wing parties, the Committee could not coexist with the Soviet regime. The fate of the Committee was sealed after the Communist Bund [Kombund] quickly addressed a memorandum to the Bolsheviks.[121] The Soviet regime issued a directive to close the Committee. And so, the only institution that at least somewhat helped the pogrom victims was closed in May 1919 while rivers of Jewish blood continued to flow.

---

[118] See Polly Zavadivker, "'Jewish Fever': Myths and Realities in the History of Russia's Typhus Epidemic, 1914–1922," *Jewish Social Studies* 26, 1 (2020): 101–12.—Trans.

[119] The Central Committee [of Kiev] to Aid Pogrom Victims was registered in Kiev on February 3, 1919.—Trans.

[120] *Di Yidishe avtonomye un der natsyonaler sekretaryat in Ukraine*, 291–92.

[121] When the Bolsheviks occupied Kiev and Komenetz in spring 1919, the Jewish noncommunist left was excluded from aid work. The Jewish section of the Communist Party of the Soviet Union (Yevsektsye) insisted that aid should be handled by party institutions. In May 1919 the Bolshevik authorities in Kiev dismantled the Central Aid Committee.—Trans.

This was a great misfortune. Every day new victims arrived and we were not allowed to provide aid. The activists from EKOPO and members of the left wing of the defunct Committee demanded that the Soviets establish a new institution that would address the suffering of Jewish victims. But new impediments arose.

The Communist Bund did not want to give aid work to the Jewish socialists, activists from EKOPO, OZE, and others. The Bolsheviks in general were against creating an autonomous Jewish organization to aid pogrom victims. They maintained that the work should be under the department called "Division to Aid the Victims of Counterrevolution" in "Sobes."[122]

During these events, I happened to be in Kiev to speak with M_ko, the administrator for the entire Ukraine of the Division to Aid the Victims of the Counterrevolution. This M_ko was a young Christian man who had absolutely no idea how to manage aid work, nor did he know anything about the Jewish population. And imagine: he was given this great responsibility. In his opinion the greatest danger to the Jews was the "nationalist" politics of the Communist Bund, which demanded an autonomous Jewish section in the Division to Aid the Victims of the Counterrevolution.

After many negotiation sessions the Soviet regime established a Soviet Red Cross with a Jewish section that only Communists could join.[123] This was easy to do in Kiev, but in Vinitza—at that time the center of Podolia—this was very hard to accomplish. And in the province this plan would simply be regarded as laughable.

I traveled to Litin and met with an inspector from Yevsektsye. He brought funds that were supposed to be distributed to victims and wanted to hand the money over to the Jewish activists in Litin. But the activists categorically refused to take the money.

Major confusion broke out because the committees in the Jewish Section [of the Yevsektsye] and the Red Cross had to do the same exact work. The Russian Red Cross's Aid Committee for Jewish Pogrom Victims was established after the original pogrom committee was dissolved at the initiative of the so-

---

[122] Sobes or SoBez was the Commissariat of Social Welfare (Narkomsobes)/Department of Welfare. It operated a Division to Aid the Victims of the Counterrevolution (Pomzhekhor), which had a section dedicated to pogrom victims.—Trans.

[123] In August 1918 the Bolshevik government nationalized the Russian Red Cross under the same name—the Russian Society of the Red Cross. A new aid committee known as the Kiev Pogrom Aid Committee (or All-Ukrainian Committee for Pogrom Victims) was established in May 1919 that worked with the reorganized Red Cross. It was headed by Elias Heifetz and staffed by people from the older prewar aid organizations.—Trans.

cialist and democratic activists. But the Jewish Communists looked with disapproval at the Red Cross and interrupted its work as much as they could.[124]

In summer 1919 I served as a fully authorized representative of the Red Cross. Everywhere in Podolia I faced great danger when we visited the towns where insurrections had occurred and could reoccur. Funds from the Russian Red Cross were very limited. We did not receive help from the Soviet institutions, and the need among the victims remained very great.

In July, Vinitza experienced pogroms. I went to Kiev and demanded more resources from the Red Cross but did not get a positive answer. I was only given underwear, which with great effort I distributed in Vinitza. All together I received 300,000 Soviet rubles for the entire region of Podolia.

Every communal institution in Vinitza, Litin, Kolenivka, and Orinin was closed except for a children's home, which exists to this day in Proskurov. The homeless were in a terrible situation. In Vinitza alone there were thousands of homeless Jews who could only be helped by massive aid activity. Typhus spread among the refugees and in the small towns that had been plundered. Groups of Jews moved into various communal buildings in Vinitza, increasing the spread of disease.

Many Jews, mainly the orphans and widows of pogrom victims, wandered in the forests asking for alms from the peasants, who would occasionally have mercy and give them something. And the sole organization that had enough money to help—the Yevsektsye—lacked the ability to establish a large relief effort. As a Red Cross representative, I requested a million-ruble loan from the Vinitza Yevsektsye without which it would be impossible to conduct relief work. The local Yevsektsye agreed, but the Kiev Yevsektsye categorically forbade a loan to the Red Cross. Consequently, Yevsektsye took millions of unutilized funds during the Bolshevik evacuation in 1919.

In June [1919] the Jewish Ministry in Komenetz established a [local] Jewish Central Committee for Pogrom Victims. The Central Committee was made up of various political and communal groups, including Ahdut, Zionists, Tseire Tsiyon, artisans, Poale Tsiyon, Fareynitke Bund, and Central Bureau of Professional Associations. It received funds from the Ukrainian regime and worked within the territory that was controlled by the Ukrainian army. Two million hryvna/kopecks were especially designated for the victims in Proskurov. At first the Jewish community refused to take money from the government, which it held responsible for Proskurov's great tragedy. But it finally agreed to take the funds and later accepted even more money.

---

[124] The aid committee administered by Yevsektsye and the reconstituted Red Cross committee were in competition.—Trans.

The Mood of the Jewish Population under the Soviet Regime (Summer 1919)

Amidst such a hell, it was no wonder that the Jewish population in the Ukraine in summer 1919 was in a terrible state of mind.

Pogroms, pogroms, and pogroms without end … and there did not seem to be any hope that the situation would get better. A small number of Jewish intellectuals were able to smuggle themselves to Russia.

We gradually became convinced that nobody would come to help us. On one side stood the Ukrainian army, which under the fog of war perpetrated pogroms. Insurgents also terrorized and perpetrated violence against the Jewish population. On the other side stood the powerless Soviets. Anarchy swept across the land. Larger cities were poorly defended, and small towns were entirely abandoned.

We were unable to organize aid for the pogrom victims. The Jewish population was imbued with a pogrom-fear. Our anxiety and exhaustion were at a peak. Feelings of hopelessness took hold not only of the everyday Jews, but also of experienced political and communal activists.

I happened at that time to attend a conference of prominent Jewish activists in Kiev. We tried to agree on the question of collecting pogrom evidence and also to consider the question of guilt.[125] Our mood during these deliberations was very gloomy. We do not even know, said one delegate, whether we will survive this year. Let us print the material about the pogroms so that at least something will be passed to the coming generations.

Nobody believed that we would survive the waves of pogroms. When I went to the region of Orinin on behalf of the Red Cross, people bid me farewell as if I were going off to war. And at the same time, the Jewish Communists began to conduct a campaign for political hegemony in the Jewish street. [As I wrote above], they succeeded in shutting down the kehillah, the Committee to Aid the Pogrom Victims, and tried to close EKOPO (KAPE). They did not allow Jewish socialists to participate in the activities of the Jewish Sections [Yevsektsye]. Protests from Jewish socialists at the meetings did not help (at this time Jewish socialists did not even have their own press). The Jewish Communists took over aid work. But they were all talk because they were unable to undertake such a huge initiative by themselves.

The situation meanwhile continued to worsen. News arrived of antisemitic sentiments among certain segments of the Red Army, and the news of

---

[125] In May 1919, representatives from the Jewish National Secretariat, the publishing house Folks-Farlag, and the Central Committee of Kiev for Relief of Pogrom Victims met to establish an Editorial Board for Gathering and Researching Materials Regarding the Pogroms in the Ukraine. The group would later change its name to the Historical Archive of Eastern Jewry.—Trans.

violence on the part of the Red Army was confirmed. Even the mood among members of the Komfarband gradually fell, especially among the activists in the province.

Disturbing news arrived about Denikin's assault on Ukraine. He had taken Kharkov and was approaching Kiev.[126] It felt like the Soviet authority in the Ukraine was falling and a dark Russian reaction was approaching that would bring new pogroms.

The Bolsheviks lost ground and started to evacuate. Many Komfarband members decided not to evacuate with the Bolsheviks and remained in Podolia. At that time, I was in Proskurov trying to organize aid for the Jewish victims as a representative of the Red Cross.

Under assault by the Ukrainians allied with the Galicians, the Bolsheviks were forced to leave Proskurov.[127] After long deliberation some friends and I decided to stay in Proskurov. The road between Proskurov and Zhmerinka was cut. It was impossible to travel by train, especially in civilian clothes, because Red Army soldiers were terrorizing Jews. Furthermore, I had instructions from the Central Committee of the Red Cross in Kiev not to leave the region when the Ukrainians entered and to guard the institutions. Several Komfarband members also remained in Proskurov.

The Jews of Proskurov experienced a terrible day and night waiting for the Ukrainians to enter. [As they retreated,] the demoralized Red Army troops plundered the town and murdered two Jews. Nevertheless, Jews did not hide. Quite the opposite: every man left his house and patrolled the streets the entire night in groups.

Galician troops entered Proskurov quietly at the end of August. The haidamaks, who also entered the town, killed a young Jewish man denounced by a prostitute. Generally, however, the situation was calm.

Meanwhile, Ukrainian counterintelligence agents from Komenetz came to Proskurov searching for young men who had fled in June with the Bolsheviks. Several colleagues and I hid for eight days because the authorities in Komenetz knew that we were in Proskurov illegally. Thanks to the successful intervention of the Jewish Ministry we were able to go to Komenetz.

A new chapter in my story began when I returned to Komenetz. It was very quiet in the town. Political parties were active. Jews were in business and money was made. The pogrom was almost forgotten. It felt as if I had arrived

---

[126] The White Army took Kiev in August 1919.

[127] Galician regiments had evacuated Galicia under the pressure of Polish troops. They had entered Podolia and allied with the Ukrainians. [With the collapse of the Hapsburg monarchy, Galician Ukrainians established the Western Ukrainian National Republic (ZUNR) in Lvov in November 1918. It comprised eastern Galicia, northern Bukovina, and Transcarpathia.—Trans.]

in another world. People asked me about the situation and mood among Jews who were on the other side of the front. I told them that Ukrainians were regarded as "Petliurans"—pogromists—and that in general the Jewish intelligentsia stayed clear of them. As for Jewish communal activists who worked with the Ukrainian regime, the relationship was more than negative.

But in Komenetz there was an entirely different mood. During my absence, a certain rapprochement between the Ukrainian and the Jewish socialist parties emerged. The Folkspartey, Poale Tsiyon, and the Fareynikte Bund took an active role in the Jewish Ministry. Many Zionists were also among its officials. I was even offered a post in the Jewish Ministry. I thought this was a strange situation and declined to participate in any fashion in the Jewish Ministry until the Fareynikte party conference would clarify our position vis-à-vis the Ministry.

The Situation of the Jews in the Komenetz Period of the UNR[128]

Jews remained depressed for a long time after the June 3 to 6 pogrom. Active antisemitism had not quieted. A horrendous terror began. Jews were kidnapped for forced labor—even those in their 70s. If a Jew walking down the street saw a haidamak with the red fringe on his hat, he would retreat fearfully.

The news from the province was also bad. Murderous gangs lurked on the roads and it was dangerous to travel even a few versts from town. The "counterintelligence" agents arrested people without cause, and innocent Jews sat in prisons in Komenetz and in the province. The Jewish community was particularly terrorized by a regiment called the "Death Squad" that captured Jews in the street and beat them mercilessly.

The Jewish kehillah was very active during this difficult period. The representative of the kehillah, L. Kleiderman (Ahdut), energetically defended the Jews before the authorities. With the help of the Jewish Ministry the kehillah saved many Jews from death. But normal communal work in such circumstances was hardly possible. The splendid site of the Workers' Club where the Kultur Lige was located was totally plundered and ruined. This was the situation until the civil administration replaced the ataman (in whom lay the actual authority) and his troops.

---

[128] The UNR established itself in Komenetz after the Red Army retreated from the city. It was in authority intermittently from May/June–November 1919.

There was a significant disparity between reality and the democratic declarations and promises of the new [Directory] socialist regime.[129] As a result,
the situation did not change. The socialist supporters that rallied around the
new cabinet made great efforts to gain the sympathies of the Jewish masses
and negotiated with the Jewish socialists for their support.[130] To this end, the
leaders of the Ukrainian Social Democratic Party, Chekhivsky, Mazepa, Bezpalko, and Fedenko, were especially active.[131]

In order to quiet the Jewish population and above all gain the sympathy
of the Jewish workers, a meeting was called by the Ministry of Labor, headed
at that time by Bezpalko, at which Ukrainian socialists, Jewish socialists, and
Tseire Tsiyon appeared.

The Ukrainian Social Democrats petitioned the Jews to work actively as
a united front against the dark forces. The Jewish activists at the meeting related the terrible terror that threatened the Jews.

The idea was raised to send a delegation to Petliura, the chairman of the
Directory, consisting of the rabbi of Komenetz [Israel Gutman], a representative of Ahdut, the Zionists, the artisans (Folkspartey), Poale Tsiyon, and Fareynikte Bund.[132]

The delegation emphasized that the Jewish population did not op-
pose Ukrainian independence but was against pogroms perpetrated by the
Ukrainian military. These pogroms pushed the Jewish population towards the
Bolsheviks. They demanded that the bloody pogroms and the terror stop.[133]

After these events the atmosphere was somewhat better. Jews began to
travel on the roads and on trains. Life became more or less normal. A notice-

---

[129] In April 1919, Borys Martos (1889–1977) headed a new socialist cabinet in Rovne. In
August, it was replaced by a cabinet led by Isaak Mazepa.—Trans.

[130] In April 1919, a new socialist cabinet was established in Rovne.

[131] Yosyp Bezpalko (1881–1950) was a member of ZUNR. In 1919–20 he served as UNR's
minister of labor in Mazepa's cabinet. In 1918 he briefly was mayor of Chernevtsy
(Tshernevits, Yid.), a town in Bukovina on the border between Romania and Ukraine,
41 miles southeast of Komenetz. Panas (Opanas) Vasylyovych Fedenko (1893–1981)
was active in drafting the policy that approved the reunification of the UNR and the
ZUNR in January 1919. He served as a political commissar of the Ukrainian army in
Mazepa's government. Fedenko relocated to Poland as the Red Army advanced into
Ukraine. He was a member of the UNR's government in exile.

[132] The principal activists from the Fareynikte Bund distanced themselves from the
Bolsheviks and were not in Komenetz for the meeting. B_D, however, appeared in
the name of the Fareynikte Bund. After the party conference in August 1919, he was
a Folkspartey member. Later he became a member of the Ukrainian delegation in
Warsaw.

[133] This meeting took place on July 17, 1919.—Trans.

able increasing closeness between the Jewish and Ukrainian socialist circles occurred after the Galician army, which was aligned with the Ukrainians, occupied a large area of Ukraine without committing an inordinate amount of violence (Proskurov, Vinitza, Barditchev).

But then Denikin took Kiev and proceeded to march further into Ukraine. His military perpetrated new slaughters in Kiev and Chvostov.[134] In the face of these new developments the war between Bolsheviks and the Ukrainians stopped.[135]

Jewish political groups on the side of the front whose towns were occupied by the Ukrainians began to be active. The Fareynikte Bund held a conference in Komenetz at the end of August. At this conference the Fareynikte and the Bund from Komenetz, Proskurov, Mohilev-Podolsk, Litin, Haysin, Horodok, Yarmolintz, and other places were represented. Resolutions were drafted concerning the general political situation and the Jewish question. In the resolutions the Jewish socialists declared that they were ready to join the Ukrainian socialists only if the latter would clearly distance themselves from the petite bourgeois reactionary elements that brought so much misfortune on the Jewish population. The Fareynikte Bund also denounced the dictatorship of the Bolsheviks and its myopic politics in Ukraine that had brought complete ruin to the land and prepared the fertile soil for the coming reaction. It took a stand against the Entente for its support of reactionary forces [the White Army] in the territory of former Russia. The Fareynikte Bund also demanded a stop to political terror. The pogroms had to stop and the guilty parties, without exception, must be punished. The ruined Jewish cities and towns had to be rebuilt. At the conference the delegates demanded that the Jewish Ministry listen to the voices of Jewish democracy. The resolution to unify Fareynikte and the Bund was also accepted. A central bureau was established at the conference, in which Proskurov, Vinitza, Mohilev, and adjacent regions were represented.

After the conference a celebratory meeting was held in the city theater. Bezpalko, the Social Democrat from Galicia, extended greetings in the name of the "Ukrainian Socialist government" and recognized the demands of the Fareynikte Bund.

The Jewish minister Krasny announced that his ministry would accede to the voices of Jewish democracy. Representatives from the Central Commit-

---

[134] Denikin's offensive lasted from August/September 1919 to December 1919. The Volunteer Army occupied Kiev and most of Ukraine. In December 1919, the Red Army mounted a counteroffensive and overran most of Ukraine, reestablishing a communist government that remained in power until May 1920. Chvostov (Yid.), Fastov (Rus.), Fastiv (Ukr.) is located 177 miles northeast of Komenetz in Kiev gubernia.—Trans.

[135] See *Vil'na Ukraïna* (Lviv, 1 August 1919), 120.

tee to Aid Pogrom Victims, the Komenetz committee of the Ukrainian Social Democrats, the Central Committee of the Ukrainian Socialist Revolutionary Party, Poale Tsiyon, the Inspector General (a special body to monitor order in the army), the Folkspartey, the Kultur Lige, and the artisans were also present at the conference.

Shortly after these events, a Poale Tsiyon conference was held. Vinitza, Proskurov, Komenetz, Podolsk, Letichev, and other towns were represented at the conference. A regional (Podolia-wide) conference of Zionists and Tseire Tsiyon also took place. They were positive towards the Ukrainian national movement, though one felt their sharp opposition to the Jewish Ministry [with its socialist majority]. They invited the leaders and representatives of Ukrainian parties to this celebratory session, but only the Socialist Federation (Ukrainian Kadets) attended.

After the Fareynikte Bund and Poale Tsiyon conferences, Ukrainian socialist parties made several attempts to connect government leaders [in the Directory] with Jewish democratic circles. The Jewish democratic and socialist parties, however, did not have a general plan for how to cooperate. Each party worked in its own area of responsibilities. Thus, Poale Tsiyon took for itself the post of assistant minister of labor (Goldelman) and the Folkspartey took the assistant minister of commerce (Solodar).

In autumn 1919, Tseire Tsiyon, Folkspartey, Poale Tsiyon, and Fareynikte Bund participated in several governmental meetings in Komenetz. At these meetings the various parties announced their official position towards the UNR. Tseire Tsiyon and Folkspartey came out positive for Ukrainian sovereignty. The representative from Fareynikte Bund (and in the name of Poale Tsiyon) stated that while they respected the Ukrainian people's movement in general, after what had happened in Ukraine, after the bloody pogroms, no stronger enthusiasm could reasonably be asked of them than what had already been shown. They had done more than was realistically possible.

Until the Ukrainians evacuated, the months of August through November, when the Galicians were in Ukraine, were more or less a quiet time for the Jewish population. Trade picked up; Jews traveled freely on the roads and trains; the artisans had work. Two hundred Jewish youth—men and women—worked in the Jewish Ministry's Central Committee to Aid Pogrom Victims and in other ministries.

Jewish communal life revived at a faster pace. The waves of pogrom terror stopped almost completely. Komenetz-Podolsk became the center for the entire district. Various Jewish delegations arrived with requests and demands from various corners of Ukraine on the right side of the Dnieper. Komenetz had business connections with many large towns from that part of Ukraine: Barditchev, Uman (Kiev district), Olt-Kostin, Sepetovka, Tchan, Polona (Volhynia district), Proskurov, Zhmerinka, Vinitza, Mohilev-Podolsk, Litin, Haysin, Bratslav, Mezbizh, Letichev (Podolia district), and so forth.[136]

But despite the superficial quiet and relative order, Ukrainian and Galician counterintelligence agents did not stop their repressive activities. The Ukrainian counterintelligence police even arrested Goldelman (assistant minister) in Zhemerinka. In Komenetz, the chairman of the main bureau of the Fareynikte Bund was arrested twice. In general, the counterintelligence police attacked the Jewish socialists mercilessly. And in the province the situation was worse. At least in Komenetz the Jewish socialists were under the protection of the Jewish Ministry and were more or less secure.

The Jewish Ministry in August–November 1919 (Komenetz Period)

The Jewish Ministry in this period was not anything like the organization envisioned by the builders and creators of national personal autonomy in Ukraine. It was ultimately transformed into a kind of Jewish Red Cross. The activists in the Ministry were almost entirely engaged as "intercessors" [shtadlanut] to the powers that be in order to save Jews from pogroms, decrees, and sorrow.[137]

The Jewish Ministry did a lot to defend the Jewish population against pogroms. At its initiative Ukrainian authorities promulgated a series of edicts against the pogroms. It also played a large part in creating the so-called office of the "state inspector." Established in summer 1919, the state inspectorship had representatives in every military unit. The role of the inspector was to ensure that military units act lawfully and not tolerate criminal activities. When the Jewish Ministry received news about excesses against the Jews, it vigorously responded by calling upon the appropriate authorities to actively manage the situation. Knowing that there was an agency that defended the interests of the Jews, the pogrom elements did not behave as brazenly. The Jewish Ministry also began to demand that the guilty participants in the pogrom be punished. Admittedly, it was very unsuccessful with this goal.

---

[136] Uman (Yid., Rus., Ukr.) is 253 miles east of Komenetz. Olt-Kostin (Yid.), Starokonstantinov (Rus.), Starokostyantyniv (Ukr.) is 90 miles northeast of Komenetz in Volhynia gubernia. Sepetovka (Yid., Rus.), Shepetivka (Ukr.) is 107 miles north of Komenetz in Volhynia gubernia. Polona (Yid.), Polonnoye (Rus.), Polonne (Ukr.) is 107 miles northeast of Komenetz in Volhynia gubernia. Mohilev-Podolsk (Yid.), Mogilev-Podolskiy (Rus.), Mohyliv-Podilskyy (Ukr.) is 57 miles east of Komenetz. Mezbizh (Yid.), Medzhibozh (Rus.), Medzhybizh (Ukr.) is 82 miles northeast of Komenetz.—Trans.

[137] *Shtadlanut* (intercession) was the premodern relationship between the Jewish community and gentile powers. The *shtadlan* was a person of standing in the Jewish community who had access to the non-Jewish authorities.—Trans.

The pogrom atmosphere cooled bit by bit. With the help of the Galician army the Ukrainians occupied a number of Jewish cities in the summer of 1919 (Proskurov, Vinitza, Barditchev, and others) that by and large did not experience pogroms. Even when the Ukrainian troops withdrew under the pressure of Denikin's army in November 1919, there were few incidents of violence.

Besides the pogroms, however, there was another issue to be addressed, namely, the illegal acts against Jews perpetrated by the civil administration in Komenetz. Every day there were complaints about extortions, requisitions, and illegal demands (especially from the representatives in small towns). At the initiative of the Jewish Ministry, the military and civil authorities issued a series of orders to ameliorate these problems. Further, many Jewish towns (for example, Lantzekronia, Grayding, Nei-Ushitz, and others) demanded that the Jewish Ministry intervene with the government to obtain from the civilian administration the promised support and rights for the victims in the Jewish population.[138]

The Jewish Ministry was also besieged with requests from individual persons, especially from the Jewish socialists, who were terrorized by the Ukrainian counterintelligence police. Some Zionist representatives from a small town told the following story: When the Bolsheviks took their town, they demanded that a revkom be established. Usually, if they demand, we must obey. And since there had to be representatives of the working class in the revkom, the Jews approached a worker and asked him to save the town and become a member. The worker joined and did a lot of good for the town. But when Ukrainians came to power they arrested the worker for being a Bolshevik and now he is in great danger. The Jews called upon the Ministry in the name of the entire town not to abandon this worker for fear that something bad will happen to him. In such cases the Jewish Ministry made every effort to save innocent people accused of these sorts of "crimes." It generally energetically defended Jews who were involved in the Bolshevik movement. It demanded that where there was no concrete evidence of criminal activities, Jews accused of Bolshevism should be treated like Ukrainians and not be put on trial so long as they did not take part in direct activities against the local population.

The Jewish Ministry focused great attention on defending Jews from various criminal elements. Because it was overwhelmed, however, the Ministry accomplished very little in the area of national education and national self-government. The political situation was dire, and it was impossible for the

---

[138] Lantzekronia (Yid.), Lyantskorun (Rus.), Zarechanka (Ukr.) is 18 miles northwest of Komenetz. Grayding (Yid.), Gorodok (Rus.), Horodok (Ukr.) is 153 miles northwest of Komenetz.—Trans.

Ministry to develop a broad policy in these areas. Besides, advocates for [national] culture did not exist in a provincial town such as Komenetz. We could no longer use the more abundant resources of the Jewish Ministry that had been available in the Kiev period [1918]. We were forced to start everything anew. The Department of National Education supported the existing Jewish schools as much as it could, helped to rebuild ruined schools (e.g., in Grayding, Yarmolintz, and Polona), drew up projects for a larger school network for national education, and initiated professional education.

Thanks to the aid of the Jewish Ministry, the Komenetz Kultur Lige established Froebel courses [early childhood education] and teachers' courses.[139] It also supported several other institutions (kindergartens and orphanages). On the language question, the department was tolerant towards the Hebrew schools, though it demanded that Yiddish be the language of instruction.

The Jewish Ministry implemented elections (in Lantzekronia, Smotritch, Grayding, and Nay-Kosntin and re-established the old kehillot which had not functioned during the period the Bolsheviks were in Podolia.[140] The financial situation of the kehillot had been very grave for some time. Even the largest kehillot in Podolia (i.e., Komenetz-Podolsk, Proskurov, and Mohilev-Podolsk) were not capable of collecting the mandatory contributions as required by the law of April 17, 1919.[141] The Jewish upper class had strenuously hindered the undertaking. In Komenetz, 28 wealthy Jews submitted a writ against the kehillah (the Vaad HaPoel was composed of Ahdut and Zionists) claiming that the contributions were illegal.[142] The Komenetz circuit court ruled that the contribution tax was indeed illegal. During this period the socialists did not participate much in the kehillah. In fact, very often they were against the kehillah (e.g., in Smotritch), as were the workers, artisans, and the petty bourgeois (Ahdut). Many kehillot turned to the Jewish Ministry for support, but without funds, it could not satisfy them.[143]

Regarding the language question, the Jewish Ministry's Department of National Self-Administration demanded that the kehillot's administrative

---

[139] Friedrich Wilhelm August Fröbel or Froebel (1782–1852) was a German educator who created the concept of "kindergarten" and coined the word. In 1917 the Froebel Pedagogic Institute in Kiev established a Children's House. Between 1917–19, nurseries funded by local governments opened throughout Ukraine.—Trans.

[140] Smotritch (Yid.), Smotrich (Rus.), Smotrych (Ukr.) is 18 miles north of Komenetz.—Trans.

[141] Directory law that established taxation of Jewish communities.—Trans.

[142] The Vaad HaPoel was the governing institution of the Zionist groups.—Trans.

[143] Proskurov, Komenetz-Podolsk, Mohilev-Podolsk, Vinitza, Olt-Kostin, Barditchev, and many more towns.

business be conducted in Yiddish and sent a special circular to this effect.[144] A statutory solution was also worked out: Yiddish was recognized as the language of instruction in schools and would be the official language in the Department of National Self-Administration. Jews had the right to utilize their language. For violators of the law (i.e., prohibiting people from speaking in Yiddish) there would be a penalty (prison).

[As mentioned,] in summer 1919 the Jewish Ministry had established a central aid committee in which all Jewish parties were represented (Ahdut, Zionists, Tseire Tsiyon, Folkspartey, Poalei Zion, Fareynikte Bund). But aid work stalled because the committee was unable to administer such a difficult task. Consequently, the committee transformed into a private organization with its own board.

The Jewish Ministry also had a council whose task was to unify the activity of its various departments, and to consider policy and other important questions. The following people were involved in council meetings: the Jewish minister Krasny (Folkspartey), the director of the Department of General Matters (Folkspartey), the director of the Department of National Education (Mr. T., a town councilman from Poale Tsiyon), and I, as deputy to the director of the Department for National Self-Administration (Fareynikte Bund), and also as a member of the city council. In the council there were two right-wing votes (Folkspartey), two left-wing (Fareynikte Bund), and a Poale Tsiyonist whose vote determined the majority. Poale Tsiyon usually voted with Fareynikte Bund, but when negotiating a compromise with the right-wing Jewish parties, it would vote with the Folkspartey.

In general, the Ministry was popular with the Jewish population. During difficult moments Jews turned to it for help. The various political groups, however, had a different attitude towards the Ministry.

Poale Tsiyon and Folkspartey actively supported the Ministry. Fareynikte and the Bund first vacillated over the question of their relationship with the Ministry, and after the August 1919 conference held in Komenetz-Podolsk, their position was more or less determined. They were in a unique situation. They exited the kehillah and distanced themselves from the right-wing Jewish groups but did not support the [Ukrainian] Bolsheviks after the Soviet regime retreated from Ukraine. As a result, they were completely isolated and severely terrorized by the counterintelligence agents. The Jewish Ministry, however, which from the beginning of its existence was tied to the Jewish socialists, brought them into its fold and defended them. Various workers' organizations also turned to the Jewish Ministry for support.[145] The Jewish

---

[144] See Appendix 4.

[145] See Appendix 5.

Ministry was the only place where the Jewish socialists could, as it were, find respite. Several left-wingers even worked in the Jewish Ministry.

Despite the fact that the Jewish Ministry employed many Zionists and several members from Ahdut, the Zionists and the Tseire Tsiyon led a campaign against it, bringing their old claim from the Kiev days that the left had grabbed the Ministry. Pressured by the Komenetz kehillah, where the Jewish socialists did not play a part, a delegation was sent to Ukrainian authorities with the goal to undermine the Ministry. The delegates claimed that a large majority of the Jewish population was against the Ministry because it was not an elected body. Thus, no laws regarding the Jewish population could be issued by the Ministry. The delegates also stressed that Zionists represented the majority of the Jewish population. But in fact, the Ministry employed many Zionists and several members of Ahdut.

The Second Death Throes of the UNR

During the great assault against the Bolsheviks in August 1919, Denikin's army encountered the Ukrainians in Kiev.[146] Denikin did not want to negotiate with the Ukrainians and war started between the two armies. At the same time, and virtually without any resistance, the Bolsheviks lost the right bank of the Dnieper (Podolia, Volhynia, and a part of Kiev province), and Denikin began to attack the Ukrainian troops. The battles between the Ukrainians and the Bolsheviks halted of their own accord. The struggle now was between Denikin's troops and the Bolsheviks, and between Denikin and the Ukrainians.

The Ukrainian army was in a critical situation. It had neither ammunition nor supplies. In addition, typhus felled thousands of troops from the Ukrainian Galician army. The Ukrainian army yielded to Denikin's significantly smaller forces.

In November, rumors spread in Komenetz-Podolsk that the Galician army with its headquarters in Vinitza had made a treaty with Denikin. As usual, the rumors were officially denied, but very soon we learned that they were true. The Galician betrayal was catastrophic for the Ukrainian People's Army and brought an end to the existing UNR.[147]

---

[146] Denikin's and Petliura's forces arrived in Kiev at the same time. After a few days Petliura retreated in the face of Denikin's superior forces.—Trans.

[147] In July 1919 the Ukrainian Galician army had settled in Komenetz and Vinitza. Ravaged by typhus and lacking supplies, it signed an alliance with Denikin in November. The UNR nationalists considered this pact treacherous. Eastern Galicia, however, had already been conquered by Poland, and in 1920 the ZUNR left Galicia to establish a government-in-exile in Vienna. It collapsed in 1923 when the Entente recognized Galicia as part of Poland. Until the UNR forged an alliance with Poland,

In the city the mood was very dismal. We had grown more or less accustomed to the Ukrainians and suddenly there was a new caesar [in Podolia] with new decrees. The Jewish population was frightened of the change and of the new ruler, Denikin—known for his pogroms in Kiev, Chustov, and other places.

The Ukrainian socialists looked for a way to save the situation. But it was too late. They had missed the moment. Instead of acting to conclude a treaty with the Bolsheviks who were then under pressure from Denikin and would have been open to certain concessions, the Ukrainian nationalists were entangled in the intrigues of the reactionary Ukrainian Directory and the Galician dictator Petrushevych.[148]

When they appeared at socialist party meetings, the Galician Social Democrats were concerned above all with sloganeering and trying to organize demonstrations against Petrushevych. They did not offer any helpful proposals. Unable to organize, they convened a large meeting. The most distinguished Ukrainian socialists and even Ukrainian Communists attended. A representative from Fareynikte Bund also participated. At the meeting, the Ukrainians complained about their bitter fate and bid farewell to [the so-called] "sovereign Ukraine" [ZUNR].

Meanwhile it became known that the Ukrainian regime was leaving Komenetz and that the city would be occupied peacefully by the Poles.[149] The Jewish population was relieved. It had been worried that the Ukrainians would instigate violence during the transition and was also concerned about what would happen if Denikin's troops entered the city. The transition from Ukrainian to Polish rule occurred quietly.

The Jewish socialists, however, were unsure about what to do. At first many decided to evacuate [from Komenetz] with the Jewish Ministry but then changed their minds. I decided to make my way to the part of Volhynia that was occupied by the Polish military and from there I figured that I would be

---

Petliura's forces were limited to guerilla warfare against both the Red Army and the Volunteer Army.—Trans.

[148] Petrushevych, who was called "dictator," had authority over the Galician army. [Yevhen Petrushevych (1863–1940) was president of ZUNR from October 1918 to November 1919. As Gumener notes, the relationship between Petliura and Petrushevych was poor. Petliura regarded the Bolsheviks as the great threat; by contrast, Petrushevych considered Poland a greater threat. Gumener implies that Western and Eastern Ukrainians should have joined forces against Poland and not against the Bolsheviks.—Trans.]

[149] After the ZUNR troops retreated, the Polish army moved into Podolia and Volhynia, making Komenetz their headquarters in November.—Trans.

able to return home to Vilna, where I had not been in four years. Since the Ukrainian troops were evacuating in that direction, I decided to go with them.

For three days the Ukrainians traveled in a special train from Komenetz to Proskurov (93 versts). One could see that the officials were greatly demoralized; the journey went very badly. The train stopped in Hrechana [?], 7 versts from Proskurov. The officials consulted among themselves. I became frustrated with the trip and decided not to go any further with the Ukrainians and to stay in Proskurov.

I went to Proskurov and visited the community. The town was relatively quiet. The Ukrainian commander only demanded clothing from the Jews. The town was uneasy because of the uncertainty about who would take Proskurov after the Ukrainians left. I remained with the Ukrainians for four days during this uncertain time. Everything was disorganized. Everyone had to look out for themselves even to get food.

On shabbes morning the train began to move. At first I thought that we were travelling again, but I was mistaken. The peasants did not allow the officials from the UNR to go through Olt-Kosntin (Volhynia) and we had to choose another direction. At the same time the unsettling news came that Denikin was not far from Proskurov.

The train arrived at the Proskurov station from Hrechana [?]. People were saying that we should go to the border towards Volotchisk. There was not much time left. We ran around, appealed, and transferred funds from other trains to the ministerial train. A sick worker from the Jewish Ministry crept off the train and entered the town. I personally considered going into town but worried lest I fall from one trouble to a greater one.

Meanwhile, the train started to move. Suddenly—boom, boom, boom! At first I thought that our train was under fire. But finally, it was clear that one of Denikin's supporters had set on us a "wild machine" (a locomotive without an engineer) that had crashed into the car in which I was travelling. Luckily, the car was very strong and sustained the crash. This saved me.

We boarded another car and continued on. We came to a station not far from Volotchisk. The station was in a neutral zone and did not belong either to the Poles or to the Ukrainians. Denikin was still far away. A deadly silence lay over the station. No officials were in sight.

I had decided to go to Volotchisk, but since the situation was precarious and one could not know what the next hour would bring, I continued according to my original plan. We left the train and went with horse and wagon across Jewish towns and villages.

We came across Ukrainian soldiers. I looked at their wild faces. They were dressed in torn clothes, were barefooted and hungry, and looked dejected. I

found the provincial Jews wonderful. The peasants, however, were antagonistic towards the [Ukrainian] officials.

We arrived finally at Olt-Kosntin. The remnants of the UNR gathered in
a large, friendly, and warm Jewish home. There were representatives from
the socialist ministry cabinet, the Central Committee of the Ukrainian Social
Democrats, and the Social Revolutionaries. The hosts were very hospitable
towards the Ukrainians.

I spent the day in Olt-Kosntin and then we continued forward. It was
dark when we arrived in the next village—dark and cold. The peasants did
not want the Ukrainian officials in their homes. In virtually every town a sick
person lay with typhoid fever. We spent the night and could not wait for it to
become light to continue onward.

We arrived at a tavern not far from Lieber Tov (Volhynia district) and
discovered that there were insurgents in the town who were aligned with
the Bolsheviks and were robbing the retreating Ukrainians.[150] Some of the
ministers thought of hiding in the village. My patience had come to an end.
I considered returning to Olt-Kosntin. Finally, I decided that if I managed to
arrive in Lieber Tov, I would no longer travel with the Jewish Ministry.

We received calming news, however, and traveled on. We arrived in
Lieber Tov on Friday night. The workers from the Jewish Ministry proceeded
to the relief agent of the Lyubar kehillah. As employees of the Jewish Ministry, the activists in Lieber Tov who knew us from Komenetz behaved warmly
towards us.

Lieber Tov is a large Jewish town in Volhynia. It gives the impression of a
place of culture. It is powered with electrical lights. There was also a significant Jewish social life, including a Jewish gymnasium.

I told the local activists how I and my colleagues, who were desperately
trying to get to their homes in Barditchev, arrived here. We made it known
that we no longer wanted to travel with the Jewish Ministry. The local activists assured us that we could remain in Lieber Tov no matter which authority
arrived.

Meanwhile Lieber Tov found itself under the control of insurgents aligned
with the Bolsheviks. What would happen was hard to say. On one side (around
Chudnov) the Bolsheviks were fighting against Denikin and not bothering the
Ukrainians. On the other side (Olt-Kosntin) Denikin was attacking, and on the
third side (in Polona) were the Poles.[151]

---

[150] Lieber Tov (Yid.), Lyubar (Rus., Ukr.) is 99 miles northwest of Komenetz in the
gubernia of Volhynia.—Trans.

[151] Chudnov (Yid., Rus.), Chudniv (Ukr.) is 117 miles northeast of Komenetz in the
gubernia of Volhynia.—Trans.

The Ukrainian army and the Ministry fell apart. Sympathy for the Bolsheviks was evident, and different elements began to go over to the Soviet regime. Ministry officials hired buggies and went to the Bolsheviks and were well received. A military division under the leadership of Ataman Volach attacked the government treasury and took it to the Bolsheviks.[152] The Ministry was afraid and fled to a small town, Nay-Tshertriye.[153]

Several colleagues and I parted company from the Jewish Ministry and remained in Lieber Tov. There was unrest in the town; there was no longer an official governmental authority. Denikin's troops were coming closer. The Bolsheviks remained in their positions. The remaining remnants of the Ukrainian army continued on their way; some gave themselves up to the Poles.

I rented a wagon, which they [?] tried to take from me forcefully. Seated with me were a young Ukrainian noncommissioned officer and two Jewish women. We traveled 30 versts from Lieber Tov to Polona, where the Poles were. In Polona I met friends who provided proper papers that allowed me to go to Vilne. After other difficulties that are quite natural in such a situation, I arrived in Vilne.[154]

Old Vilne, Yerusholayim d'lite [Jerusalem of Lithuania], made a strong impression on me.[155] I had not been there since 1915, and in my mind hovered the scenes of the city that I knew in the years 1911–13. I sought the Jewish communal organizations. Desolation ruled. The Vilne kehillah did not make a better impression than kehillot in Ukraine. An exception was the celebration of the school week in Vilne, organized by the school organization. This was a splendid celebration of everything that the Jewish teachers' union had created by their own efforts.

---

[152] Omelian Volokh (1886–1937) was a commander of several UNR military units from 1917 to 1919. Facing a desperate situation at the front, he tried twice to defect with his troop to the Bolsheviks. In December 1919 he rebelled against the Directory, seizing the state treasury, but was allowed to join the Red Army only in February 1920. After the Civil War he pursued a career in the Ukrainian Soviet Socialist Republic but was arrested in 1933 and charged with counterrevolutionary activities. He was sentenced to ten years in the Gulag but was shot in 1937.—Trans.

[153] Nay-Tshertriye (Yid.), Novaya Chartoriya (Rus.), Nova Chortoriya (Ukr.) is 131 miles northeast of Komenetz in the gubernia of Volhynia.—Trans.

[154] The German army occupied Vilne from 1915 to 1918. Bolshevik Lithuanian and Belorussian troops occupied the city in January 1919. Lithuanian nationalists demanded sovereignty, but Polish nationalists with expansionist goals wanted to annex Lithuania. In April 1919, the Polish army moved into Vilne. Alleging that the Jews were pro-Lithuanian and pro-Bolshevik, troops perpetrated pogroms. Vilne was in Polish hands when Gumener visited.—Trans.

[155] Vilne (Vilnius in Lithuanian) was called the "Jerusalem of Lithuania" in honor of the important role it played in Jewish learning and culture.—Trans.

I did not remain long in Vilne and went to Warsaw. After the quiet half-dead Vilne, Warsaw impressed me as a vibrant city. It was festive in the Jewish streets. They were bustling with Jewish newspapers, political parties, and organizations. At the same time, one felt the underlying brokenness and weakness of the Jewish community.

I had to return to the Ukraine. I could not acclimate myself to Poland and Lithuania. I was pulled back to Ukraine. I arrived in Komenetz-Podolsk and found old friends—only in a very different situation.

Under the Polish Occupation (End of 1919–July 1920)[156]

Komenetz had suddenly become still. This [calm] was especially evident after getting used to the notion that Komenetz would become a [Polish] residence. Except for Tseire Tsiyon, Jewish communal organizations were inactive. Komenetz's isolation made a strong impression. On one side the Bolsheviks remained near Proskurov and Nei-Ushitz, and on the other side stood the Romanian border. The Galician border was not in better shape. Only smugglers received passes with ease. But activists [aid workers] suffered a lot before they got passes.

The wounds of the pogrom victims were still fresh. The consequences of recent events were terrible. The Jewish population required quick and meaningful support. At the beginning we waited. Perhaps help would come from somewhere. We were sure that Polish-Jewish activists, who were able to travel to a portion of the territory of Ukraine [held by Polish troops], where so many Jews suffered, would certainly appear soon. But the hope was for naught. An important lease on life was brought by an American delegate, B_R [James Becker]. He played a role in restoring the Committee to Aid the Pogrom Victims.[157] Some political work began, but only for a short time.

Ukrainian and Jewish socialists gathered in Komenetz to discuss the situation. Sympathy everywhere was towards the left factions that wished to rebuild the basic principles of the UNR. The question of liquidating the Directory was seriously raised. This demand was emphatically supported by the Jewish socialists.

---

[156] The Polish Seventh Division occupied Komenetz from November 1919 to July 1920. Petliura retreated to Volhynia and then went to Warsaw, hoping for an alliance with Poland that would halt the advance of the White Army and the Bolsheviks.—Trans.

[157] See the following section, "The Komenetz Jewish-American Aid Committee for the Pogrom Victims."—Trans.

These meetings, however, were interrupted in an original manner when the Polish authorities began to arrest the representatives.[158] At the beginning, the Ukrainian socialist ministers were arrested. They were immediately released, but then the Jewish socialists were arrested. Some managed to flee; the rest served time in prison. But calm was restored again, and life flowed monotonously for several months.

The news of the decision at San Remo created a great commotion in the Jewish community.[159] The Zionists decided to mark the event with a big celebration. The event was very impressive. The heart that was so anguished and that fought for survival looked for a way to express itself. The Polish administration did not hinder the celebration. A few days prior to the event all Jewish homes were decorated. The bourgeois parties and Poale Tsiyon participated in the holiday. Even the Folkspartey joined in.[160]

A grand march was organized. There were young men on horses, and many rode on bicycles. Thousands of Jews from Komenetz and adjacent towns took part, among them rabbis, artisans, small shopkeepers, merchants, women's organizations, gymnasiums, university students, children from Folkspartey schools, and representatives from various parties. Two gatherings were organized: in the street and in the town theater. Greetings were extended by representatives from the UNR, the Polish authority, and from foreign missions. The Jewish minister, who had just been released from Bolshevik imprisonment, also arrived.[161]

In general, this was a quiet period for the Jewish population in the Polish-occupied sections of Podolia and also in more far-flung districts. But in the spring of 1920 Denikin's army was forced to retreat from Ukraine by way of Podolia, and with that began new pogroms. Podolia was not really under the control of any specific power. The remnants of Ukrainian troops were in the area of Yampol. The Bolsheviks remained passive and only partially drew closer to the Polish front line. The demoralized Volunteer Army, which the Bolsheviks had driven out of Odessa and Kiev, retreated further and further into Podolia. As it went through the towns of Podolia on the way to Galicia,

---

[158] The Poles ordered the house arrest of UNR ministers who were still in Komenetz: Bezpalko, Livytskyi, Ohienko, and Prime Minister Mazepa.

[159] At the San Remo Conference (April 19–26, 1920) the Entente reiterated the promise contained in the 1917 Balfour Declaration. The British Mandate in Palestine had already been created in February 1920.—Trans.

[160] This was significant because the Folkspartey ideology advocated nonterritorial autonomy.—Trans.

[161] The Bolsheviks had arrested Krasny. They released him and allowed him to reside in Barditchev. After the Poles occupied Barditchev, he relocated to Komenetz-Podolia.

it terrorized and robbed the Jewish population. A small village called Zamichov (seven versts from Nei-Ushitz) suffered greatly.[162] There were many
victims, and many houses were burnt down. The Mohilev-Podolsk region also
suffered much.

Denikin's troops employed the following ruse. They would pose as Bolsheviks before taking a town. [Thinking that they were Red Army troops], the
Jews were not afraid and did not go into hiding. The troops would then exploit
this ruse to rob and beat the Jews. Such stories occurred in Kalis (situated near
the Dniester), which found itself between the Ukrainian-Polish and Bolshevik
front. A former White Army regiment arrived in Kalis and surrendered to the
Ukrainians who were under the command of Frolov [?]. The troops posed as
Bolsheviks, and the local Jewish population were not particularly afraid. By
chance a worker, a Jewish Bolshevik named SR from Komenetz, initiated a
conversation [with some soldiers whom he thought were Bolsheviks]. They
immediately took him from the town and shot him. The army then plundered
the town. When Denikin's army entered an area that was occupied by the
Poles, they disarmed and interned the Polish soldiers in POW camps.

The Komenetz Jewish-American Aid Committee for Pogrom Victims

Komenetz and the area around it were cut off from the rest of the world. In
November 1919, on the eve of the Ukrainian evacuation, a representative from
the aid committee in Kishinev (S_N, a Zionist), visited Komenetz-Podolsk. At
this point, the Central Committee for Aid to Pogrom Victims had removed itself from the Jewish Ministry, and in June the left and the right party factions
established an independent aid committee in Komenetz.

Feeling that they could get outside support from Kishinev, the Zionists,
particularly the Tseire Tsiyon, demanded that the aid committee be administered by the Komenetz kehillah. And they insisted that it be comprised of
members in the same proportion as the National Assembly in Kiev (Ahdut 14
representatives, Zionists 24, Tseire Tsiyon 14, Folkspartey 4, Poale Tsiyon 11,
Fareynikte 12, Bund 23). S_N created an aid committee with a secure majority
in the Komenetz kehillah.

The socialists, however, ultimately decided not to join a kehillah-run committee and established the independent committee. Thus, two [aid] committees were established in Komenetz-Podolsk: one independent, with a demo-

---

[162] Zamichov (Yid.), Zamekhov (Rus.), Zamikhiv (Ukr.) is 39 miles northeast of
Komenetz.—Trans.

cratic majority, and the other run by the kehillah with a Zionist majority.[163] The former was organized and experienced in aid work (and had accumulated resources); the latter had support from abroad, and the opportunity of receiving sufficient funding.

In January 1920, B_R [James Becker] arrived in Komenetz from Bucharest—the first American representative. He brought a large sum of money (around a million Rumanian leu and several hundred thousand tsarist rubles) and announced that he would distribute funds only after both committees (the democratic and the one from the kehillah) united.

The concern that the wealthy "uncle" might leave without distributing the needed money was effective. A compromise committee was established in the following manner.

Nine representatives in the committee came from the left (three each from Folkspartey, Poale Tsiyon, and Fareynikte Bund), nine representatives came from the right (three each from Ahdut, the Zionists, and Tseire Tsiyon) and three came from the kehillah—one from the right wing, one from the left and one from the center (Tseire Tsiyon and Folkspartey). The last two groups chose a Tseire Tsiyon representative who was also introduced into the presidium, consisting of three representatives from the right wing, three from the left and the seventh from the center—the representative from Tseire Tsiyon.

Since a plenum of all the groups seldom met, decisions were made in the committee, which had a secure majority from the right. It became obvious that the left had not made a good deal. It had relied on an agreement between the Folkspartey (left) and Tseire-Tsiyon (right) about parceling out aid work. In reality, most of the work was taken away from the left because Tseire Tsiyon maintained an expressly hostile attitude and constantly opposed the left's proposals. There were moments when the left was able to have conversations with Ahdut and the Zionists. But it was impossible to forge agreement with Tseire Tsiyon regarding aid work. The committee finally concluded that practical aid work required trained and experienced managers who had to be invited without regard to party membership. The experts familiar with this sort

---

[163] This situation is confirmed by a JDC report dated July 1920: "In January 1920, the Poles captured the city of Komenetz-Podolsk; two Jewish relief committees had been functioning here, the Central Committee for Relief of Pogrom Sufferers (organized by the Ukrainian Jewish Ministry) and a relief committee organized by the Kehilla.... James Becker, who was then working for the JDC in Roumania [sic], came to Kamenetz-Podolsk, organized a united committee of all parties and factions and left one million Roumanian Lei and four hundred thousand Russian Roubles [sic] (Romanoff) to be distributed by this committee in the city and the surrounding district." Report of Activities of JDC in Occupied Parts of Wohlynia and Podolia, October 1, 1919–April 1920. Report by Shohan., folder 22.92.

of work were mainly from left groups. In the end, most of the practical work was given to them.

Tseire Tsiyon then began a campaign against the committee. After many debates it was decided to divide the work between the parties. And that was how in the worst way politics was introduced into the core of essential work in such areas as medical and social aid—needs that had nothing to do with political platforms.

The two sides constantly fought, and it is no surprise that hundreds of millions of funds were distributed without much rationale. Still, a great deal was accomplished through the significant amount of money and the large amount of clothes and products that was received. We opened distribution points for children (in Komenetz-Podolsk, Kitaigorod, Zvanchik, Orinin, Lantzekronia, Chemirovits, Husiatyn, Smotritch, Zamichov, Slobkovitz, Balin, and other places).[164] Orphans and the elderly were cared for. An entire array of centers were dedicated to medical aid. There was support for cooperatives, and help with credit was also organized, as well as aid to a variety of schools.

During the period that the Jewish-American [Aid] Committee was providing help, Denikin's retreating army continued to perpetrate pogroms, such as the large one in Zamichov, where many victims fell, and a large part of the town was burnt down. The [Jewish-American Aid] Committee worked under the banner of the Ukrainian Red Cross. A unit of ten people with two doctors was sent to the devastated region. In Zamichov a children's club was established (it was open from morning to night) for 100 children, as well as a nutrition center for the elderly.

The aid work went on more or less smoothly, but there was no overall plan and no clear direction. Each group tried to use the American committee for its own purposes. For example, the Zionists received a million *karbovantsi* (Ukrainian currency) for a kindergarten, attended by many children from the wealthy classes, despite the fact that priority should have been to address the essential concerns of the victims who had not yet received any help. The left demanded funds for a model workers' school for children of the poor. When it was given the funds from the community ORT, the right demanded an even larger sum for the "He-Halutz." L'appetit vieut en mangeant—the appetite comes with the eating.

The Zionists, and especially Tseire Tsiyon, who had a secure majority in the central aid committee, began to use the American money for necessities that had no relation to the pogrom victims. For example, a large sum was used

---

[164] Chemirovits (Yid.), Chemerovtsy (Rus.), Chemerivtsi (Ukr.) is 26 miles northeast of Komenetz. Husiaty (Yid.), Gusyatin (Rus.), Husiatyn (Ukr.) is 43 miles north of Komenetz. Balin (Yid., Rus., Ukr.) is 15 miles northeast of Komenetz.—Trans.

to celebrate Lag B'Omer at the Maccabee sport center.[165] Tseire Tsiyon also forcefully demanded subsidies for the musical group Kadimah that were rejected by the vote of the left and Ahdut. The committee's right-wing majority fiercely opposed every attempt by the left—which administered welfare—to turn the nutritional centers into orphanages and to create an appropriate environment for the local activists. The end result was sad. When the Jewish American [Aid] Committee in Komenetz closed, the children's institutions fell apart. The right was also against expanding aid work into the province. Representatives from the Zionist faction in the kehillah were also included in the central committee's council.

The Komenetz community was in a serious financial crisis. Rather than raise the appropriate funds in Komenetz-Podolsk itself, the leaders of the right in the kehillah found it more convenient to utilize the American funds. They took money from Komenetz institutions meant for poor people and for the support of the kehillah administration. Komenetz alone received 50 percent of the available funds, while the worst-off victims of the region—Litin, Haysin, and Broslev—received very little.

Representatives from the left energetically protested against such right-wing politics and considered leaving the committee. Given, however, that the responsibility for the children's institutions was mostly their responsibility, they voted to remain. The American representatives, who from time to time would come to Komenetz with needed funds, did not do anything to alleviate the tense situation. After B_R nobody else came from Romania.

The first representative from the Warsaw "Joint" [JDC] came to Komenetz in February 1920, and until the Poles left, several representatives and two more missions arrived in Komenetz. It is difficult to criticize the American representatives, especially when contrasting the work they did for the Ukrainian Jews to the work of the Polish Jews—neighbors who did not even bother to appear in Ukraine. We should also note that because Ukrainians wanted to avoid [Jewish] party politics they were mostly uninvolved in aid work even when there was no need for them to remain passive.

The first mission to Ukraine was that of Mr. [Max] Pine (New York) and Judge [Harry] Fisher (Chicago).[166] They spent several days in Komenetz to

---

[165] Lag B'Omer is a minor holiday celebrated in the spring. The Zionist movement elevated the holiday because of its association with the last great Jewish revolt against the Romans.—Trans.

[166] Max Pine (1866–1928), an American labor leader and relief worker, went to Ukraine in March 1920 as part of a Joint Distribution Committee mission to study the situation of the Jews. He was accompanied by Harry Fisher (1882–1955), an American superior court judge in Chicago and an active Zionist.—Trans.

properly familiarize themselves with the local conditions and took with them a lot of material.

We were from two different worlds. They were the representatives of a new fully developed Jewish community, and we were the remnants of a Jewish society. On their shoulders stood Jewish kehillot with large populations; on our shoulders—destroyed towns and villages. They were the free citizens for whom the whole world was open; we could not find any place to rest. "What is life like here?" they asked us. We remained silent. How could we answer the question what life was like...?

At a plenary meeting of the central aid committee, Pine and Fisher demanded that the wealthy Jewish classes in Komenetz support their own poor. Fisher made it clear that while American Jews were obligated to aid the destroyed Jewish kehillot, "why should the wealthy Jews from Chicago worry more about the poor of Komenetz than the wealthy [citizens of] Komenetz?" Pine and Fisher were generally oriented more towards the left but were reluctant to introduce fundamental changes in Komenetz.

The second delegation, which had such a tragic end, included Professor [Israel] Friedlaender, Moshe Kass, and Dr. [Meyer] Leff.[167] They came to Komenetz before the arrival of the Bolsheviks [July 1920]. The right wing, thinking that it could gain support from abroad, began a strong attack on the left in order to eliminate it from communal activities.

The American delegation was in a difficult position. On the one hand it did not want to break apart a committee that included different political parties in the Jewish community; on the other hand, the right threatened to leave the central committee if it was not given the main role in aid work. Their demand was not accepted by the American delegation.

Seeing that there was no end to the in-fighting, the delegation decided to visit Proskurov and Mohilev-Podolsk. The Ukrainians were evacuating

---

[167] Israel Friedlaender (1876–1920) was a commissioner of the JDC to the Ukraine. A renowned biblical scholar, he served on the faculty of the Jewish Theological Seminary in New York. In January 1920, Friedlaender traveled to Poland with Overseas Unit Number 1 of the JDC and reached Warsaw in February 1920. The unit was made up of 23 volunteers from the United States. Its task was to provide aid to Jewish communities in Poland that had been ravaged during World War I. A typhus epidemic raged in Ukraine, and the American Red Cross had withdrawn from the area after some of its staff died. Maurice (Moshe) Kass (1887–1933) was the editor of the paper *Jewish World* in Philadelphia. He was a member of the JDC's special Ukraine Commission with Pine, Fisher, and Friedlaender. They first visited Polish-occupied Ukraine, where they submitted a situation report to the JDC in April. Kass and Friedlaender stayed in Polish-occupied Ukraine, while Fischer and Pine continued on to Soviet Russia. Gumener's published Yiddish memoir has the name as "Katz," which is a typo. Meyer Leff (1888–1982) was the medical director of the JDC's Overseas Unit Number 1.—Trans.

from Mohilev-Podolsk, and the city was preparing for the Bolsheviks. The delegates had the opportunity to see for themselves the hell that the Jewish population lived in. For us this was a normal experience. For the Americans, it made a terrifying impression. They then understood that aid must come from inside and not from an external power.

At the moment, the relationship between the Ukrainian army and the Jews was better, though during the army's evacuation from Mohilev-Podolsk, there was a rumor that the Jews had killed a Ukrainian. There was a panic in the city, but thanks to the intervention of the American delegates the incident was dismissed.

The Americans returned to Komenetz depressed. Applying pressure, the right wing denounced the delegation's demands and the situation in the committee remained the same. The committee's days were numbered.

In short order, the Bolsheviks took Komenetz and liquidated the Jewish-American Committee. The remaining articles meant for the Jews were taken and distributed to Red Army soldiers and even to the peasants in the villages. Despite the efforts of some former members of the left from the central committee, the resources that had been designated for the Jewish community could not be saved.

Before the Bolsheviks arrived, a large part of the aid committee's assets had already been divided among various institutions. Some of those assets were lost. Even after the Ukrainians retook Komenetz [from the Bolsheviks], it was not possible to get an accounting either of the items distributed or the funds that these institutions owed the central committee.[168] The institutions, cooperatives, credit institutions, and the Halutz did not fulfill their obligation to return the funds they owed. An exception was the workers' cooperative "Proletari," which reimbursed the funds and provided an accounting despite the fact that the socialists had not taken part in the work of the Jewish-American Committee. This was the end of the Jewish-American Committee, an unsuccessful coalition of the right and the left. There had been every possibility to do great work because there were significant amounts of money, and 30–40 employees in the aid committee, some experienced, but very little was accomplished.

---

[168] The Ukrainians had retaken Komenetz and the region for a very short time in September 1920.

The Polish Assault on Kiev (April–May 1920)

After the arrests of the communal and political activists, Komenetz grew calm.[169] There was no political activity.

In April, news arrived that the UNR was signing a treaty with the Poles.[170] The socialist circles reacted negatively to the Polish-Ukrainian treaty. Firstly, they were against any intervention by a foreign power in Ukrainian affairs; secondly, they saw danger in how the treaty addressed the interests of the peasants. The socialists were also against the agreement to establish borders without a plebiscite and in general were against the secret character of the treaty.[171] They decided to recall the socialist members who were in the government. The Ukrainian Social Democrats and the Ukrainian Socialist Revolutionaries also recalled their representatives.[172] The Poale Tsiyon representative, Goldelman, who was assistant minister of labor, resigned. The Fareynikte Bund debated whether to withdraw from the Jewish Ministry. The supporters of withdrawing, besides citing general political concerns, made it known that they were motivated by the fact that the Ministry was increasingly orienting itself to the right and drawing closer to the kehillot; meanwhile, parties from the right were grouping themselves around the kehillot. The majority in the Fareynikte Bund maintained that supporting the Jewish Ministry was an entirely separate matter [than the question about supporting the Directory's alliance with the Poles]. After long debates it was decided that the representative from the Fareynikte Bund would remain in the Jewish Ministry until a party conference that was to take place on May 26 [1920] in Vinitza.

---

[169] See the section "Under the Polish Occupation (End 1919–July 1920)," in Gumener, *A kapitl Ukraine*, 108–12.—Trans.

[170] On April 21, 1920, Josef Piłsudski, head of the Polish army, and Petliura signed the Treaty of Warsaw, an alliance in which Poland promised to commit forces in the campaign to regain Ukrainian territory from the Red Army. The Polish army launched a major offensive on April 25 (the Kiev Offensive) and quickly overran much of Ukraine, including Kiev in May. But in June the Red Army drove back the Poles, retook Kiev, and in November occupied Komenetz.—Trans.

[171] As part of the Treaty of Warsaw, the UNR ceded Polish territorial gains in western Ukraine. In return, Poland would accept Ukrainian sovereignty and a Polish–Ukrainian border on the River Zbruch. Polish landlords in Volhynia (who owned much of the land) were allowed to retain land until a future date, when the UNR would address the issue of Polish landed property in the region.—Trans.

[172] The Ukrainian Social Democrats quickly changed their minds. Within a few weeks they voted in Vinitza to participate in the right-wing cabinet of [Prime Minister] Prokopovych (Mazepa, Bezpalko). When they met with the Poles, they decided with the socialists from Proskurov to withdraw from the regime.

The treaty between Poland and Ukraine was signed at the end of April and the attack on the Bolshevik army began. The Polish army took Kiev, and all the Ukrainian ministries, including the Jewish one, were transferred to Vinitza. The local administration in Vinitza was taken over by well-known bandits. The terrorized Jewish population remained silent, observing the situation with fear and trembling and waited to see how this "wedding" between Poles and Ukrainians would end. But at least no pogroms occurred in this period.

Despite their decision to remain in the Jewish Ministry until the party conference, Jewish socialists in Podolia continued to be oriented to the left. At the same time, the Jewish Ministry and the Vinitza Tseire Tsiyon drew closer to one another. The provincial committee of Tseire Tsiyon crafted a resolution for Krasny, the minister for Jewish affairs, declaring that due to the tense situation it was prepared to support the Jewish Ministry if all the democratic groups (?) [sic] within the Jewish community would participate. In general, the Jews of Vinitza forged a warm relationship with the Ministry and tried to help it acquire a residence, furniture, and apartments for its officials. The Fareynikte Bund, however, broke with the Jewish Ministry and Tseire Tsiyon became the dominant player.

Jewish communal life in Vinitza began to revive. The kehillah established an American-Jewish Committee with different groups from within the community. The need among the impoverished and dejected Jewish population was very great. Most critically, the small towns in the districts of Vinitza, Litin, and Haysin, needed help. For many months the situation had been unstable and sometimes there was not even a governing authority in these cities and villages. They lived cut off from the entire world—town Jews with broken windows, waiting for a miracle that would relieve their tragic situation. Having survived various conquering powers, the Jews of Podolia despaired that a government could be forged in Ukraine that would create the conditions for them to return to their peaceful occupations.

Jews had heard that Americans brought funds, and in every new person they hoped to see a delegate. I visited several towns. A terrible stillness pervaded. Some houses were burnt down and the rest stood with broken windowpanes. Jews in torn rags went about the towns with depressed faces. Seeing an outsider, they surrounded the wagon and asked with voices full of both hope and despair: "Are you a delegate?" Many petitioners from the towns came to the Jewish Ministry and to the Vinitza kehillah to ask for aid. But the Ministry did not have any funds, and no American delegation visited Vinitza.

The Vinitza kehillah could not even manage the 20 or so orphans that had ended up there by chance. The orphans were relegated to the poorhouse with a kindly nurse who accidently ended up in Vinitza because she was cut off from Kiev. The Komenetz committee sent a large sum of money (up to 200,000 tsar [rubles]), medicine, and equipment. After a short time, I left Vinitza and went to Volhynia province for some private matters.

In June I learned that the Polish-Ukrainian army was withdrawing. I met the remnants of the Jewish Ministry in Proskurov. I also met and spent several days with the Jewish-American delegation: Professor Friedlaender, Moshe Kass, and Dr. Leff.

The delegation deliberated the situation in Ukraine with Krasny, in particular the question concerning Jews in Ukraine.

The evacuation continued. The Poles retreated quietly, as did the Ukrainians, though in several places Ukrainian insurgents perpetrated violence. But it was not like the pogrom mood of 1919, when the air was filled with Jewish blood. The Ukrainians sensed that thanks to the pogroms they had lost the sympathy of the Jewish population for many long years to come. After spilling so much Jewish blood, they realized the harm it had caused not only to the Jewish community but also to their national movement. The Ukrainians now took measures to fight against the pogromists.

All the ministers relocated from Proskurov to Komenetz-Podolsk. The town was completely quiet. The Poles had withdrawn, and authority was transferred to the Ukrainians but for only a few days.

Suddenly we received terrible and unbelievable news: Professor Friedlaender, Dr. Cantor, and a third person—unknown—were killed in Yarmolintz, a town 25 versts from Proskurov, as they were travelling from Komenetz to Proskurov. A special committee was sent from the Komenetz American-Jewish Committee to investigate. The murder happened in the following way.

On Yod Tet Tammuz, July 5, 1920, a Bolshevik intelligence unit entered Yarmolintz, a town that lies on the road between Komenetz and Proskurov. Seeing from afar an automobile with people in military uniform, the unit mistook them for Polish officers and killed all of them and distributed the booty. Shortly after, a Bolshevik official came on order from Moscow to investigate the incident. In Komenetz a large group, including representatives from both the right and left, attended a memorial. Far, far away in the small town of Yarmolintz, Professor Friedlaender and Dr. Kantor lie in the cemetery without even a headstone.[173]

---

[173] Friedlaender, who was distributing JDC funds, met up with Rabbi Bernard Cantor in Komenetz. Cantor (1892–1920) was a rabbi in Flushing, New York when he became a JDC aid worker. He was assigned to eastern Galicia. The JDC understood the danger of being so close to the front, but they hoped to meet with Pilsudski to negotiate his help in getting aid to the Jewish population. Travelling by car towards Lvov on July 5, 1920, they were attacked and killed by Red Army troops on the highway leading from Komenetz-Podolsk to Yarmolintz. The driver escaped. The third person who was killed was a community leader from Tarnopol named Grossman. Friedlaender's

I considered leaving Ukraine, bidding farewell to Dr. Leff and Mr. Kass, who were terribly upset by this great misfortune. Dr. Leff prevailed upon me to remain and insisted that it would be a sin for me to abandon Ukraine under these circumstances. As a Jewish activist, I did not have the right to abandon the Jewish population in such a moment. After long sleepless nights and considering the situation from various perspectives, I decided to remain in Komenetz-Podolsk.

We were in the hands of the Ukrainians again. And again, the old well-known conversations about protecting Jewish life began. But the Ukrainians left Komenetz-Podolsk quietly, and after a year the Bolsheviks took over again.

Bolsheviks Again in Podolia (Summer 1920)

Well before they retook Komenetz and the region, there were many rumors about the Communists. Some people held that these Bolsheviks were nothing like the Bolsheviks who had occupied Komenetz in 1919; that they would not bother the local population, except for the merchant class, whom they would execute; and that they would be mainly controlled by the Cheka. Others said the opposite, that lately the Bolsheviks had abandoned their extreme tactics and had adapted themselves to local conditions. In any case, this time the Jews welcomed them quite coldly. The enthusiasm that had greeted the Bolsheviks in 1919 was gone. They waited to see what the new authority would do.

And the Bolsheviks indeed took to their "work." Like strangers in a strange land, they now behaved as occupiers in Podolia. They had prepared their policy, and everything was decreed from above.

Their manner of ruling was very simple. At the head were the party Communists (partkom), who were nominated by the central executive committee.[174] To become a member of the Communist Party was quite difficult. All responsible positions were given to officials who were sent by central. The chairman and revkom members were either affirmed by the occupying army or by the central committee.

In a matter of a few months the authorities issued a constant stream of declarations that placed the population in a difficult situation. The local professional unions, the workers' cooperatives, workers' clubs, and worker activists could not initiate even the smallest matter. The workers' club, which had 600 members of various political shades and had been decimated under the Ukrainians in 1919, remained closed. All efforts to open the club were unsuc-

remains were reburied in Jerusalem. Michael Beizer has concluded that they were probably mistaken for Polish officers.—Trans.

[174] The partkom was the local party committee.—Trans.

cessful. The Bolsheviks planned to establish a communist workers' club and
were against a multiparty club where they could not play a majority role.

The Bolsheviks did not initiate terror against the noncommunists. Gradually, however, the military Cheka—called the "Special Division"—began its
work. On a beautiful morning we suddenly learned that 16 Zionists from Mohilev-Podolsk had been brought to Komenetz. They included Y_Ki (the chairman of the Mohilev community council), members of Tseire Tsiyon, representatives of the community council "B," and workers from HeHalutz. These
Zionists were accused of being counterrevolutionaries, deserters, having con-
cealed weapons, and so forth. They had to appear before a judge of the military revolutionary tribune of the "N" division.[175]

The Jewish socialists immediately became involved and secured a team
of attorneys to defend the Zionists; however, no attorneys or defenders were
permitted. The situation was very serious. A day earlier the Bolsheviks had
shot as deserters 3 Jewish workers who had not immediately made themselves
available for the required mobilization. We also received news that the Revtribunal intended to transform the trial of the 16 Zionists into a sensational
showcase of a "revealed Jewish counterrevolution."

The Zionists and Tseire Tsiyon in Komenetz were despondent. Only a few
of them still mustered any energy for communal action. The Jewish socialists
took vigorous steps to defend the Mohilev Zionists. Unable to speak directly
with the authorities in whose hands the fate of the men lay, we quickly appealed to the Jewish Communists. We argued that it was simply ridiculous
to accuse as counterrevolutionaries men whom we knew were loyal and who
had even saved many Jewish Communists from death. Ukrainian pogromists
turned all Jews into Bolsheviks and based on this accusation committed great
atrocities. Now Russian Bolsheviks want to transform all Jews into counterrevolutionaries, and antisemitism again found favorable soil. Fortunately, the
local Jewish Communists took an interest in the situation and did everything
to save the arrestees. But it was challenging to do anything because of the
Revtribunal's peculiar jurisdiction in Komenetz.

Power was in the hands of the Division's military courts, whose judges
consisted of three Red Army personnel, one of them the chairman. The judge
nominated an investigator, who was also a prosecutor. The investigation was
based on written material. The prosecutor did not always appear in court.
And as long as the prosecutor did not appear (as was the case with the 16
Zionists), no defense attorney was permitted to argue the case. There were
no rules that regulated the procedures by which the court rendered a verdict.

---

[175] Revolutionary tribune, special court, a sort of field court law. [The Revtribunal
(Extra Military Revolutionary Tribunal) was a judicial body established in April 1919
to deal with cases of counterrevolutionary activity.—Trans.]

Judgment was rendered by the formula: "revolutionary consciousness and socialist justice." The same division of the judiciary that rendered verdicts carried out the verdicts. The Revtribunal was staffed by outsiders whom nobody, even the local Communists, knew. The chairman was a Latvian. In such a situation it was very difficult to know what to do, but we continued to try everything we could.

We did not know the date the trial would begin. For three days we stood at the site of the court and waited for them to bring the 16 Zionists who were held in a railcar prison wagon. The father of four of the arrestees, a butcher from Mohilev, made a strong impression on us. He sat the entire time at the site of the court and recited t'ilm [psalms].[176] "I gave them two sons; give me two," he pleaded. The situation was very difficult because his sons were accused of remaining in Ukraine during Denikin's attack while they were members of the Red Army. The Revtribunal held that the mere fact that they remained indicated that they went over to Denikin.

The accused pleaded: "How could we, Jews, go over to Denikin, who was responsible for such terrible pogroms against us? He would kill us for being members of the Red Army." "Indeed, that is why your guilt was even greater," retorted the chairman of the court. "The Soviet regime had defended your parents, brothers, and sisters, and you did not evacuate with the Red Army but remained in Denikin's territory."

Despite these serious accusations, all the arrested men were successfully saved from the death penalty. The chairman of the Mohilev kehillah and a few others were released even before the trial started. Some others were given light punishments. A few were sentenced to 10 years forced labor (on the condition that they will not repeat their offense). The rest were released and sent to the front. The court justified the light sentence for those accused of desertion by the fact that they were not from the "idle class" and had worked in agriculture as "pioneers." The large crowd that attended the trial greeted the verdict with warm applause.

The trial of the 16 Zionists was the only victory for the Komenetz community during this period. The Bolsheviks continued to act with impunity and absolutely did not consider the sentiment of the local population and even the workers.

The relationship between the Jewish Bolsheviks, the Jewish population, and the Jewish socialists was not the same as in 1919. It was especially bizarre to see that the Jewish Communists, who had once been socialists, were estranged from their former colleagues. Not long ago many of them hid under the wing of the Jewish socialists and thus saved themselves; now they ar-

---

[176] *Zogn t'lim* (reciting Psalms) is a common religious response to a hardship or danger.—Trans.

rived with administrative portfolios from the center, exchanging their Jewish names for Gentile ones and leading an almost personal attack against former comrades and friends.

It was a difficult situation for the Jewish socialists. In 1919 every Jew had immediately turned to the socialists whenever he encountered misfortune and much had been accomplished; now the socialists were powerless. In reality, the strong socialist organizations that we had in Podolia in the years 1917–19 no longer existed. The transition period, the waves of pogroms, and the Bolsheviks had all undermined their existence. Their ranks were increasingly thinned and their impact on communal life weakened. The Fareynikte Bund did not resonate with the Jewish workers. Dejected, persecuted, and exhausted, the Jewish workers were indifferent to political and social issues. Some individuals remained with the socialist parties, and some joined the Bolsheviks. The masses however, remained directionless.

When news came from Kiev that the Social Democratic Bund still existed, the Fareynikte Bund in Komenetz immediately called a general meeting to decide whether to liquidate itself as an organization.[177] The executive committee chose to stop the party's activities. Within a short time, the old Social Democratic Bund was restored in Komenetz, and Fareynikte no longer continued as an organization. By contrast, Poale Tsiyon was more active, and although there was also a split between the right and left Zionists, they still were able to work together in the Borochov Club.[178]

For the Jewish socialists in Komenetz-Podolsk a new question arose, namely, its relationship to the Jewish Public Committee.[179] An agreement between the Soviet authorities and the American delegation (Pine and Fisher) had been reached to establish a Jewish Public Committee (Yidgeskom) that would aid the pogrom victims with American funds. The committee was supposed to include representatives from the Jewish Communists and socialists, the Jewish communal organizations (EKOPO, ORT, OZE, Kultur Lige), the Jewish workers, and Jewish representatives of some city organizations. They were required to establish commissions, and through an agreement between

---

[177] The Social Democratic Bund was the non-Bolshevik faction of the Bund. Gumener states that its revival made the existence of Fareynikte, also a non-Bolshevik socialist group, redundant.—Trans.

[178] The Borochov Club was named after Ber Borochov (1881–1917), the founder of Poale Tsiyon.—Trans.

[179] The Kiev Regional Commission of Yidgeskom began its work in July 1920. Yidgeskom quickly shed its "ecumenical" beginnings as the Jewish Communists within the organization purged noncommunist aid workers and dictated policy. See Beizer, *Relief in Time of Need,* 96–98, 101–04, 106–08; and Granick, "First American Organization in Soviet Russia," 61–93.—Trans.

the Communists and socialists in Komenetz a commission was formed. The Jewish Communists had even taken measures to legalize the local Yidgeskom as a communal organization.

The chairman of the Yidgeskom (E_N) arrived from Kiev and suddenly issued an edict, ordering that the commission could only be composed of Communists. The Komenetz Jewish Communists argued in vain that this policy greatly damaged aid activity. But E_N was angry and wanted to take revenge on the so-called Komenetz "counterrevolutionaries." Even the Kultur Lige was against this demand but in the end gave in.

ORT decided not to recognize the purely communist Yidgeskom. The Komenetz communal organizations engaged in an angry conversation with Mr. E_N. They felt that the Communists had abandoned Ukraine for Moscow and had concluded an agreement with the Jewish-American representatives on behalf of the millions of Ukrainian Jews without even consulting the Jewish workers. Further, they reneged on the agreement, and created a purely communist Yidgeskom. The local activists who remained in Ukraine and worked for the good of the Jewish masses would not agree to be bullied in such a manner.

E_N, however, signed away two ORT institutions: a shoemaker and a carpenter workshop. It was interesting to note that he did not find it necessary to demand that the Bolsheviks return 7 pud [about 252 pounds] of leather soles that had been requisitioned from the ORT. The material was supposed to have gone to Yidgeskom upon his arrival.

The commission, however, found itself in an uncomfortable position and could get virtually nothing accomplished. Despite their antagonism towards the socialists, the Jewish Communists needed them for cultural activity because there were few workers in that field. The Jewish section of Folkspartey-Bildung [National Education] was already in the hands of the Jewish socialists.

The Zionists, however, were completely isolated. At the beginning they tried to dialogue with the Jewish socialists, but as usual nothing was achieved, so they resorted to personal connections to maintain their institutions.

The Ukrainians Retake Komenetz-Podolsk and the Region (September 1920)[180]

As usual, a day before the change of regimes we had no idea what was going to happen. A student whom I knew announced at my door, early in the

---

[180] Ukrainian forces regained Kiev and Komenetz between July and September, until the Red Army definitively conquered Ukraine in 1921. The UNR held its last session on Ukrainian soil on November 22, 1920.—Trans.

morning, that the Bolsheviks were leaving Komenetz. Nobody knew what was going to take their place, who would come in their stead, and why there was such a quick evacuation. Although there was a general commotion in the town, the Jewish population remained calm.

The Red Army quietly left Komenetz. A local militia was organized to maintain order. Jews and non-Jews alike displayed an antagonistic attitude towards the Bolsheviks. Soon there was not a Bolshevik military presence. Some retreating Red Army soldiers were stopped but quickly released before continuing to the front.

In a few days Ukrainians appeared in town. This time Jews were not afraid, and they did not hide. On the contrary, they walked down the street freely and openly. The kehillah sent representatives to greet the Ukrainians. A Tseire Tsiyon representative made a welcoming speech. Several times we went outside to look at the military as it entered, even on the day of Yom Kippur. The volunteer firemen (mostly Jews) greeted the troops with music. At their head was the rabbi. The Ukrainians took Komenetz without violence. Quiet was also reported from the surrounding area. Among the Jewish citizens there was a good feeling. The Jewish socialists, however, remained cold and passive as did some Ukrainian socialist circles.

In the first days, the Tseire Tsiyon made a lot of noise. As time went on, however, their mood also fell. They no longer believed that the Ukrainians would restrain themselves. Tseire Tsiyon activists began to leave Komenetz in droves, as did those from the central aid committee, without giving an account of the remaining American funds that they had received before the Bolsheviks came in July.

As soon as the Ukrainians arrived in Komenetz, Tarbut issued an announcement in Yiddish and Hebrew with a mogen dovid ["Jewish star"] and "tzion" [Zion] at the top, which was posted in the streets of Komenetz.[181] The announcement said that the kindergarten had been seized by the Jewish socialists and by the Kultur Lige (the leaders of Narobraz) and was not under the control of Tarbut.[182]

In other circumstances, such behavior from the Komenetz Tseire Tsiyon would have surely spelt tragedy for the Jewish socialists. But the Ukrainains remained relatively calm and the issue passed without incident.

---

[181] Tarbut was a Hebrew primary school. —Trans.

[182] The original is located in the Komenetz community, Kiev Kultur Lige. It was published at the Gusyatins' press. [Narobraz (Department of Public Education) was a unit within Narkompros (the People's Commissariat of Enlightenment). This Bolshevik agency was in charge of education, and responsible for the administration of public schools. It included a Jewish section.—Trans.]

The bourgeois Jews now felt that their moment had arrived: the socialist circles were apathetic and the Tseire Tsiyon activists had fled. Now the "elect" from the *batei midrashim* began to "deal."[183] Their representatives were a Jew who had become wealthy in the war, a shyster lawyer, a community activist, an ordinary Jew, and a scoundrel who had stumbled into communal work. For them even the Ahdut Zionist group was too left, and they strove to liquidate the kehillah and take its place. Their attention was mainly focused on the American funds. And while this was happening people in the old age homes were literally starving to death, and the Talmud Torah schools were about to be closed.

The Jewish socialists who were not activists in politics remained indifferent. They did not take part in the Jewish-American Committee. The remaining members (the others having fled) were busy liquidating the committee.

Through an initiative of the socialists who were activists, a new committee was established made up of the Kultur Lige, EKOPO, OZE, and the ORT. It provided funds for all institutions, especially for the orphanage and kindergarten. The institutions were in a dire situation. The committee connected with the Joint Distribution Committee in Warsaw and distributed funds borrowed from private individuals.

In this period the Ukrainians took Proskurov and Olt-Kostin, and were closing in on Vinitza. Komenetz and its region were quiet. We had no idea about the intention of the Ukrainian regime. We only knew that the Directory (Petliura) was in control and that its cabinet was right wing. Six or seven weeks after Ukrainian troops took Komenetz, the Ukrainian government entered. The Jewish Ministry arrived with it. But two days later the Ukrainians again were forced to leave Komenetz under pressure from the Bolsheviks.

Bolsheviks in Komenetz-Podolsk (End of 1920–Beginning of 1921)[184]

When the Bolsheviks arrived in November 1920 the Jewish population was very depressed. The propertied class had emigrated abroad, and the simple Jew just wanted to pack his suitcase and hit the road to America.

The entry of the Bolsheviks in Komenetz-Podolsk did not start well. The cavalry troops that took the town immediately robbed the population. Antisemitic slogans were often heard. Many homes were looted on the first night, among them the OZE colony for sick children. When the administrators of the

---

[183] Literally, the "houses of study," a metaphor for the religious parties.—Trans.

[184] In November 1920, the Red Army drove the remnants of the Ukrainian army and the Petliura government into exile in Galicia. Komenetz-Podolsk was now permanently under the Bolsheviks.—Trans.

colony came to the commander to complain, they were received very coldly, and nothing was done to discover the culprits. There was nobody to whom to appeal or with whom to lodge a complaint.

Unlike 1919, there were none of the usual processes in place when the Red Army entered. There were no meetings, no summons, and no revolutionary slogans. This was not like the Red Army that had occupied Komenetz the last two times. It was as if a foreign military power simply entered and occupied the area. The Jewish population was very frightened. At night one did not see a living person in the streets. Doors and gates were locked, and a dread took hold of everyone.

The cavalry quickly continued on its way and the town was relatively calmer.

But the central executive committee remembered well "counterrevolutionary" Komenetz and sent three Chekists to "clear" it out. Why they needed three Chekists was not apparent since the true counterrevolutionaries had already fled with the Ukrainian intelligentsia and only the middle classes, the worker, and the poor remained. But this was not the point: they could not sit idle, and soon created work for themselves. It did not matter to them whether through proper or contrived methods.

For example, a Chekist demanded a Jew procure gold coins. The Chekist reassured the Jew that he needed it for himself, for his teeth. The Jew bought the gold, and when he brought it to the Chekist, he was arrested and jailed and forced to report those people from whom he had obtained the coins. He had been assured that he would not be punished if he told. The Jew confessed, and everyone that had sold the gold to him was arrested, even for as little as one or two coins. Their trial was short. The Cheka court for Komenetz district sentenced all of them to death, including the entrapped broker, Feldman. Those in the court that made the decision included the Cheka agent who provoked the entire episode.

Other Jews and Christians were also sentenced to death for different "crimes." Among them was a 72-year-old Jew, Moshe Hochman, who was accused of paying a bribe to a Chekist after haberdashery goods were found in his possession. In total, according to the announcement in the *Komenetz News*, 14 people were shot. Among the victims were the prominent Komenetz citizens Yokim Weinboim, 55 years old, Srul Feldman, Moshe Hochman, and several other people.

The town was very aggrieved by the death of Yokim Weinboim. He was an educated, well-mannered businessman impoverished by the war. The Bolsheviks had mobilized his son-in-law, who was a surgeon and his only support. His economic situation was very grave. Weinboim's entire guilt was that he had sold a Jewish acquaintance—a broker—two gold five-ruble pieces. And for this they shot him. The execution of the fourteen made a shocking impression in the town.

Thanks to its geographical location Komenetz-Podolsk and its vicinity had been relatively calm under the bourgeois-democratic [Ukrainian] regime. By contrast, the newly arrived Bolsheviks wanted to push through in one shot all the decrees promulgated in the past months by the Russian Soviet authorities in Moscow. These were physically impossible for the Komenetz inhabitants to bear.

The Bolsheviks first enforced the decrees on the townspeople; for villagers and peasants, they imposed the policies more slowly. They began with the decree to register various handwork, musical instruments, furniture, and other objects. Then there were decrees to hand over merchandise that had been registered. This was followed by the requisition of furniture. Obviously, merchants, shopkeepers, artisans, and others hid their wealth. Then the real work of the Cheka began: they inspected private homes, communal organizations, churches, and synagogues and found hidden merchandise, gold, silver, and cash.

The situation for the Jewish masses became very difficult; almost all Jewish incomes were severely curtailed. Five to six hundred small shopkeepers were without livelihood. The authorities then threatened to requisition the wooden stalls in which the merchants stored their few meagre items of merchandise for market.

There was no work for the artisans, and the Jewish workers, who were employed by them, lost their jobs. The intellectuals (doctors, lawyers, engineers, and teachers) were mobilized. The privileged class was engaged in the national [sovietization] enterprise. They included the mobilized intellectuals, along with the workers and employees of Soviet organizations. They were paid a salary of 6,000 [*sic*] a month, for which at the most one could buy 30 pounds of bread; in addition, they received a ration. The Bolsheviks then announced a policy prohibiting private businesses without giving the local population options to obtain products.

The economically weakened Jewish workers, and the Jewish masses in general, played no role in politics. They were completely indifferent to politics. Besides the military authority, the policy was in the hands of the general Communist Party (partkom).[185] They did not engage with Kombund (Communist Bund) or with EKOPO (Poale Tsiyon Communists).

The Jewish division of partkom, which was run by six or seven Jewish Communists, was the sole authority for Jewish issues. It was responsible for appointing an administrator to the Jewish section of the Department of Na-

---

[185] The general Communist Party refers to the party of the Ukrainian Bolsheviks, whose allegiance was to the Soviets.—Trans.

tional Education. All Jewish organizations in Komenetz and in the region were placed under the authority of the Jewish division of partkom. All policies of the Yevodal [Yidgeskom/Evobkom] that touched upon the interests of the Jewish population were reviewed by partkom and revkom.

The few Jews that belonged to the general Communist Party were employed in Soviet posts and so did not work in the Jewish section of partkom. In any case, there were few suitable people in the Jewish section. Thus, partkom was left with two options: either attract people from other parties (national Communists and socialists) or do not participate at all in the Jewish organizations.[186]

Such a situation occurred in Komenetz with the head of the Jewish section of the Department of National Education, who was a member of Poale Tsiyon (an Ekopist).[187] A consultation was called by the Jewish section in which national Communists took part, as well as Jewish socialists and some Zionists but none from the general Communist Party. No activists from the Kultur Lige or teachers from the Komenetz district participated.

Central knew the situation in the provinces and sent a nonlocal Jewish Communist over whom the local activists, especially the Jewish socialists, could not have any control. This also happened in Vinitza, where the Jewish section of the Department of National Education sent a young man who exhibited a special hatred for the Kultur Lige, where Jewish socialists were in the majority. This was the environment in which the Jews lived—always racking their brains on how to adjust to a new tense situation.

As time went on, things went from bad to worse. The population stopped accepting Bolshevik currency and the Cheka answered with terror. The situation in Komenetz became unbearable. Every day there were new arrests and searches with no end in sight. I met a well-known Communist, a former Bundist, who came to Komenetz for a few days. He wondered how we could live in such a situation. Komenetz, he said, resembles an insane asylum.

The terror increased. They arrested the chairman of the town duma—Miransky—a Jew, a right Socialist Revolutionary—and the former town mayor Kylymnyk, a left Ukrainian Social Democrat who was very popular with the Jews for his activity during the Komenetz pogrom. The Jewish socialists, however, were not harassed by the Cheka.

Meanwhile an order was issued regarding elections in the worker and peasant soviets. Precisely where and when the elections were supposed to

---

[186] National communism refers to the Jewish communist parties such as the Kombund.—Trans.

[187] Ekapist refers to a member of the communist wing of Poale Tsiyon. Gumener means that the head of the local Department of National Education was from Poale Tsiyon.—Trans.

take place was not determined. Besides the general Communists no other political party offered to take part in the election. No group wanted to participate in an atmosphere of terror. The exception was that in some professional
clubs elections spontaneously took place and politically unaffiliated workers
and Jewish socialists were elected. The electoral polling stations were open
everywhere and conducted according to instructions in leaflets that the Communist Party had prepared.

Opposition grew from a significant worker and peasant group, but without the backing of a political party that could lead, it quickly fell apart. There
was little interest in organizing. We were convinced that in the existing conditions the same people would be selected again. In reality our belief was
confirmed.

The Christian population was still mobile and could move to villages
where the impact of Soviet power was very weak. Jews began to flee abroad
en masse: the petty merchant, the shopkeeper, the craftsman, the laborer, the
intellectual, the teacher, lawyer, doctor, and engineer fled. They all fled. People of different beliefs fled, even Communists. They went to Galicia and to
Bessarabia. Their anxiety reached the highest pitch. The tiniest rationale was
enough to abandon all one's belongings and travel the 18 to 30 versts that separated Ukraine from the rest of the world. But not everyone could go. Very few
individuals were able to get permission; most could not even go to another
town within Ukraine or Russia. We were cut off from the entire world.

The aid organizations were in crisis. For six months we lived on the remnants of the American Committee [JDC] funds and the products that we received from the Soviets. The local councils tried with all their power to maintain the children's institutions, but what could they achieve when they too
had little to give?

The chairman of the Komenetz landsmanshaft in New York, who was sta-
tioned in Bessarabia, instructed the Jewish activists to continue their relief
activity on a limited basis, and asked us to help evacuate the relatives, wives,
parents, sisters, and brothers of American citizens for whom there were funds
and documents to travel to America waiting for them in Bessarabia.

After long deliberation we agreed to help. We also decided to administer
aid activity through the Yidgeskom, the Jewish Public Committee. With the
help of the Jewish Communists in Yidgeskom, we held discussions with revkom about legalizing this work. Revkom said that it would make every effort
to help Yidgeskom. The Komenetz revkom gave the American delegation permission to come to Komenetz and took upon itself the responsibility for the
personal safety of the delegation and for the security of its possessions.

The representatives of the Komenetz landsmanshaft had explicit direc-
tives to distribute the funds under the rabbinate's supervision. It was clear

that the members of the Komenetz landsmanshaft in New York had an an-
tiquated idea of the Komenetz that they left many years ago. They were not
attentive to the fact that Komenetz, like all cities in Russia, had lived through a
world war followed by the great Russian Revolution.[188] Though the American
representatives of the landsmanshaft attempted to engage them in relief work,
the rabbinate feared repercussions from the Bolsheviks and kept its distance.

After many negotiations and adamant demands from the delegation that
aid work should include representatives from all strata of the Jewish population, Yidgeskom established a council in which all groups from the Jewish
community took part, e.g., Ahdut, Zionists, Tseire Tsiyon, Folkspartey, Jewish
socialists, Communists, and also representatives from communal [kehillah]
organizations and members of Yidgeskom itself. The executive bureau of this
council was made up of two Communists from Yidgeskom. A Jewish socialist
represented the communal organizations.

Yidgeskom achieved a lot with funds from the Komenetz landsmanshaft.
The children in the orphanage, kindergartens, and schools were no longer
cold and hungry. The situation of the old age home improved. With the aid
of "SoBez" (Sobes/Social Welfare Department) and Yidgeskom, a nominally
priced kitchen opened for 250 persons. The OZE colony for disabled children
that had been plundered had been reestablished, and it was decided to open
new children's institutions (in the Polish estate Timkovitz and in Krivazer).[189]

Yidgeskom also helped immigrants who were going to join their families in America. An information bureau was established that distributed
emigration information. In general, this bureau was politically diverse. The
work of the Yidgeskom grew. It was the only organization that provided aid
to the Jewish community. Yidgeskom and the communal organizations that
belonged to it (KOPE, ORT, OZE, Kultur Lige) were the only legally existing
Jewish institutions.

The Jewish Section of the Department of National Education consisted of
personnel who were close to Yidgeskom. Consequently, almost every question related to the Jewish population was decided through national Communists and the Jewish socialists. There was a tremendous difference between
the general conditions in towns where Yidgeskom operated and the towns

---

[188] Gumener means that the representatives from New York imagined the old
prerevolutionary social structure when the rabbis exercised authority in local
communities.—Trans.

[189] Timkovitz (Yid.), Timkovichi (Rus.), Cimkowicze (Pol.), Tsimkavichy (Bel.) is in
present-day Belarus. Krivazer (Yid.), Krivoye Ozero (Rus.), Kryve Ozero (Ukr.) is 179
miles southeast of Komenetz. The Timkovitz rural commune was located in the Minsk
district and in 1919–20 was administered by the Polish authority. Krivazer was a village in Podolia.—Trans.

without Yidgeskom. Towns where the Cheka was the master trembled in terror. Towns where Yidgeskom existed were protected by agreements between the Americans and the higher Bolshevik authority. Its activities were not subject to anyone's control.

Unfortunately, the situation could not last. This was felt by all those who worked in Yidgeskom. The rumor spread that the Cheka were preparing to act against the Yidgeskom. For example, it claimed that there was sufficient evidence that the committee had purchased products for welfare institutions that had not been approved; consequently, punishment was called for.

The unravelling came with the first announcement from partkom. Seeing that the work of Yidgeskom was being done without them, the Jewish Communists (members of the general Communist Party) placed in authority a young Jewish man who had a Christian family name and who spoke only Russian, despite the fact that everything in Yidgeskom was conducted in Yiddish. He took the role of defender of the interests of the Soviet authority. One of his first demands was that funds sent by the American landsmanshaft to Komenetz be sent in dollars or in other foreign currency and not as was usual, in Soviet currency. The difference resulted in a deflation in value of more than 100 percent. Yidgeskom found it impractical to demand that the delegation bring its funds in foreign currency. Then an order came that foreign currency be deposited in the government bank and exchanged according to the official rate of exchange back into Soviet currency.

This was only the first conflict. Soon it was clear that the work of the communal organizations could not continue. Every new order brought impossible consequences. On the one hand, Yidgeskom did not have the right to buy products at market prices; on the other hand, the Soviets were unable to provide food to Yidgeskom despite an agreement between them and the Americans. Immigration work also had to stop: Yidgeskom's work in this area was so successful that immigration from Red Russia and Red Ukraine was now forbidden. In addition, Yidgeskom had internal problems. The Communists who were nominated by central behaved as if they were privileged and did not always feel the responsibility that lay on their shoulders as the directors of the only aid organization in the Komenetz region. We felt that such a situation could not last long.

Meanwhile news came that the central committee and executive bureau of the Kultur Lige in Kiev were disbanded and would be replaced by an "administrative committee" consisting of members from the general Communist Party and Kombund. In addition, the remaining communal organizations were to be liquidated. We understood that shortly the end of the line would be coming to Komenetz and we too started to think about liquidation.

Dismantling the Kultur Lige in Kiev elicited anger in the province. The Kultur Lige was the only organization that at every crucial moment had identified with the democratic elements. In several places in Podolia the Kultur Lige blossomed nicely. In Mezbizh, for example, it owned a meeting hall, movie theater, schools, a library, a cooperative, a theater, and even its own electric generator station that served its institutions as well as several houses in the town. In Komenetz-Podolsk the Kultur Lige owned three schools, among them a model school—a crafts school—that visitors from Kiev admired. The nursery school section (OZE) of the Komenetz Kultur Lige ran three orphanages and two kindergartens. In addition, it owned a library and had a choir. It periodically organized teacher courses, courses for preschool teachers, and lectures for adults. The Kultur Lige also ran evening classes for workers.

A democrat, a socialist, and a Communist worked together peacefully in the administration of the Kultur Lige. We understood, however, that the existence of the Komenetz Kultur Lige was short-lived; they would probably soon become part of the Jewish Section of the Department of National Education [and thus lose their independence to the Soviet institutions]. In a meeting of the Komenetz Kultur Lige (that was halted by the authorities) a resolution was unanimously adopted declaring solidarity with the dismantled central committee of the Kultur Lige. In addition, the Komenetz Kultur Lige refused to perform its mission in the "communist spirit."

The work of the committee continued for the time being. Yet with each passing day it became clearer that dark clouds were gathering over the communal organizations and that in a short time its work would end. News arrived that the Cheka in Komenetz had cast its eyes on the Yidgeskom, the national Communists (Kombund, EKOPO), and on the Jewish socialists. The Cheka took a special interest in the American delegation. There was even an attempt to intimidate the delegation. No official permission was granted to go abroad, but at the same time permission was not refused.

The atmosphere was becoming darker. Yidgeskom reported that many immigrants—men, women, and children—were detained on the Bessarabian border. The delegates from the landsmanshaft were forced to leave Komenetz clandestinely and cross the border illegally, despite the fact that they possessed documents given to them by the chairman of revkom.

An internal struggle between revkom and the Cheka began, and the situation worsened. I remember my last shabbes in Komenetz. I went through the streets and at each step was stopped by acquaintances who related the latest news: one person told me that the Cheka demanded as witnesses the members of the Kultur Lige choir who had submitted a request to release their arrested choir leader. I was told that they had mobilized a well-known young Jewish bookkeeper to work for the Cheka who simply went crazy.

Another person reported that a well-known worker, a member of Poale Tsiyon and of the workers' council, was forced to leave Komenetz. The Cheka was totally out of control, and no one could restrain it. We expected that it would also turn on us, the Jewish socialists. Despite this concern we remained calm because we had not done anything for which we felt culpable even from the standpoint of the Soviet authority.

We learned that the Yidgeskom treasurer, the former administrator in the medical camps (and a Communist from Kiev), abandoned Komenetz and went abroad without telling anyone, even his friends and colleagues. We sensed that we were in an untenable situation. The Cheka was angry that a Communist had fooled it, and we feared that it would certainly attack anyone who had the slightest connection to Yidgeskom (we learned later that we were not mistaken). Besides, we were absolutely unable to understand what had driven a very responsible activist to run away so quickly without discussing this plan with even his closest colleagues. We surmised that something terrible had happened. But we could not think long about these matters. At night we left Komenetz by foot to the border without saying goodbye to relatives and to our closest friends. After suffering small obstacles, we arrived in Galicia with many other Jews.

Our Wanderings in Galicia and Poland

One thousand Jews from Komenetz were gathered in "S," the closest guard station from Komenetz to the Zbruch. The majority were merchants, but among them were also artisans and university-trained intellectuals. At first they were fearful when they saw us: "Is it that bad in Komenetz that even you, the Jewish socialists, could not remain there?"

These Jews were antagonistic towards us. They were mainly wealthy Jews, now homeless, who were angry and blamed us, the Jewish socialists, for all their troubles. They were now 30 versts from home where they had left their possessions and their families. They even threatened to turn us over to the authorities.

This kind of welcome affected us strongly. We were at that time virtually the only advocates for the Jewish population in the Soviet regime, and many of those who now threatened us had been entirely dependent upon the Jewish socialists in their hour of need. But there were also some among the refugees who made a real effort to ease our situation.

We left immediately. We were received in a friendly manner by the Jewish youth in the small Galician towns that lay near the border. They received us with great warmth and devotion. But it was an entirely different situation when we entered Galicia; and the difference was even more immediately apparent when we arrived in Poland.

In the years 1914 and 1915, aid workers saw how Ukrainian Jews warmly received the homeless Jews of Galicia and Poland who had suffered in the war. Now they could not help themselves from asking what would happen if the Ukrainian Jews were homeless and needed help from Galician and Polish Jews—how would the latter treat them? The bitter answer was provided by life itself. It was simply difficult to comprehend and to believe that the Polish Jews, who in their time of need received such material and moral support from the Ukrainian Jews, would forget so soon. The Jewish bourgeois philanthropists did something for the homeless, but the Jewish working class in Poland did absolutely nothing. Among the hundreds of thousands of Jewish immigrants from Ukraine were tens of thousands of workers, thousands of former members of professional organizations, and yet the Jewish worker in Poland and Galicia remained indifferent to them. Not long ago they were friends, members of the same party, and belonged to the central committee. Now their former Russian comrades were like strangers to them.

Meanwhile, the stream of immigrants grew. Escape was a kind of psychosis; one ran at the slightest provocation. People fled from Ukraine towards Galicia or to Poland. Some telegraphed relatives in America, acquired dollars, exchanged them for marks, and banged on the doors of various institutions, in order to acquire the appropriate documents. There was a new Jewish employment: "We are going to America." Meanwhile, no good news was coming from Komenetz. The Komenetz Ispolkom tried to resist the criminal activity of the Cheka.[190] After a long fight, the Cheka gained the upper hand and arrested the chairman of Ispolkom, who had been selected at the last meeting of peasants and workers.

Conclusion

My scant memories are finished. I have published everything that I could publish. I expressly focused on the group of Jewish socialists who were isolated from the entire world and on their own had to carry out a responsible policy. There was no other solution. We, the Jewish socialists, held that the only way to work for the Jewish masses was to live among them and to remain with them. Consequently, we refused every opportunity to leave Ukraine and go to Moscow or Western Europe and from afar send various prescriptions to heal the very sick Jewish invalid. We had to stay in place and actively help the Jewish masses. Understandably, this required compromises and resulted

---

[190] Ispolkom (executive committee) was the name of the administration in local soviets.—Trans.

in some great mistakes. We lived in a period in Ukraine when every word, every step from the various Jewish groups could cost tens, hundreds, and even thousands of Jewish lives. We therefore could not hold fast to established principles and positions when the very existence of the Jewish population was at stake. Perhaps it was easier for those who left Ukraine and emigrated to Moscow, Paris, London, Berlin, Warsaw, and other places. Being at home, however, we could actively take part in local political and communal life, and we took full responsibility for our actions.

Now, as we are forced to leave Ukraine in general and specifically Podolia, perhaps for a long time, we can no longer give advice to our comrades and friends who remain there. We can only send them our deepest brotherly love and compassion.

Appendix No. 1

From the Directory of the Ukrainian National Republic

In several locations in Ukraine, groups of Cossacks committed acts of violence against the Jews. Research showed that the Cossacks were misled by the Hetmanates, Volunteers, and those who called themselves "Bolsheviks." Their goal was to elicit hatred towards the Cossacks among the population, and to create divisions and chaos in the land. In this way they hoped to regain the old power of the bourgeoisie. Some of these provocateurs and pogromists were caught and shot, others were handed over to military field courts.

The Directory commands the Cossacks in the People's Army and all loyal citizens to stop violent provocations. Anyone who agitates for violence should immediately be handed over to the authority of the military tribunals. The Directory emphatically warns the Hetmanates, those counterrevolutionaries who hide under the name of "republicans": he who dares tarnish the good name of the army of the Workers' Revolutionary Ukrainian People will be punished severely.

The Directory calls upon the entire democratic Jewish nation in particular to energetically fight against the anarchistic Bolshevik members within the Jewish nation who agitate against the working people of Ukraine and its political existence. These elements provide the Hetmanates and provocateurs an excuse for demagogy and harmful agitation against the non-Bolshevik Jewish nation. They provoke Ukrainians, the fiery defenders of all working people, against the Jewish democrats, who are faithful to the Ukrainian state and are not anarchistic Bolsheviks.

Signed: Chairman of the Directory: V. Vynnychenko
Members of the Directory: Shvets, Andrievsky, Makarenko, Petliura[191]

---

[191] *Di Yidishe avtonomye un der natsyonaler sekretaryat in Ukraine.*

Appendix No. 2

A Declaration from the Working Group (Artisans) of the Komenetz Jewish Kehillah (July 6, 1919)

The history of the Jewish working class in Ukraine is closely bound with the history of the Ukrainian people. Every inch of Ukrainian earth is soaked with the sweat and blood of Jewish people. The pressure on Ukraine from various imperialists is also pressure on the Jewish working masses.

In the time of the tsar, the Jewish masses, together with the Ukrainian people, were robbed of their rights and chased into the former Pale. The centuries of suffering that was the common fate of both peoples gave the Jewish working class the certainty that the Ukrainian earth belonged to both. In the Ukrainian "cottage" the Jew is not a stepson, not a temporary guest, but a full-fledged equal citizen in Ukraine side by side with the Ukrainian working people. Therefore, the Jewish working class will not remain neutral in this great revolution—this moment of political, national, and economic freedom for Ukraine. The Jewish working masses, together with the Ukrainian working class, will fight for an independent Ukrainian National Republic.

We are sure that the best solution for our centuries of suffering can only be a free Ukraine devoid of exploitation and built with the participation of Jewish democratic forces. The Jewish democrats must have complete opportunity to participate and demonstrate their own initiative in all state and social institutions.

The fought-for 20th-century principle of self-determination upon which the Ukrainians built their sovereignty must become the foundation for all peoples in Ukraine. Thus, we demand that the proclaimed national-personal autonomy, whose realization [has the highest priority] for the Jewish working class, should develop broadly and strongly with participation by the Jewish Ministry, as well as with local and central Jewish autonomous institutions. We support the Jewish Ministry in the Ukrainian National Republic, and we will actively participate in the realization of national-personal autonomy for which the Jewish democrats have fought long and hard.

The existence of a Ukrainian socialist regime gives us the guarantee that Ukraine will be built upon the principles of the working masses. We, the toilers, actively support and demand that a war be waged against the dark and instigating elements that forced themselves into the government and civil institutions and directly participated in the bloody massacres of Jews in Ukraine.

The tens of thousands of Jews that were killed in the pogroms in Ukraine, the damage to the Jewish population that reached into the hundreds of millions, the violence that still goes on to this day in Jewish cities and towns calls for the strongest protest from the Jewish laboring masses. The destruction of Jewish towns and villages also brought the destruction of Ukraine, a country underdeveloped from an industrial point of view in which the Jews represented its greatest hope for the development of manufacturing and industry.

Appendix No. 3

The Unification of the Bund with the Fareynikte in Ukraine

The representatives of the Bund and the Fareynikte, who were active in every area of Ukraine during Petliura's regime, held a meeting in Komenetz-Podolsk. It was decided to unite both organizations under one name: the "Fareynikte Bund."

The conference of the Fareynikte Bund was attended by 26 groups and organizations from Komenetz-Podolsk, Mohilev, Proskurov, Vinitza, Olt-Kostin, Zhmerinka, and many other smaller towns. (Not all the towns that were invited were represented because not all invited delegates came.) The conference passed resolutions relating to the political situation, the pogroms, the Jewish ministries, personal national autonomy, and the subject of unity for both organizations. A temporary central bureau was established, and district offices were created in Proskurov, Mohilev, and Komenetz-Poldosk.

In the resolution we declared that the traitorous policy of the Russian bourgeoisie on the one side, and the Hetmanate reaction on the other, had prepared the soil for Bolshevism in Ukraine. The Communists exacerbated the split between city and village, totally destroyed workers' democracy, and in turn created conditions for the dark reaction reflected in the coalition between Denikin and the Poles.

To save the last fortresses of the revolution, Jewish workers must join the social democratic forces in the land. These forces must initiate the following actions: (1) separate themselves from the chauvinistic petty bourgeois elements; (2) re-establish workers' organizations and give amnesty to every arrested worker and Communist; (3) build workers' councils in order to control production and to develop worker legislative councils; (4) prepare a constitutional assembly; (5) give the final voice to the Jewish worker democrats for policies related to the Jewish population.

Regarding the pogroms, we assert that tens of thousands of Jewish souls were slaughtered, numerous towns were destroyed, and we demand that the state rebuild destroyed communities, end the storm of pogroms and the poisonous antisemitic incitements, and forcefully punish the guilty parties irrespective of their other accomplishments.

Resolution published in *Lebensfragen*, Warsaw, October 21, 1921, No. 227 (396)

Appendix No. 4

Ministry for Jewish Affairs
Department for National Autonomy.
Administrative Division.
No. 290 Komenetz-Podolsk, 2nd Zhovten (October)

Circular

As reported to us from various kehillah councils, only Hebrew is being utilized in community business. We declare that the exclusive use of the Hebrew
language is illegal.

   According to the National Personal Autonomy law of January 1, 1918,
and articles 12—18 regarding autonomous Jewish community promulgated
17th Kviten [April] 1919, all minutes of the sessions of the kehillah councils
and all bookkeeping must be kept in the two languages: Ukrainian and Yiddish.... The use of Hebrew instead of Yiddish for kehillah council business is
completely illegal and forbidden. This notice is for your strict and complete
implementation.

Director of the Department of National Autonomy (signature)
Administrator of Organizational Administration Division (signature)

Appendix No. 5

Petition to the Jewish Ministry

During the transitional period it was impossible for the club to exist normally. The library is in ruins. There are no funds for rebuilding. The apartment has not been paid for the coming summer. Money shortage does not allow us to invite people. Thus, we ask for ten thousand rubles.

The funds were legally received on September 12, 1919.

Chairman (signature)
Berditchev Jewish Workers Club (Bronislav Grosser)

Selected Bibliography

Primary Sources

An-sky, S. *1915 Diary of S. An-sky: A Russian Jewish Writer at the Eastern Front*. Translated by Polly Zavadivker. Bloomington: Indiana University Press, 2016.

Babel, Isaac. *1920 Diary*. Translated by H. T. Willetts. New Haven: Yale University Press, 1995.

Batchinsky, Julian et al. *The Jewish Pogroms in Ukraine: Authoritative Statements on the Question of Responsibility for Recent Outbreaks Against the Jews in Ukraine*. Washington, DC: Friends of Ukraine, 1919.

Cohen, Israel. *A Report on the Pogroms in Poland*. London: Central Office of the Zionist Organization, 1919.

The Destruction of Proskurov: In Memory of the Sacred Souls Who Perished During the Terrible Slaughter of the Haidamaks (Khmelnytskyy, Ukraine). New York: Proskurover Relief Organization, 1924. https://www.jewishgen.org/yizkor/ Khmelnytskyy/Khmelnytskyy.html. [Translation of *Khurbn Proskurov: Tsum ondenken fun di heylige neshomes vos zaynen umgekumen in der shreklikher shkhite, vos iz ongefirt gevoren durkh di haydamakes*]

Drakhter, Yisroel. *Mayses fun a kleynem vanderer: Erinerungen fun a yidishn yingl in ukrayne beys der milhome un pogromen* [Stories of a little wanderer: The experiences of a Jewish boy in Ukraine during the war and pogroms]. Vilna, 1928.

De Lubersac, Jean. *The Ukraine Inferno: Recital of an Eye-Witness*. London: Fund for the Relief of the Jewish Victims of the War, 1922.

Faygenberg, Rokhl. *Bay di bregn fun Dniester* [On the banks of the Dniester]. Warsaw, 1925.

———. *A pinkes fun a toyter shtot: Khurbn dubove* [A record of a dead city: The destruction of Dubove]. Warsaw, 1926.

Federation of Ukrainian Jews. *The Ukraine Terror and the Jewish Peril*. London: Federation of Ukrainian Jews, 1921.

Goldelman, Solomon. *Jewish National Autonomy in Ukraine, 1917–1920*. Translated by Michael Luchkovich. Chicago: Ukrainian Research and Information Institute, 1968.

Gumener, Elijahu. *A kapitl Ukraine: Tsvey yor in Podolye* [A Ukrainian chapter: Two years in Podolia]. Vilna: Sreberk Publisher, 1921.

Heifetz, Elias. *The Slaughter of the Jews in the Ukraine in 1919*. New York: Seltzer, 1921.

Kamianets-Podilskyi Memorial Book. Edited by L. S. Blatman. New York: Sponsors of the Kamenetz-Podolsk Memorial Book, 1966.

Khrystiuk, Pavlo. *Zamitky i materialy do istoriï ukraïns´koi revoliutsiï, 1917–1920 rr.* [Notes and materials on the Ukrainian revolution, 1917–1920]. Vienna: Ukraïns´kyi sotsiologichnyi instytut, 1921–22.

Kipnis, Itsik. *Khadoshim un teg: A khronik* [Months and days: A chronicle]. Vilna: B. Kletskin, 1929; Tel Aviv: Y. L. Perets, 1973. https://www.yiddishbookcenter.org/collections/yiddish-books/spb-nybc200477/kipnis-itzik-hadoshim-un-teg-un-andere-dertseylungen.

Koren, Y. *Yehudei Kishinev* [The Jews of Kishinev (Chişinău, Moldova)]. Tel Aviv, 1950. https://www.jewishgen.org/yizkor/kishinev/kishinev.html.

Margolin, Arnold. *Ukraine and Policy of the Entente* [Ukraina i politika Antanty]. Translated from Russian by V. P. Sokoloff. Berlin: S. Efron Izdatel´stvo, 1921.

Mazepa, Isaak. *Ukraïna v ohni i buri revoliutsiï, 1917–1921* [Ukraine in the fire and storm of revolution, 1917–1921]. Prague, 1942.

Navaredok Memorial Book (Navahrudak, Belarus). Edited by Helen Cohn. Tel Aviv: Navaredker Relief Committee, 1963. https://www.jewishgen.org/Yizkor/Nowogrodek/Nowogrodek.html.

"The Polish Relief Unit." *Jewish Social Service* 10, 7 (January 1920): 155–57.

"Relief for Europe's Jewry." *Jewish Social Service* 10, 6 (December 1919): 127–29.

Revutsky, Abraham. *In di shvere teg oif Ukraine: Zikhroines fun a yidishn ministr* [In the terrible days in Ukraine: Recollections from a Jewish minister]. Berlin: Yidisher literarisher farlag, 1924.

Sadikov, Max. *In yene teg: Zikhroynes vegen der Rusisher revolutsye un di Ukrayner pogromen* [In those days: Memoirs of the Russian revolution and the Ukrainian pogroms,]. New York: [o. Fg], 1926. https://www.yiddishbookcenter.org/collections/yiddish-books/spb-nybc208816/sadikoff-max-in-yene-teg-zikhroynes-vegen-der-rusisher-revolutsye-un-di.

Shalit, Moses, ed. *Oyf di hurves fun milhomes un mehumes: Pinkes fun Ge-gnt-komitet "YEKOPO" 1919–1931* [On the ruins of wars and turmoil: Records of the Regional Committee YEKOPO, 1919–1931]. Vilna: Gegnt-komitet, "YEKOPO," 1931.

Shtif, Nokhem. "The Pogroms in Ukraine: The Period of the Volunteer Army." Translated by Maurice Wolfthal. *In geveb: A Journal of Yiddish Studies*, 15 September 2016. http://ingeveb.org/texts-and-translations/the-pogroms-in-ukraine-the-period-of-the-volunteer-army.

The Pogroms in Ukraine, 1918–19: Prelude to the Holocaust. Translated by Maurice Wolfthal. Cambridge: Open Book Publishers, 2019.

Silberfarb [Zilberfarb], Moshe, and David Lincoln. *The Jewish Ministry and Jewish National Autonomy in Ukraine.* Translated by Lincoln. New York: Aleph Press, 1993.

Tcherikower, E. *In der tkufe fun revolutsye: Memuarn, materyaln, dokumentn* [In the era of revolution: Memoirs, materials, documents]. Berlin: Historical Archive of Eastern Jewry, 1924. YIVO Institute for Jewish Research Microfilm collection 1989-Y-1264.1.

Tcherikower, E. [I. M. Cherikover]. *Antisemitizm un pogromen in Ukraine, 1917–1918: Tsu der geshikhte fun Ukrainish-Yidishe batsiungen* [Antisemitism and pogroms in Ukraine, 1917–1918: A history of Ukrainian-Jewish relations]. Berlin: Yidisher literarisher farlag, 1923.

———. *Di Ukrainer pogromen in yor 1919* [The Ukrainian pogroms in 1919]. New York: YIVO, 1965.

Di Yidishe avtonomye un der natsyonaler sekretaryat in Ukraine: Materyaln un dokumentn [Jewish autonomy and the national secretariat in Ukraine: Materials and documents]. Kiev: Idisher folks-farlag, 1920.

Secondary Sources

Abramson, Henry. "Historiography on the Jews and the Ukrainian Revolution." *Journal of Ukrainian Studies* 15, 2 (1990): 33–45.

———. "Jewish Representation in the Independent Ukrainian Government of 1917–1920." *Slavic Review* 50, 3 (1991): 542–50.

———. *A Prayer for the Government: Ukrainians and Jews in Revolutionary Times, 1917–1920.* Cambridge, MA: Harvard University Press, 1999.

Adams, Arthur. *Bolsheviks in the Ukraine: The Second Campaign, 1918–19.* New Haven: Yale University Press, 1963.

Alroey, Gur. "Documenting the Pogroms in Ukraine, 1918–1920: Eliezer David Rosenthal's *Megilat Hatevah*." *Gal-Ed: On the History and Culture of Polish Jewry* 24 (2015): 63–102.

Astashkevich, Irina. *Gendered Violence: Jewish Women in the Pogroms of 1917–1921*. Brookline, MA: Academic Studies Press, 2018.

Atkinson, Dorothy. "The Zemstvo and the Peasantry." In *The Zemstvo in Russia: An Experiment in Local Self-Government*, edited by Terence Emmons and Wayne S. Vucinich, 79–132. Cambridge: Cambridge University Press, 1982.

Bauer, Yehudah. *My Brother's Keeper: A History of the American Jewish Joint Distribution Society, 1929–1939*. Philadelphia: Jewish Publication Society, 1974.

Beizer, Michael. *Relief in Time of Need: Russian Jewry and the Joint, 1914–24*. Bloomington, IN: Slavica, 2015.

Bemporad, Elissa. *A Legacy of Blood: Jews, Pogroms, and Ritual Murder in the Lands of the Soviets*. New York: Oxford University Press, 2019.

Budnitskii, Oleg. "Jews, Pogroms, and the White Movement: A Historiographic Critique." *Kritika: Explorations in Russian and Eurasian History*, n.s., 2, 4 (2001): 1–23.

———. *Russian Jews Between the Reds and the Whites, 1917–1920*. Philadelphia: University of Pennsylvania Press, 2012.

Davis, Natalie Zemon. *The Return of Martin Guerre*. Cambridge, MA: Harvard University Press, 1983.

Dekel-Chen, Jonathan et al., eds. *Anti-Jewish Violence: Rethinking the Pogrom in East European History*. Bloomington: Indiana University Press, 2011.

Doroshenko, Dmytro. *A Survey of Ukrainian Historiography*. New York: The Ukrainian Academy of Arts and Sciences, 1957.

Eley, Geoff. "Remapping the Nation: War, Revolutionary Upheaval and State Formation in Eastern Europe, 1914–1923." In *Ukrainian-Jewish Relations in Historical Perspective*, edited by Peter J. Potichnyj and Howard Aster, 205–46. Edmonton: Canadian Institute of Ukrainian Studies, 1990.

Engel, David, ed. *The Assassination of Symon Petliura and the Trial of Scholem Schwarzbard 1926–1927: A Selection of Documents*. Göttingen: Archive of Jewish History and Vandenhoeck & Ruprecht, 2016.

———. "Lwów, 1918: The Transmutation of a Symbol and Its Legacy in the Holocaust." In *Contested Memories: Poles and Jews during the Holocaust and Its Aftermath*, edited by Joshua D. Zimmerman, 32–44. New Brunswick, NJ: Rutgers University Press, 2003.

Engel, David. "What's in a Pogrom? European Jews in the Age of Violence." In *Anti-Jewish Violence: Rethinking the Pogrom in East European History*, edited by Jonathan Dekel-Chen, David Gaunt, Natan M. Meir, and Israel Bartal, 19–37. Bloomington: Indiana University Press, 2011.

Engelstein, Laura. *Russia in Flames: War, Revolution, Civil War, 1914–1921*. New York: Oxford University Press, 2018.

Estraikh, Gennady. "The Yiddish Kultur-Lige." In *Modernism in Kyiv: Jubilant Experimentation*, edited by Irena Makaryk and Virlana Tkacz, 197–217. Toronto: University of Toronto Press, 2010.

Fink, Carole. *Defending the Rights of Others: The Great Powers, the Jews, and International Minority Protection, 1878–1938*. Cambridge: Cambridge University Press, 2004.

Fischer, Lars. "The *Pogromshchina* and the Directory: A New Historiographical Synthesis?," *Revolutionary Russia* 16, 2 (2003): 47–93. http://dx.doi.org/10.1080/09546540308575772

Frankel, Jonathan. *Prophecy and Politics: Socialism, Nationalism, and the Russian Jews, 1862–1917*. New York: Cambridge University Press, 1981.

Freiden, Gregory, ed. *The Enigma of Isaac Babel: Biography, History, Context*. Stanford, CA: Stanford University Press, 2009.

Garbarini, Alexandra. *Numbered Days: Diaries and the Holocaust*. New Haven: Yale University Press, 2006.

———. "Power in Truth Telling: Jewish Testimonial Strategies before the Shoah." In *Kinship, Community, and Self: Essays in Honor of David Warren Sabean*, edited by Jason Coy, Benjamin Marschke, Jared Poley, and Claudia Verhoeven, 170–84. New York: Berghahn, 2015.

———, ed. *"A Terrible and Terribly Interesting Epoch": The Holocaust Diary of Lucien Dreyfus*. Lanham, MD: Rowman & Littlefield, 2021.

Gatrell, Peter. *A Whole Empire Walking: Refugees in Russia during World War I*. Bloomington: Indiana University Press, 1999.

Gergel, N. "The Pogroms in the Ukraine in 1918–21." *YIVO Annual of Jewish Social Studies* 6 (1951): 237–52.

Gilley, Christopher. "Beyond Petliura: The Ukrainian National Movement and the 1919 Pogroms." *East European Jewish Affairs* 47, 1 (2017): 45–61. https://doi.org/10.1080/13501674.2017.1306403.

———. "Fighters for Ukrainian Independence? Imposture and Identity among Ukrainian Warlords, 1917–22." *Historical Research* 90, 247 (2017): 172–90. https://doi.org/10.1111/1468-2281.12168.

Ginzburg, Carlo. *The Cheese and the Worms: The Cosmos of a Sixteenth-Century Miller.* Baltimore: Johns Hopkins University Press, 1980.

Gitelman, Zvi, ed. *The Emergence of Modern Jewish Politics: Bundism and Zionism in Eastern Europe.* Pittsburgh: University of Pittsburgh Press, 2003.

Gitelman, Zvi. *Jewish Nationality and Soviet Politics: The Jewish Sections of the CPSU, 1917–1930.* Princeton, NJ: Princeton University Press, 1972.

Granick, Jaclyn. "The First American Organization in Soviet Russia: JDC and Relief in the Ukraine, 1920–1923." In *The JDC at 100: A Century of Humanitarianism,* edited by Avinoam J. Patt, Atina Grossmann, Linda G. Levi, and Maud S. Mandel, 61–93. Detroit: Wayne State University Press, 2019.

———. *International Jewish Humanitarianism in the Age of the Great War.* Cambridge: Cambridge University Press, 2021. https://doi.org/10.1017/9781108860697.

———. "Waging Relief: The Politics and Logistics of American War Relief in Europe and the Near East (1914–1918)." *First World War Studies* 5, 1 (2014): 55–68. https://doi.org/10.1080/19475020.2014.901183.

Gurevitz, Baruch. *National Communism in the Soviet Union, 1918–1928.* Pittsburgh: University of Pittsburgh Press, 1980.

Guthier, Steven. "The Popular Base of Ukrainian Nationalism in 1917." *Slavic Review* 38, 1 (1979): 41.

Holquist, Peter. *Making War, Forging Revolution: Russia's Continuum of Crisis, 1914–1921.* Cambridge, MA: Harvard University Press, 2002.

———. "Violent Russia, Deadly Marxism? Russia in the Epoch of Violence, 1905–21. *Kritika: Explorations in Russian and Eurasian History* 4, 3 (2003): 627–52.

Horowitz, Brian. *Jewish Philanthropy and Enlightenment in Late-Tsarist Russia.* Seattle: University of Washington Press, 2009.

Jacobs, Jack. *Bundist Counterculture in Interwar Poland.* Syracuse, NY: Syracuse University Press, 2009.

Johnson, S. "The Daily Lives of Civilians in the Russian Civil War." In *Daily Lives of Civilians in Wartime Twentieth-Century Europe,* edited by Nicholas Atkin, 49–72. Westport, CT: Greenwood Press, 2008.

Kagedan, Allan L. "American Jews and the Soviet Experiment: The Agro-Joint Project, 1924–1937." *Jewish Social Studies* 43, 2 (1981): 153–64.

Kaplan, Deborah. *The Patrons and Their Poor: Jewish Community and Public Charity in Early Modern Europe.* Philadelphia: University of Pennsylvania Press, 2020.

Karlip, Joshua. "Between Martyrology and Historiography: Elias Tcherikower and the Making of a Pogrom Historian." *East European Jewish Affairs* 38, 3 (2008): 257–80.

———. *The Tragedy of a Generation: The Rise and Fall of Jewish Nationalism in Eastern Europe.* Cambridge, MA: Harvard University Press, 2013.

Kenez, Peter. *The Defeat of the Whites: Civil War in South Russia, 1919–1920.* Berkeley: University of California Press, 1977.

Kuchabsky, Vasyl. *Western Ukraine in Conflict with Poland and Bolshevism, 1918–1923.* Edmonton: Canadian Institute of Ukrainian Studies Press, 2009.

Lederhendler, Eli. *The Road to Modern Jewish Politics: Political Tradition and Political Reconstruction in the Jewish Community of Tsarist Russia.* New York: Cambridge University Press, 1989.

Lohr, Eric. "The Russian Army and the Jews: Mass Deportation, Hostages, and Violence during World War I." *Russian Review* 60 (2001): 404–19. https://doi.org/10.1111/0036-0341.00177.

Lukin, Benyamin. "Kam'ianets'-Podil's'kyi." In *The YIVO Encyclopedia of Jews in Eastern Europe,* https://yivoencyclopedia.org/article.aspx/Kamianets-Podilskyi.

Marrus, Michael R. *The Unwanted: European Refugees in the Twentieth Century.* New York: Oxford University Press, 1985.

Martin, Sean. "How to House a Child: Providing Homes for Jewish Children in Interwar Poland." *East European Jewish Affairs* 45, 1 (2015): 26–41. https://doi.org/10.1080/13501674.2015.968825.

Material Concerning Ukrainian-Jewish Relations during the Years of the Revolution (1917–1921). Munich: Ukrainian Information Bureau, 1956.

Maza, Sarah. *Violette Nozière: A Story of Murder in 1930s Paris.* Berkeley: University of California Press, 2011.

Meir, Natan. "From Communal Charity to National Welfare: Jewish Orphanages in Eastern Europe before and after World War I." *East European Jewish Affairs* 39, 1 (2009): 19–34. https://doi.org/10.1080/13501670902750261.

———. *Stepchildren of the Shtetl: The Destitute, Disabled, and Mad of Jewish Eastern Europe, 1800–1939.* Stanford, CA: Stanford University Press, 2020.

Mendelsohn, Ezra. *On Modern Jewish Politics.* New York: Oxford University Press, 1993.

Meyers, Joshua. "A Portrait of Transition: From the Bund to Bolshevism in the Russian Revolution." *Jewish Social Studies: History, Culture, Society*, n.s., 24, 2 (2019): 107–34. https://doi.org/10.2979/jewisocistud.24.2.09.

McGeever, Brendan. *Antisemitism and the Russian Revolution*. Cambridge: Cambridge University Press, 2019.

Miliakova, Lidia, and Irina Ziuzina. "Le travail d'enquête des organisations juives sur les pogroms d'Ukraine, de Biélorussie et de Russie soviétique pendant la guerre civile (1918–1922)" [The investigative work of Jewish organizations into the pogroms in Ukraine, Belarus and Soviet Russia during the Civil War (1918–1922)]. *Le Mouvement Social* 222 (2008): 61–80.

Magocsi, Paul Robert, and Yohanan Petrovsky-Shtern. *Jews and Ukrainians: A Millennium of Co-Existence*. Toronto: University of Toronto Press, 2016.

Murav, Harriet. "Archive of Violence: Neighbors, Strangers, and Creatures in Itsik Kipnis's Months and Days." In "The Pogroms of the Russian Civil War at 100: New Trends, New Sources," edited by Elissa Bemporad and Thomas Chopard. Special issue, *Quest: Issues in Contemporary Jewish History*, no. 15 (2019). https://doi.org/10.48248/issn.2037-741X/836.

Nathans, Benjamin. *Beyond the Pale: The Jewish Encounter with Late Imperial Russia*. Berkeley: University of California Press, 2002.

Nutkiewicz, Michael. "Shame, Guilt, and Anguish in Holocaust Survivor Testimony." *The Oral History Review* 30, 1 (2003): 1–22. https://doi.org/10.1525/ohr.2003.30.1.1.

Nutkiewicz, Sergei. "Eliyahu Gumener." *Oyfun Shvall* 12 (June–July 1947): 12.

Palij, Michael. *The Ukrainian-Polish Defensive Alliance, 1919–1921: An Aspect of the Ukrainian Revolution*. Edmonton: Canadian Institute of Ukrainian Studies Press, 1995.

Petrova, Olga. "The Jewish Question in the Ukrainian Revolution (1919–1920): A Reappraisal of Ukrainian-Jewish Relations Based on the Daily *Ukraina*." Ph.D. diss., Central European University, 2013.

Petrovsky-Shtern, Yohanan. *The Golden Age Shtetl: A New History of Jewish Life in East Europe*. Princeton, NJ: Princeton University Press, 2014.

Pevzner, Y. "Jewish Committee for the Relief of War Victims (1914–1921)." *Pinkas* 1 (2006): 114–42.

Prusin, Alexander. *Nationalizing a Borderland: War, Ethnicity, and Anti-Jewish Violence in East Galicia, 1914–1920*. Tuscaloosa: University of Alabama Press, 2016.

Rabinovitch, Simon. *Jewish Rights, National Rights: Nationalism and Autonomy in Late Imperial and Revolutionary Russia.* Stanford, CA: Stanford University Press, 2014.

————. "Jewish-Ukrainian-Soviet Relations during the Civil War and the Second Thoughts of a Minister for Jewish Affairs." *Studies in Ethnicity and Nationalism* 17, 3 (2017): 339–57. https://doi.org/10.1111/sena.12256.

Reshetar, John S., Jr. *The Ukrainian Revolution, 1917–1920: A Study in Nationalism.* Princeton, NJ: Princeton University Press, 1952.

Ringlee, Andrew. "The Romanovs' Militant Charity: The Red Cross and Public Mobilization for War in Tsarist Russia, 1853–1914." Ph.D. diss., University of North Carolina at Chapel Hill, 2016.

Roskies, David. *Against the Apocalypse: Responses to Catastrophe in Modern Jewish Culture.* Cambridge, MA: Harvard University Press, 1984.

Rudnitsky, Stephen. *Ukraine: The Land and Its People. An Introduction to Its Geography.* New York: Rand McNally, 1918.

Ryan, James. "The Sacralization of Violence: Bolshevik Justifications for Violence and Terror during the Civil War." *Slavic Review* 74, 4 (2015): 808–31. https://doi.org/10.5612/slavicreview.74.4.808.

Safran, Gabriella. *Wandering Soul: The Dybbuk's Creator, S. An-sky.* Cambridge, MA: Harvard University Press, 2010.

Salant, Yankl. "Frayland-Lige." In *The YIVO Encyclopedia of Jews in Eastern Europe.* https://yivoencyclopedia.org/article.aspx/Frayland-lige.

Sinkoff, Nancy. "In the Podolian Steppe." In *Out of the Shtetl: Making Jews Modern in the Polish Borderlands.* Providence, RI: Brown University Press, 2020.

Skirda, Alexandre. *Nestor Makhno: Anarchy's Cossack.* Translated by Paul Sharkey. Edinburgh: AK Press, 2004.

Snyder, Timothy. *The Reconstruction of Nations: Poland, Ukraine, Lithuania, Belarus, 1569–1999.* New Haven: Yale University Press, 2003.

Spitzer, Yannay. "Pale in Comparison: The Economic Ecology of the Jews as a Rural Service Minority" (December 2019). London: Center for Economic Policy Research Discussion Paper No. DP14262.

Stillschweig, Kurt. "Nationalism and Autonomy among Eastern European Jewry: Origin and Historical Development up to 1939." *Historia Judaica* 6 (1944): 59.

Szajkowski, Z. "Jewish Relief in Eastern Europe 1914–1917." *The Leo Baeck Institute Yearbook* 10, 1 (1965): 24–56.

The Ukrainian Congress Committee of America. *Ukrainians and Jews: Articles, Testimonies, Letters and Official Documents Dealing with Interrelations of Ukrainians and Jews in the Past and Present. A Symposium.* New York: The Ukrainian Congress Committee of America, 1966.

Von Hagen, Mark. *War in a European Borderland: Occupations and Occupation Plans in Galicia and Ukraine, 1914–1918.* Seattle: University of Washington Press, 2007.

Weeks, Theodore. *From "Russian" to "Polish": Vilna-Wilno 1900–1925.* Washington, DC: The National Council for Eurasian and East European Research, 2004.

Werth, Nicolas. *Le Livre des pogroms: Antichambre d'un génocide, Ukraine, Russie, Biélorussie, 1917–1922.* Paris: Mémorial de la Shoah, 2010.

Weinberg, David. *Between Tradition and Modernity: Haim Zhitlowski, Simon Dubnow, Ahad Ha-Am and the Shaping of Modern Jewish Identity.* New York: Holmes & Meier, 1996.

Weiser, Kalman. *Jewish People, Yiddish Nation: Noah Prylucki and the Folkist in Poland.* Toronto: University of Toronto Press, 2010.

Yekelchyk, Serhy. *Ukraine: Birth of a Modern Nation.* New York: Oxford University Press, 2007.

Zavadivker, Polly. "Fighting 'On Our Own Territory': The Relief, Rescue, and Representation of Jews in Russia during World War I." In *Russia's Home Front in War and Revolution, 1914–22, Book 2, The Experience of War and Revolution*, edited by Adele Lindenmeyr, Christopher Read, and Peter Waldron, 79–105. Bloomington, IN: Slavica, 2016.

———. "'Jewish Fever': Myths and Realities in the History of Russia's Typhus Epidemic, 1914–1922." *Jewish Social Studies* 26, 1 (2020): 101–12. https://doi.org/10.2979/jewisocistud.26.1.09.

Zipperstein, Steven. *Pogrom: Kishinev and the Tilt of History.* New York: W. W. Norton, 2019.

———. "The Politics of Relief: The Transformation of Russian Jewish Communal Life During the First World War." *Studies in Contemporary Jewry* 4 (1988): 22–40.

About the Translator

Michael Eli Nutkiewicz earned his Ph.D. in History from UCLA. He taught Jewish history at the University of Missouri–Columbia, San Diego State University, and the University of New Mexico. Nutkiewicz served as director of the Los Angeles Museum of the Holocaust, senior historian at the Survivors of the Shoah Visual History Foundation, executive director of the Program for Torture Victims in Los Angeles, and manager of the refugee resettlement program at Catholic Charities–New Mexico.